Feeding Winter Birds
in the Pacific Northwest

Bob Waldon

THE
MOUNTAINEERS

To Dr. Jack and Ida Waldon Guthrie and Frances Guthrie Agars
for the time they shared their home with me many years ago in
Pullman, Washington. Their generosity was to mean
more to me than any of us realized at the time.

 Published by The Mountaineers
1011 SW Klickitat Way
Seattle, Washington 98134

8 7 6 5 4
5 4 3 2 1

Manufactured in the United States of America

Edited by Kris Fulsaas
All illustrations © Peter Sawatzky
Cover design by Bookends
Book design and typesetting by The Mountaineers Books

Cover illustration: Pine Grosbeaks

Library of Congress Cataloging-in-Publication Data
Waldon, Bob, 1932–
        Feeding winter birds in the Pacific Northwest / Bob Waldon.
                p.   cm.
        Includes bibliographical references and index.
        ISBN 0-89886-405-4
        1. Birds--Northwest, Pacific. 2. Birds--Northwest, Pacific--Feeding and feeds. 3.
Bird feeders. 4. Birds--Northwest, Pacific--Identification. 5. Birds--Wintering--
Northwest, Pacific.
        I. Title
QL683.N75W35   1994
598'.07234795--dc20   94-23145
                                                                            CIP
Printed on recycled paper

Contents

Preface

This is a nontechnical, nonacademic book. It is intended for the information and enjoyment of the thousands of householders in the Pacific Northwest who feed birds in winter and who enjoy their birds through a picture window.

My own feeding experience began in Manitoba, in winter conditions that tax survival capabilities to the limit. It was not unusual for the chickadees to arrive at my feeders about the time the morning radio was reminding me that the wind chill of the moment would freeze exposed flesh in thirty seconds or less.

In such conditions it was impossible for me to watch those tiny, bare-footed birds without marveling how they could possibly survive on the other side of that sheltering pane of glass. My search for the answer led to the discovery of much that was fascinating in the world of birds and, in time, to the idea that other people would be interested in hearing what I had found out. There seemed to be a place for handy-sized references, each focusing on a discrete region, its particular winter birds, and the feeding of them.

Writing this book has been a lot of fun, an admission one probably ought not to make. My research was essentially painless, consisting of foraging through the popular literature, constantly on the sniff for those neat bits of lore that we information junkies love to collect. Although these sources are readily available, not everyone has the determination to muster them, nor the time to wade through the resulting piles of books and periodicals. In assuming the task, I have tried to assemble a truly absorbing collection of information and to present it from a fresh perspective.

There are few source references; most of my reading was from books and periodicals whose authors and writers themselves gave no sources. I therefore relied on my own judgment and cross-checking to determine the reliability of the information I selected. Where material was obviously an author's own, or in rare cases where the statements bent credulity a little, I accorded in-text credit.

In conclusion, this is not the work of a scholar, nor even of a respectable birder. Rather, it is the offering of a writer with an abiding sense of excitement about nature and a shameless compulsion to infect others with it. I hope my fellow birdwatchers enjoy reading this book as much as I enjoyed writing it.

Acknowledgments

As a lifelong naturalist, it has been my pleasure to have worked with staff and members of the National Audubon Society, at both the state and national level. In accumulating the background that in time led to this book, these relationships were valuable for the knowledge and information they imparted, and for the encouragement they afforded.

I must also extend thanks to the Cornell Laboratory of Ornithology, especially Erica Dunn, coordinator of Project FeederWatch. Through participation in their many programs and services, and in personal communications, I have grown and benefitted as an observer of the world of birds.

Over the many years that I have known artist and woodcarver Peter Sawatzky, the illustrator of this book, I have greatly enjoyed both his work and his friendship. Working with Peter is a pleasure not only because of the high level of his interpretive skill, but also because he brings to his profession a good business sense and an enthusiasm for developing new projects and for working in a partnership.

During my travels in the Pacific Northwest in preparation for this book, I visited or phoned a number of people, bird feeders and otherwise, who were generous with their personal observations, or who simply offered the kind of encouragement authors seem to need. I owe a special nod of appreciation to Ken Bevis of Ellensburg, Washington, who checked the species list and offered helpful suggestions on cavity-nesting bird species. Dr. Dennis Paulson of the Slater Museum at the University of Puget Sound in Tacoma, Washington; Howard Ennor of Richland, Washington; and Bill Tweit of Olympia, Washington also checked my species list and offered helpful suggestions. Due to the limitations of time and space, I couldn't do full justice to all of the recommendations. Therefore, such omissions or errors as there may be, and the ultimate choice of species, are entirely my responsibility.

I would also like to thank Bob and Serene Haugen of Lynden, Washington; Elva and Paul Nibbelink of Issaquah, Washington; Linda A. Easley of Portland, Oregon; Priscilla Dauble of Milton-Freewater, Oregon; Frances Agars of Ellensburg, Washington; and Dan Stouter of Redi-National Pest Control of Seattle, Washington.

Golden-crowned Kinglet

Introduction

Everyone knows that in autumn most of the birds leave, and in spring they return. It may seem contradictory, therefore, to point out that in fact far more people spend far more time watching greater numbers of birds in winter than in the warm seasons. Although there are many more species around in summer, they are scattered, busy with domestic chores amidst the concealing foliage. Certain dedicated birders arise in summer before dawn and prowl amidst the dewy tangles and the mosquitoes. This is admirable beyond words, but exceeds the resolve of most of us. Besides, many of us are just as busy in summer as the birds are.

Winter, though it banishes most of the birds, also strips the concealing foliage from the deciduous trees and from much of the ground cover, clearing the view. Winter also changes the remaining birds' social habits. Many species gather into large flocks, roving widely in search of food. Most of these will congregate readily around feeders that can be placed near a convenient window where the birds can be continuously, closely, and comfortably observed. In effect, instead of having to seek out birds, winter birders can manipulate the birds into seeking out *them*!

Selecting what species of wintering birds to include in a book is a challenging task. It is especially complicated if the subject is the Pacific Northwest. There are many "Pacific Northwests." On the balmy coastline of northern California, hummingbirds search out flowers while Gray Jays in the Selkirk Mountains of northernmost Idaho retrieve the food they stashed away in summer. On the Cascades' highest ridges the Willow Ptarmigan plucks buds from arctic plants. Between the beaches and the peaks is strewn a landscape of wet rain forest, ice-age–carved basins, volcanic giants, plateaus, canyons, and sagebrush steppes. It is a complicated mosaic.

This mosaic of habitats and the variety of birdlife it harbors confronts the author of a book on feeding birds with a dilemma of choices. There is no problem with gulls, scoters, shorebirds, and Bald Eagles, since they do not as a rule rate as "feeder" birds. Others, like the Sage Grouse, would be welcome guests at feeders but I am told they aren't the slightest bit interested.

The most accessible, reliable sources of information on birds that are realistic prospects as feeder visitors come from the annual Christmas Bird Count (CBC) lists (see Chapter 7, Census-Taking). The birds tallied in the CBCs fall into several categories.

Each zone has its resident, nonmigratory regulars, such as jays, woodpeckers, and chickadees. These might, or might not, be joined by flocks of nomadic northern finches whose numbers range, year to year, from abundant to absent.

Then there are the rather hesitant migrants such as goldfinches. And juncos in much of the Pacific Northwest migrate up–down as much as north–south. Some species of sparrows number in their largely migratory midst a percentage that elect to stay behind, or go only halfway. "Holdovers" are that small percentage of a normally migratory population that stays behind. These include thrushes, some sparrows, flickers, and blackbirds of several kinds.

In the minds of some, a "feeder" roster should also include stay-over waterfowl. In sheltered bays and estuaries along the coast and in stretches of open river inland, flocks of mallards are joined by other species for as long as food holds out. In most urban areas ducks, gulls, swans, and squads of Canada Geese shake down the tourists for tidbits of fast food, and mob the regular benefactors who faithfully distribute corn, peanuts, and other non-junk foods by the bucketful. These accomplished mooches may be *fed* birds, but they are not *feeder* birds.

To complicate the problem of choosing what to include and what to leave out, there are the decidedly winter birds, such as Horned Larks and Snow Buntings, that rarely visit feeders, and shrikes, owls, hawks, and other predators that come with sinister motives. One would like to include them all, but sooner or later the limitations of space in a book assert themselves, and one is obliged to muster one's biases and make arbitrary cuts.

As if cutting out some hawks and the buntings wasn't sufficient offense, I ran the risk of further angering the purists by using the space thus saved for a few mammals. "The walk-in trade" rarely gets respectful treatment in bird-feeder books, even though some of these pedestrians play a major role in the activity around feeding stations. Their natural history is, to me, just as fascinating as that of the birds.

This book is more than a field guide; as well as bird lore, this augmented guide includes practical information on the "how-to" aspects of winter feeding. There are tips on things to do, and things not to do, that will help you maintain a feeding station with less effort, and enhance your viewing pleasure.

How to Use This Book

Understanding how science classifies and names birds will clarify the organization of Chapter 8, Knowing Your Winged Visitors, and help make the material throughout the book more understandable and enjoyable.

Taxonomy

The science of describing living things and figuring out their relationships is called taxonomy. Under its direction all life is arranged into two huge family trees, one for the plant kingdom, one for the animal. All relationships in each "tree" are determined on the basis of recognizable differences and similarities in structure, physiology, DNA analysis, and (sometimes) behavior.

All plants and animals have folk names, at least one for each language. The confusion inherent in this is typified by the name "gopher." Depending on where you live in North America, a "gopher" is either a ground squirrel, a turtle, or a snake.

To bring order out of such chaos, eighteenth-century Swedish botanist Karl von Linné devised a system of giving every living thing its own, exclusive name. Knowing that using a single contemporary language would doom his idea to death in nationalistic wrangling, Linné built his system on words from Latin and classical Greek, neither of which is any longer a national language. He not only avoided bruising cultural egos, he tapped into two rich vocabularies. Linné himself is now universally known by the Latinized version of his name, Linnaeus.

Thanks to him, all known plants and animals now have a scientific name of at least two words. Species (the second name) are ranked into genera (the first name), which in turn are arranged into families, these in turn into orders, and so on.

As well as providing distinctive labels, the names try to be descriptive. They don't always succeed. Neither are they free of the signs of human error, whimsy, favoritism, and sycophancy. According to Edward S. Gruson in his book *Words for Birds*, a "madly mixed bag of British admirals, U.S. Army doctors, fur traders, wives of friends of ornithologists (and at least one Italian paleobotanist) live on in the names of common American birds."

By custom, scientific names are printed in *italics*, with the generic part of the name capitalized.

Confusianus ignoramus

The out-of-place use of scientific names, or of any kind of excluding jargon, is both confusing and irritating to non-insiders. However, there is economy and clarity to be gained through the use of descriptive terms coined for a specific discipline where everyday words would be clumsy.

Because this is not a technical book, the use of terms not familiar to the average reader has been kept under control. Applied judiciously, they need not constitute a barrier to understanding if, either in context or with definitions, their meanings are clear.

It is no accident that the bird families in almost all field guides are presented in more or less the same order, beginning with what is generally regarded as the earliest evolved (loons), ending with the most recently evolved, usually finches. I arranged my species selection more or less as they appear in the major field guides, although these differ among themselves.

Obviously, everything is easier to find in a reference book with only sixty-one bird species. Another advantage is that there is plenty of room for information that can't possibly be included in a continental guide that must cover more than 650 species. To answer the need for quick reference under standard subheads, the species accounts are condensed and formally organized. But for background information, the family write-ups are informal and open-ended, each as long as is necessary to do justice to the natural history of the subject. My intention is to present the most interesting lore I could find, to the end that beyond mere identification my readers could look at each bird or mammal in a new light, with an enriched understanding of why each behaves the way it does, and how it survives and fits into the overall scheme of life.

This regional reference is intended to supplement the major North American field guides, one or more of which many readers will already have. To make cross-referencing with these field guides easier, in each species account I have listed the page numbers where that bird can be found in the most recent editions (as of 1994) of the four most popular field guides.

Regarding the capitalizing of the common names of species, I follow a widely used, but by no means universal, style. For the full, recognized common name, all words, except those following a hyphen, are capitalized; obsolete, regional, or partial names are not, and neither are the names of groups. Thus we have: "All our juncos, sometimes called 'snowbirds,' are members of the sparrow family and are variants of the Dark-eyed Junco." This also avoids confusion over name words and descriptive words: "Like the Blue Jay, Steller's Jay is also a blue jay."

Regarding some related terminology: "Birdwatcher" is part of the language and clearly applies to someone whose hobby is looking at birds, although the term is considered passé by serious aficionados who refer to themselves as "birders." The older term evokes a caricature—the ditsy spinster in pith helmet and tennis shoes. Birders include in their midst those highly motivated types referred to as "listers," "twitchers" if you're British. These people are preoccupied, often obsessively, with accurately identifying and adding to their lists as many species as they can find. In their eternal quest for rare birds, the listers are aided by a communications network called the Birding Hot Line. Thanks to this hot line, news of every rare bird spotted in North America flashes right around the continent within a matter of hours.

A final word on style: I greatly wish there were a single, universally accepted word to use in place of "people who feed birds" or "feeding-station operators." Trying to avoid tedious repetition of these cumbersome phrases is a constant vexation. Coined words, such as "feedor" or "feedist," didn't work. With no ideal terminology to fall back on, I decided to use "feeder" for the receptacle and "bird feeder" for the person, hoping that in context I could make the difference clear enough not to baffle my readers.

CHAPTER 1

Principles of Feeding Birds

At its basic level, feeding birds is blessedly uncomplicated. It can remain that way, and be easier in the long run, however, if you take stock before heading off to the shopping center of a late fall afternoon to fetch a bag of seeds. Depending upon where you live and with whom, and who your neighbors are, questions could arise to cloud your apparently innocent intentions.

What about the mice and rats that spilled seeds will attract? What about weed seeds from your feeders that will invade our flower beds? What about the noise of the birds? What about sanitation concerns, such as droppings and disease? Will we now have to put the cat in solitary confinement? What about the squirrels?

If you live in a small village, in a lakeside cottage, or on a farm or spacious acreage where you have only your own household to answer to, most of these queries are irrelevant. But on a street in a town or a suburb, these questions should be addressed honestly. There *have* been cases where bird lovers have brought the hostility of their neighbors, and civic wrath, down upon their heads by going overboard with their enthusiasms. Some advice on how to head off difficulties, and how to deal with them if they occur, is offered in Chapter 5, The Downside.

All considered, however, problems are the rare exceptions; millions of urbanites happily feed birds winter after winter without a single hitch in neighborly relations.

Why Feed Birds?

There is a healthy feeling of self-satisfaction to be had from feeding birds. It fulfills admirably that urge in all of us to be good Samaritans. It titillates our sense of curiosity and has in it the tingle of a modest adventure. What, if anything, will show up when I hang up a feeder?

Along with all those positive vibes, the happy giver gets a ringside seat at an ongoing natural wonder: winter survival. When you develop a knowing relationship with birds, you can't help but marvel how such tiny, fragile creatures are able at all to live through our cold and windswept winters. Not only do they survive, they bring to our yards their graceful beauty, color, and vitality in what would otherwise be a bleak, lifeless landscape.

There can be intellectual stimulation as well. Even the most casual of us will develop a keener appreciation for wildlife. And if we give our sense of curiosity at least half a chance, we will find ourselves learning more about these engaging creatures and how they fit into their environment. Feeding birds has, in fact, converted some of its unsuspecting beginners into lifelong students of nature.

Charity, entertainment, and intellectual growth acknowledged, there is as well a gut-level element of self-esteem involved. A forlorn, unattended feeder stands for the expectant beginner as a symbol of rejection, a minor one, to be sure, but perplexing. Doubts smolder as time passes: "Is there something wrong with my feeder? the seeds? Are the birds all over at the neighbors'? What are they doing better than I?" But let the first chickadee alight on that brand-new feeder, and a moment of triumph ignites and every doubt is forgotten. You've been accepted!

That feeling persists, with variations, for as long as you feed birds. Even those of us who consider ourselves hard-bitten and jaded develop a bit of an ego trip from having a yardful of all the northern finches, every nonmigratory regular in the book, a mob of quail, a visiting pheasant, and maybe a Sharp-shinned Hawk or a shrike that swoops in from time to time. The feeling of superiority is keenest if one's bird-feeding associates are not quite so well blessed. Even the highest-minded charity isn't immune to the temptations of one-upmanship.

Along with the pleasures of bird feeding, and the attendant birdwatching, there is always the exciting prospect of inadvertent fame. Amongst birds, essentially very conservative creatures that unfailingly follow instinctive imperatives, there are always a rare few that depart from ancestral patterns. Thus, strays from Europe, Asia, or Central America unexpectedly show up from time to time far beyond their normal haunts.

Depending on their rarity for a given region, when they show up they can instantly become the center of attention of birders from right across the continent. Alerted on the communication network called the "Birding Hot Line," birders rush to see the rarity and add it to their life lists (the total species of birds seen during the lister's lifetime) before it disappears. If the bird happens to be staying around someone's feeder, that person could become an instant celebrity of sorts.

This is a mixed blessing. Basking in the envy of a succession of callers and being written up in the press is heady stuff. But having people constantly phoning, being polite to a stream of unannounced visitors, and generally acting the good host to total strangers can be a bit wearing after a week or so.

The odds against becoming the host to a really sensational rarity exceed even those against winning a major lottery. However, there are locations where those odds improve. Birds on the move tend to navigate along major geographical features such as coasts, river valleys, and escarpments. For coasting birds, quiet bays, estuaries, peninsulas, and islands offer food and shelter. If you're lucky enough to live in such a location, keep an eye on your feeders, and in the back of your mind plan what you would do if the world started beating a path to your door.

Some guidance on this matter might be sought in the life of an Italian friar, Francis Bernardone, who lived from 1182 to 1226. As well as founding the Franciscan Order, St. Francis of Assisi is renowned for his love of wild birds and his mystical powers of attracting them; there are countless medieval paintings of "St. Francis and the Birds." His day is October 4, a fitting anniversary for a bird-feeders' patron saint, because it could serve as a reminder to us North-westerners that it is high time our feeding stations were readied for action.

You can actually have a little fun doing a pre-audit of your prospects, preferably on a summer's day long before the first chickadee has cracked a single sunflower seed. This assessment can proceed from the general to the specific, i.e., from zone to habitat to site.

Zone Assessment

It adds to your sense of anticipation if you know in advance the species resident in your ecological zone of the Pacific Northwest. This part of the world is a fascinating mosaic of geological and vegetative zones. From the coastal marshes and beaches, up the rain-soaked slopes of the Coast Range and the Cascades, into their rain shadows on the high, dry central plains and sagebrush steppes, to the towering peaks of the Rockies, this is a jigsaw puzzle of habitats.

A very few really adaptable mammals and birds can find a place in a variety of these, particularly since modern settlement has drastically altered almost all the landscape. But the more specialized species may be limited to one or two zones.

For many of these distinctive zones, the chore of assessing the bird populations has already been done and has been published in the form of a local checklist or even, in some cases, a full-fledged book. These references list all of the regional species and rate their frequency. The designating terms vary, but "abundant," "common," "uncommon," "rare," "occasional," "accidental," and "escapee" (a parakeet or tropical duck that has flown the coop) are the standbys. In some guides, the occurrence of each species is given for each season, or even for each month.

If no regional guide is available for your area, the information in the "Range" category in each species account in this book gives you an idea of whether that bird is likely to show up in your yard. Keep in mind that in mountainous terrain, climate and vegetation, and hence animal life, are markedly affected by altitude. A town on a valley floor and an alpine resort, though they may be in sight of each other, will have very different populations of birds.

Modern-day human impact almost invariably inflicts severe environmental shock. Clear-cut logging obliterates huge expanses of mature forest; its replacement is a totally different ecological mix. The transformation of dry bunchgrass prairie into irrigated fields is an economic miracle; the ecological costs are open to debate.

Habitat Assessment

Is your neighborhood within a quarter mile of a lake, a river, a marsh, or a tract of undeveloped woodland? In such places, unless compulsive civic tidiness, heavy recreational vehicle abuse, or overgrazing have denuded them, there should be ribbons or patches of good cover. Shoreside and/or floodland willow groves, scrubby gullies, and blocks of forest with an understory of shrubbery are good bird habitat. So is a large park with generous plantings of hedges and ornamental trees. The closer your house is to tangled tracts of the wild country that birds require, the better are your chances of attracting some of them to your yard.

Is your immediate neighborhood well blessed with tall trees, thick hedges, an occasional vacant lot, plenty of ornamental shrubbery? As subdivisions age, the trees get bigger, hedges and ornamentals expand. If you live on a circular bay where all the backyards, and perhaps a little park or playground, combine to provide a modest continuum of shrubby growth and reasonable tranquillity, your chances of getting some action are improved.

The less your neighborhood resembles any of the foregoing, the poorer are your chances of attracting winter birds. Prepare yourself for modest returns if you live in a spanking-new subdivision where every square foot of natural growth has been landscaped out of existence, where the neat ornamentals are barely out of their root-ball diapers and the boulevard trees are spindly adolescents still in braces. If the wildest habitat around is the convenience store in the mall, you may have to be content with a clientele of House Sparrows and starlings.

Site Assessment

If your review of your neighborhood is encouraging, and other bird feeders in the vicinity report good results, your own property has potential.

It helps if you can look at the place from a small bird's point of view on a January morning when it's well below zero and the equivalent temperature, thanks to a brisk northerly, is twenty below. The main thing you would want to do is find shelter from that nose-freezing wind as quickly as possible, and stay there. If there was a cafeteria in that sheltered spot, you would want a place to stand back and wait your turn, and a spot to sit down once you had picked up your tray.

The best windbreak on most lots is the house itself; in this latitude of prevailing westerlies, the best shelter is on the south or southeast side. An alcove formed by walls on the west and north is ideal. The waiting places, in the bird world, are simply trees or shrubs where they can perch, out of the worst of the wind, above the reach of cats. They might have to wait their turn in their own flock, as chickadees do, the "alpha" one first, the others in descending order of dominance. Or, they might have to bide their time while the big guys—Steller's Jays, Evening Grosbeaks, or a squirrel—have finished pigging out.

There are easy ways of augmenting the bird-friendly features of your yard. Putting up a temporary holdover zone of dead trees or branches, making a brush pile, "planting" a grove of discarded Christmas trees, or tacking up a plywood baffle to cut the wind are all Good Deeds we can perform. However, unless your yard is truly bleak, before rushing off to muster the raw materials it might be just as well to wait and let experience, i.e., the birds themselves, suggest specific, short-term local improvements.

For long-term modifications such as fences, hedges, and plantings, the Bibliography in the back of this book includes books that give yard plans and varieties of trees and shrubs that will attract birds.

There are people-friendly aspects to setting up your yard that bear keeping in mind. The naturalist club in your area may conduct an annual Christmas Bird Count (CBC), which requires them to survey a specified area as quickly and thoroughly as possible. Experienced bird feeders familiar with the CBC will try to locate feeders where those doing the count can see them from the road. For more on the CBC, see Chapter 7, Census-Taking.

In the event of your becoming the host to a truly rare bird, the local birders will immediately see to it that the event is heralded on the Birding Hot Line. Your yard could overnight become a destination for literally hundreds of intensely motivated listers. If you are a people-watcher, their antics could be a source of amusement.

However, zeal being what it is, there may be amongst the questers the kind of intrusive personality who, in the name of his mission (the obsessives do tend to be male), totally ignores your privacy, demands accountability if the bird is not waiting for him, and in general operates under a self-declared moratorium on common courtesy. At such times, having your feeder out front, where visitors can see it without having to tramp through your living room, could save you a lot of hassle.

The Ethics of Feeding

Serious, thoughtful bird feeders have always been aware that their hobby has ecological implications beyond what goes on in their own yards. In this environmentally sensitized world, those implications have from time to time become public issues. These have included concern about whether feeding promotes the spread of epidemics among birds, controversy about whether it encourages "nuisance" species like rats and crows, and questions about whether it is wise to "lure" birds out of their natural habitat and into suburban yards.

One can expect increasing challenges. Many species of birds are suffering alarming population declines. Even as this happens, however, bird feeding grows apace, rating second only to gardening as America's most popular outdoor pastime. It now supports chains of specialty shops that cater exclusively to it. Being so visibly commercial can of itself draw criticism, and the presence of so strong an element of vested interest can polarize and intensify debate.

Will offering food to birds tempt some of them to delay migration until it is too late to leave, thus luring them to an untimely death from cold and starvation?

This question may be prompted in part from the many instances where wild geese and ducks have forsaken migration in return for handouts. No matter how cold the weather, they stick around enjoying easy feed and protection from hunting and predators.

In reply I would point out that large waterfowl are one thing, small songbirds another. Canada Geese and mallards can afford to be casual about migration. Even without the incentive of free feed, many delay migration until after freezeup. Their large bodies and heavy layers of fat allow them ample reserve to migrate in midwinter if they have to. This is an option that small birds simply do not have.

A large proportion of our summer songbirds are insectivorous and have to migrate once cool weather eliminates their food source. These birds do not eat seeds and would not be tempted to stay if there was a feeder nailed to every tree.

Rare, solitary holdovers of confirmed migrants such as thrushes or warblers may have stayed behind because of some abnormal factor in either their behavior or physiology. An unfit bird may not have the vitality to join the hustle and commotion of large pre-migratory flocks and will simply "miss the boat" when the rest of its fellows abruptly vanish on some frosty, moonlit autumn night. Most of these unfortunates die. A few, lucky enough to find good shelter and a plentiful source of food, will survive to greet the reduced ranks of their returning relatives the following spring.

For those that *are* seed eaters, migration is not so pressing. Many simply move southward, keeping ahead of advancing winter, stopping whenever and wherever they find conditions acceptable. In some years great numbers of goldfinches and juncos, among others, elect to winter in parts of their breeding range well north of their usual winter haunts. Where they ultimately stop is a response to natural conditions of weather and food. It is a long-evolved, instinctive response that has nothing to do with the presence of feeders. Once committed to stay, however, they will flock to feeders, to the delight of everyone.

In the final analysis, as much as we like to think how important our feeding stations are, we influence only a small percentage of the total populations of even the hesitantly migratory species. It is a matter of record, however, that birds lucky enough to winter at feeders have much better survival prospects than those that do not. The male Anna's Hummingbird that has been visiting my feeders since early September isn't supposed to be anywhere near here in midwinter. The population center for his kind is somewhere in California, and the northern extremity of their range is the southerly tip of Vancouver Island, a couple of hundred miles south of where I live. I'm certain he didn't fly up here because he'd heard about my feeders, or that he was "lured" into risking winter here because of them. I *am* very sure that, without the sugar he sips at least a half dozen times a day, he would have been dead long ago. The fact that he is still zooming in, occasional snow and much rain notwithstanding, pleases me greatly, and troubles my conscience not a whit.

Another question is whether you are morally bound to keep at it once you have started feeding. If you stop, won't the birds that have come to rely on your food starve to death?

Definitely, yes! You *are* ethically obliged; qualifiers come later. Of late, however, some writers have been keen to dismiss this position as a quaint "folk myth." At the risk of falling out of step with a trend, I point out that birds wouldn't flock to our feeders unless it gave them a better chance of survival. This bit of common sense is supported by the finding of Margaret Clark Brittingham of the University of Wisconsin, who discovered that during severe winters the survival rate of Black-capped Chickadees with access to sunflower seeds was twice that of those that got all their food from natural sources.

Quite aside from ethical considerations, being consistent gets better results. You are less likely to attract and hold interesting birds with on-again, off-again feeding.

Ultimately, your decision as to whether you can stop feeding in midwinter with a clear conscience depends on circumstances of climate and location. In the severe winter weather that blesses much of North America, even the hardiest birds are tested to the ultimate. Hanging on from day to day on the slimmest margin between life and death, they don't need the added uncertainties of on-again, off-again feeding. If an "off" happens to coincide with a blizzard, an ice storm, or a spell of really deep cold, the stress of relocating to another feeder or switching back to natural food could be fatal.

The obligation to stick with it is particularly pressing if your feeder is the only one for some distance around, as at a rural homestead or a backcountry cottage. Here, you will probably attract a large number of birds a long way from their home territories and hence more critically dependent on you than those from close by. In this situation, in a region of harsh winters, you really do have a moral obligation to see to it that your feeders are kept supplied once you've started.

However, the farther south you are and the closer your bird-feeding neighbors are, the less binding is your obligation to be consistent. If you stop, but several close neighbors are still feeding, there is no problem. Whatever the situation, the withdrawal process will be easier on the birds if you do it during a mild spell well before you leave. This means you will have to watch your expectant birds come to empty feeders until they give up and go away. You can of course just continue to feed until you leave, and they will run out when you're gone. Avoiding the awful moment of total withdrawal, and the forlorn gaze of your birds, may be easier on you. But if your cop-out coincides with the worst blast of the winter, some of your trusting little dependents could be not only forlorn, but dead.

Aiding the Enemy?

There is an upwelling of concern amongst the birding constituency that by feeding birds in winter we unwittingly give aid to the "enemy." Who, or what, is the "enemy"? Well, to paraphrase Pogo's famous line, "One of 'em is us!"

We lure the birds in, then turn loose upon them our cats. We cut down old trees, we drain and fill in boggy spots, and "clean up" ditches and watercourses of untidy brush and weeds, thus depriving our songbirds of critical shelter and natural food. But squirrels, raccoons, skunks, rats, crows, ravens, and magpies have adapted to this tended habitat by substituting human-source food and shelter for the vanished natural forage and cover. To this band of versatile scrounges add the opossum, a prolific scourge aided in its conquest of the Pacific Northwest by hunters' clubs eager to broaden their sporting opportunities.

These backyard animals also prosper because their natural predators—bobcats, cougars, wolves, fishers, large snakes, most owls, and hawks—have either been totally exterminated or, if not, certainly not for a moment tolerated to the degree that we put up with Br'er Coon *et al.*

Between courses on our abundant food leftovers, all these animals turn to whatever vestiges of natural foods remain available, including, in season, songbird nests and fledglings.

Not only do we support nest predators in unnaturally high numbers, we spray, mow, and trim our yards and parks to a fare-thee-well. The result of this compulsive tidiness is an endlessly repeated pattern of close-cropped lawns, straight hedges, isolated ornamentals, and shade trees shorn of lower branches. Such closely tended cover provides nesting shelter of sorts for songbirds. But the security is largely illusory; the tightly ordered layouts are custom-designed for easy surveillance by nest predators. A brooding female may be able to hatch her eggs in the dense confines of a clipped juniper. But once she and her mate begin the busy to-and-fro demanded by nestling care, the jig's up to the first passing crow or patrolling house cat.

Just *how* vulnerable birds are in tended cover was outlined in an article, "Why American Songbirds Are Vanishing," by John Terborgh in the May 1992 issue of *Scientific American*. Terborgh drew in part on work by biologist David S. Wilcove of Princeton University. In a study ending in 1985, Wilcove stocked artificial nests with quail eggs and set them out in small, medium-sized, and large forest tracts in both rural and suburban settings in the eastern United States where raccoons and opossums abound. Half the nests were placed on the ground, half at eye level. He distributed the same number of nests in a section of undisturbed forest in the Great Smoky Mountains National Park.

Predation ranged from slightly under 25 percent for larger rural woodlots to close to 100 percent in some of the small plots, both rural and suburban. In the Smokies only one nest in fifty—2 percent—was raided.

The questions must be asked: "What can we do to prevent our suburbs and acreages from being breeding 'black holes' from which few songbird young ever emerge? Do our feeders play a part in luring birds into these reproductive booby traps?"

Before you rush out to tear down your bird feeders, please note that Wilcove's disturbing statistics would be but little changed if there were no feeders at all in either suburbia or semi-rural acreage. This is because most of us feed birds in winter. In summer most of these winter birds disperse to rural or wilderness breeding grounds. Those songbirds that do stick around town in summer, whether migrants or year-round residents, distribute themselves on the basis of available nesting territories, not on the presence of feeders. Largely insectivorous in summer, they rely on their territories to provide sufficient natural food.

Most urban predators, on the other hand, are opportunistic food generalists that do not have to rely solely on the forage within their territories. Crows, ravens, magpies, and starlings rove widely for food, and can thus take advantage of sources far removed from their nests. As already noted, whilst roving they will of course keep an eye out for songbird nests and fledglings.

Our concern should therefore focus on what we can do to improve the dismal nesting prospects offered by the tended habitat we share in summer with our songbirds.

The major factor in limiting the numbers of backyard predators is garbage and how it is managed at both the civic and private levels. Wildlife biologists discovered long ago that urbanized predators, both birds and mammals, enjoy a higher standard of living than their backwoods brethren. City-bred raccoons, skunks, opossums, and squirrels not only thrive in artificially high populations, they grow faster, get bigger, and have a higher birth rate. Therefore, you can do much for our songbirds by making sure your garbage cans are tightly lidded and cannot be tipped over. Don't leave pet food on the back step or patio where crows can feed on it by day, wild mammals by night.

Cut down on free nesting and denning shelter by making sure your buildings are claw-, beak-, and tooth-proof. Get rid of scrap piles and other ground-level refuges. If you compost, do it in a vermin-proof bin. You can add a positive note by providing nest boxes for songbirds, built to specifications that exclude the larger predators.

Feeders, unlike loose garbage, afford a means of influencing who gets access to the goodies and who doesn't, especially when it comes to separating the birds from the mammals. Methods outlined in Chapter 3, Feeders and Shelters, and in Chapter 5, The Downside, tell how this can be done. You can also make your yard more bird-friendly and less predator-friendly in all seasons by planting appropriate shrubs and trees. Check the Bibliography in the back of this book for references on how to make your yard more inviting and safer for birds.

Nest Parasites

There is nothing sinister in the actions or appearance of a Brown-headed Cowbird; the sight of it scurrying about the heads and feet of grazing cattle and sitting companionably on their backs is the very stuff of rustic innocence. It looks equally unthreatening amongst the pink flamingos on a suburban lawn, undistinguished in appearance, retiring of manner, reticent as a guest at the feeder. But this unassuming mien is in fact the quintessential cover; the forgettable public persona masks a covert life of deception, subversion, and, at times, ghoulish infanticide. We're talking nest parasitism.

Nest parasites are those that have evolved ways of tricking other birds into fostering their young. All the female does is mate and then lay her eggs in somebody else's crib. The success of the scam relies, of course, on the duped birds' (customarily, but somehow inappropriately, called the "hosts,") accepting the foster egg and incubating it along with their own.

My most memorable confrontation with cowbird parasitism was at our cabin in the country. One spring weekend I discovered that the resident pair of Eastern Phoebes had built their nest under the roof overhang that shelters the front step. The cup of mud and feathers was on a rafter right over the door. I was flattered by their gesture of trust, their previous sites having been at more removed locations.

When I came back the next weekend there were four naked baby phoebes sprawled dead on the landing below the nest. In their place above was an oversized cowbird nestling, already well covered in budding feathers.

Taken with an irrational urge for retribution, I reached up and grabbed it by one wing, whereupon it clutched the nest and began squawking loudly. This brought the phoebes, snapping their bills around my ears in such agitation that I let go and left them to finish rearing their murderous fosterling.

I readily admit that in dealing with this nestling I indulged my emotional biases, imputing human motives to this entirely blameless bird. Much as we might pity the victims of such a lethal fosterling, much as we might decry its impact on more lovable species, it is simply playing the role in which the drama of survival long ago cast it.

Or is it? Humankind has profoundly altered the face of the land, putting some native songbirds out of business altogether, putting others at critical disadvantage. Compounding the misfortune, these same alterations have created favorable habitat for the cowbird.

Just how minimal an amount of habitat alteration it takes to tip the ecological scale in favor of the cowbird is found in northern Ontario, far away from historic cowbird habitat. The *Atlas of the Breeding Birds of Ontario* notes that in otherwise cowbird-free Algonquin Park, breeding-bird surveys disclosed a line of sightings running right through it. It turns out that this line is Highway 60, a single narrow strip through uninhabited backcountry! One can ponder whether logging roads in our Northwest forests open up similar avenues of infiltration.

There are two cowbirds in North America north of the Mexican border. The Bronzed Cowbird occurs in the southern parts of the states bordering Mexico, but the Brown-headed Cowbird ranges throughout the settled parts of the continent. Once strictly a denizen of the plains, it followed European settlement to occupy a vastly expanded breeding range, including the Pacific Northwest.

When the cowbird moves into virgin territory, it meets birds that have not evolved with it and that have therefore no defenses whatever against it. Therefore, does our presence give the intruding cowbird a really lethal unnatural advantage over its victims? If so, what, if anything, can we do about it?

Habitat loss has struck our songbirds a double blow in recent times. As well as massive loss of habitat in their northern nesting grounds, they have suffered huge losses in their tropical rain-forest wintering grounds. However, the drop in their populations cannot be adequately explained solely by habitat destruction. Referring again to the *Scientific American* article, there is another "pathology" at work. A credible body of opinion is accumulating that fingers the cowbird as the critical factor.

The dilemma for us bird feeders is that, in its wintering range, which includes part of the Pacific Northwest, the cowbird comes readily to our feeding stations. Thus, the birds we help through the winter may be the agent for wiping out clutches of songbirds around our yards the following summer. But how do you feed selectively to exclude these critters? They cheerfully eat most seeds. You cannot bar them from feeders on the basis of size, as you can, for example, crows or pigeons.

The cowbird is a further dilemma for me because I am highly mistrustful of the time-worn woodlore that in the past has made "good guys" and "bad guys" out of animals on grounds that often amounted to nothing more than blind prejudice or the selfish interests of human predators. I examine this problem in Chapter 8, Knowing Your Winged Visitors, in the discussion on the crow family. But because we are no longer dealing with a "natural" world, there is room, indeed at times a need, to attempt to reestablish some degree of balance between invasive species (including ourselves) and those they are crowding out.

Our obligation is to make such manipulations as well informed and as free of irrational emotion as we know how. To this end, I have included a discussion of the natural history of the cowbird in the section on cowbirds and other blackbirds in Chapter 8.

Meanwhile, what is one to do? My own answer is nest surveillance around my own yard in spring and early summer. Any that I locate I simply check for cowbird eggs and, on finding one, throw it out. Checking is made quicker and easier with a mirror mounted on a long, light pole to hold over high-up nests.

CHAPTER 2

Seeds and Feeds

Reduced to the fundamentals, the basics of bird feeding are: 1) the feed and 2) something to serve it on. Both have been, and will continue to be, the subjects of endless debate in birding circles, and a reliable source of profits for feed outlets and nature shops.

To get started, most of us simply clump into the grocery or hardware store and pick up a bag of "Wild Bird Seed." But before doing that, it is a good idea to find out what other local feeders are using, how much feed they go through in a winter, where they get it, and the cost. Good sources of information are naturalist clubs, the nature columnist in the local paper, and the local feed store. In the last few years, nature shops that specialize in bird-feeding supplies have been springing up all over. These are a great source of advice, books, feeds, feeders, and everything you and your birds could possibly need, and more.

Another obvious source of information is your nearest nature club. See Appendix 3, Naturalist Organizations, at the back of this book.

The "KISS" Principle

Although I am taken up with the idea and pleasures of feeding birds, there are other things in my life that have a justifiable claim on my time. Therefore, I have avoided getting too fussy about feeds, operating on the "KISS" principle: "Keep It Simple, Stupid." To those who take pleasure in melting suet twice, in cooking and mixing bird cakes, in rolling balls of suet and peanut butter in cornmeal and chopped almonds, I say, "Go for it!"

Therefore, to those wishing to "go for it," a few tantalizing bird recipes are provided in Appendix 1, Recipes for the Gourmet. One of these is "bird-stone," a classic that will test the greatness of those who really get off on unusual mixtures. It is attributed to one Baron von Berlepsch.

What to Feed?

The most primitive form of feeding is found in the householder who tosses a handful or two of bread crumbs out the back door and lets the sparrows pick them off the snow. Offering bread crumbs is sometimes a very good way of initially baiting birds in, because the white fragments of bread are eye-catching. And although white bread is nutritionally impoverished, some winter birds do enjoy it, and there is usually no problem later in switching to seeds.

Baits and switches notwithstanding, the very best attractant to a feeder is a bird already busy at it. Chickadees, nuthatches, creepers, and Downy Woodpeckers commonly form loose foraging flocks. When one of these discovers your feeder, the others are quick to get in on the action. Their activity, in turn, will attract other foragers like Steller's Jays and the finches. How long they stay with you, and in what numbers, depends on the attractiveness of the setting and the quality and quantity of the feed.

Exactly what you feed may depend on what is available locally at a reasonable price. "Reasonable" is a relative term; prices for various seeds vary greatly between locations and from one season to another. The key is to shop around. Buying name-brand seed in five-pound plastic bags at the grocery store is the costliest way to buy. Purchasing directly from a grower is usually the cheapest. Good prices can usually be had if you buy fifty-pound sacks at seed and feed plants and farm feed stores. I have become a habitual nature/bird-shop hangabout ever since these specialty stores appeared on the scene. They are tough on my credit card, but I tell myself I'm just keeping professionally up-to-date, that what I'm doing is more in the nature of research than self-indulgence. Even "I Love Birds" sweatshirts have to be test-driven. I invariably walk out with an armload of goodies I never intended to buy while a friendly clerk puts a couple more bags of seeds into the hatchback.

If you have a choice of seeds, there are good reasons for making deliberate selections. Food preferences vary among species, so manipulating the kinds of feeds and where you offer them enables you, within limits, to control where various species will congregate around your yard. To help you with this, the food preferences of each bird are listed in the species accounts in Chapter 8, Knowing Your Winged Visitors.

Bird feeders are sometimes perplexed to discover that within species, preferences often vary markedly from region to region; what is a favorite in one locale may be totally ignored in another. Like young children, most seed-eating birds are very conservative in their food choices and refuse to try anything unfamiliar. Don't blame this on juvenile intransigence, but on the fact that they simply don't recognize strange seeds as food.

Authors are prone to the temptation to play the sage and solemnly hand down pronouncements as if from The Mount. But almost certainly, if you begin to talk about animals in terms of absolutes, they will immediately do something to make a fool of you in the eyes of your readers.

The nutritional worthiness of any given feed is not something to worry about that much. Birds balance their diet themselves by supplementing your feed with a continuing menu of their natural foods. I routinely see chickadees interrupt a session of to-and-fro at my feeders to search nearby shrubs, presumably hunting for insect eggs or dormants.

SEEDS AND GRAINS

Sterilizing Seeds

Winter's innocent diversion can turn into summer's aggravation if spilled seeds fall on gardens and flower borders and do what they are designed to do: sprout. Lawns are no problem as a rule; the mower looks after any errant shoots. But prepared, fertile soil can be a different matter. Does this mean you have to choose between feeding birds and gardening? Does it mean you have to put the feeders where you don't really want them because the best place is the middle of the garden?

Prevention, as always, is the best alternative. Shop for, or build, feeders that minimize spillage. Small, slippery seeds, like millet, which is quick to germinate, easily get lost in snow or duff. The larger seeds, like sunflowers, which are slower to sprout, stay visible longer. Finches, jays, sparrows, starlings, and juncos are very happy foraging on the ground and will do a good job of gleaning the fallout. Mice and chipmunks perform a similar service. You can help them by raking away leaves and duff from beneath your feeders in the fall. And during winter, pack down each fresh layer of snow so that spilled seeds don't get mixed in with it.

To be really sure there is going to be no problem, heat-sterilize your seeds. Put them a couple of inches deep in a roasting pan or a foil tray and bake it thirty minutes in the oven at just over 220° Fahrenheit. The idea is to heat the seeds, not roast them, so sniff and peek at the first batch to get the right timing and temperature for your particular oven. The microwave will do the same job in a matter of moments, depending on the amount of seed you treat and the type of oven you have.

You can do a germination test by putting a few seeds between layers of damp paper toweling in the bottom of a plastic container. Put the lid on and check in a few days' time. If a week passes by with no sprouting, you have solved the problem. As a double-check, set up a simultaneous "control" test with untreated seeds.

The Noble Sunflower Seed

I feel downright smug about feeding sunflower seeds to my birds (and squirrels). In that little black package is the closest to a universal feed that is commonly available. With more than 40 percent oil content, plus a wholesome component of carbohydrate, protein, and minerals, they are richly nutritious. Their excellent palatability is supported not only by scientific findings, but by users of mixed seed. They frequently complain that much of it is wasted by birds flicking through it to pick out the sunflowers, like party guests who eat all the cashews and filberts from the mixed nuts and leave the peanuts in the bowl.

Cultivated sunflower seeds come in several varieties, all of them arising from a Eurasian species, *Helianthus annuus*. The familiar ones we munch are referred to in the grain and processing trades as "confectionary" sunflower seeds. Whole seeds are

Large, striped "confectionary" sunflower seeds

large—up to ⅝ inch long—and striped lengthwise in buff and dusty black. Roasted, salted or unsalted, they are sold as a confection everywhere, the infamous "spits" so hated by pool hall, bowling alley, and arcade operators across the land. In a quite different role, hulled, roasted, or raw, with or without salt, they are standard items in the bulk bins of organic food shops.

Confectionary seeds are universally relished at feeders, and until 1975 were the unchallenged choice of those who fed sunflower seed. But their size and thick hulls made husking awkward for birds smaller than Purple Finches, especially if they got damp and turned leathery. Hulled or cracked, they are, of course, supremely palatable but, even at wholesale prices, expensive as bird feed.

In 1975 a particularly heavy crop of the small, black oilseed sunflower pushed it onto the bird-feed market as a much cheaper substitute for the confectionary seeds, and it quickly became the big seller. It was helped by the widely publicized findings of Dr. Aelred D. Geis of the U.S. Fish and Wildlife Service, who scientifically assessed the food preferences of wild birds that visit feeders.

Among other things, Dr. Geis discovered that all birds tested, except Tufted Titmice, Common Grackles, and Blue Jays, selected oilseeds over confectionary when given a choice between the two. It is now accepted that oilseed sunflowers are eaten readily by nearly fifty species of birds, and are the first choice of many.

Oilseeds are about half the size of the confectionary seeds and their much thinner hulls make them manageable by birds right down to siskin size. They are least expensive when bought in bulk from feed stores or seed plants, if you have one close at hand. It pays to shop around; in a busy winter, my birds and squirrels will go through more than 500 pounds.

Not quite so economical are the sunflower "hearts" (or "harts") that are advertised for sale by some seed suppliers. Unlike peanut hearts, which are the germs of peanut seeds, sunflower "harts" are the damaged and undersized kernels culled during the preparation of confectionary sunflowers for human consumption. Hulls are discarded, but there is a small percentage of chaff and milling debris mixed in.

Small, black "oilseed" sunflower seeds

Not that the birds care. As an experiment I obtained

*Whole sunflower seed head and
Evening Grosbeak*

a few kilos of hulled and cracked oil-seeds, with hulls still in the mixture, from a processing plant and tried them on my birds. My window feeder is separated down the middle by a low divider. I put crushed seeds on one half, whole on the other. That winter, siskins were abundant, and they virtually ignored the whole seeds in favor of the cracked. This is understandable; siskins are one of the smallest feeder birds, with small, lightly constructed bills. I would, however, expect all small to midsized birds to favor the easier pickings offered by cracked seeds.

This preference may create a seed wastage problem. In any sack of seeds there are always a few hulled seeds. Once the birds catch on that there are "freebies" hidden amongst the whole seeds, they will dig for them, flipping everything else aside. On a table or shelf feeder this is no problem, but in a tube or bin feeder it means an incredible waste; for every hulled seed the birds find, they dump several hundred others onto the ground.

One winter a devilishly persistent Hairy Woodpecker drove me to the verge of pici-cide. He would land on the shelf of one of the pole feeders, brace himself, and go to work as if possessed, sending a steady shower of sunflower seeds flying with rapid flicks of his bill. He would keep at it for minutes at a time, much to the benefit and convenience of the squirrels, rabbits, and mice on the ground below, and the deer that came in after dark to lick up the fallout. It took me a long time to realize that the lazy opportunist was looking for ready-husked seeds.

Since then I have run into the same problem with siskins at my tube feeders. The only way I can solve the problem is to offer either cracked or hulled sunflower seeds. I have not heard of this problem with other small species, but would not be surprised if it occurred with them also.

Sunflower "harts" would be another answer. Anyone fortunate enough to live within reach of a processing plant has the best chance of getting this premium feed at a reasonable price. Failing this, you might have seeds custom-ground, or do it yourself. I know of one ingenious bird feeder who cracks sunflower seeds with his power mower. He sets a couple of two-by-fours parallel on the concrete floor of his garage, spaced just wide enough to take the mower. Then he strews the seeds between them and "mows" them up into the grass catcher.

An advantage of hulled and cleaned (no hulls) seed, aside from waste control, is that there is no pile of husks under the feeder to contend with in spring. A disadvantage is that cracked sunflower seeds "weep" oil—the finer the crush, the faster the loss. That oil very quickly turns rancid in mild weather. Cracked seeds, with the hulls left in the mixture, might keep a little better, because the husks would tend to absorb the oil. With or without the hulls, however, broken sunflower seeds should not be stored in a hot place over the summer. If you have the space, keep them in the freezer.

Throwing a few bags of seeds into the back of the car or camper the next time you are in North Dakota or some other sunflower-growing area is the most economical source. However, seeds right out of the combine often contain a high percentage of debris—broken stems, small chunks of the heads, and lots of chaff. This will clog up the ports of small feeders and create a layer of litter at the bottom of them that has to be frequently cleaned out.

Some authors claim, by the way, that sunflower husks are plant growth inhibitors. I find that the grass under my feeders thrives just fine whether I rake up or not.

Mixed Seed

This is variously marketed as "Wild Bird Seed," "Wild Bird Mix," "Songbird Mix," and so on. Compositions vary, but millet (red and/or white) usually dominates, with cracked cereal grain (wheat, oats, barley), cracked corn, milo (sorghum), canary seed, and black sunflowers added in differing ratios. Finch mixes are generally limited to the smaller whole seeds: millet, canary, and niger.

There are no regulations about any of these; seed houses and retailers mix their own, and they may or may not declare the contents, in percentages by weight, on the package. Buying the components separately and mixing them yourself is the only way of being absolutely sure of what you are scooping into your feeders. Mixes with sunflower seeds can be very wasteful because birds flip away other seeds in search of them.

Acceptable bird fodder can be dished out in the form of "screenings," available if you happen to live near a feed manufacturer or seed cleaning plant. This is the weed seeds, damaged and undersized grain kernels, dust, and other debris winnowed out of grain when it is cleaned. It is usually very cheap, but you take your chances on what it contains. Not that the birds mind; weed seeds are part of the regular diet of many of our winter species, and may contain nutritional elements not found in cultivated seed. But many of the seeds are lightweight and blow far and wide in the winter wind, sowing the possibility of a bumper crop of objectionable weeds and neighborhood resentment. As already noted, you can easily solve this problem at home by sterilizing your seeds.

Millets

Common or proso millet, *Panicum miliaceum*, comes in white or red, and is the major constituent in commercial wild bird mixes. It is grown as human food in Asia and Europe, and as poultry and livestock feed here. Other varieties, more expensive than proso, include golden German, gold, and Siberian, which are marketed more to the cage bird trade than to wild bird feeders. All millet seeds are small, round, fairly thin-hulled; in proso, the white variety is slightly favored over the red in selection tests. House Sparrows love millet, and it is acceptable to most finches, after the sunflowers are all gone.

Canary Seed

This is a European grass, *Phalaris canariensis*, now cultivated in America as a specialty crop. The seeds are flat, small, spindle-shaped, and gray-buff with a polished, slippery coat, like flax. Free-flowing, it is excellent for tube feeders especially suited to smaller birds. Thus, while a feeding frenzy of House Finches or Evening Grosbeaks is devouring commoner fare by the pound at the main tray, the goldfinches and siskins will be extracting the high-priced canary seeds one at a time from the dainty little ports in the tube feeder. Or so the theory goes.

Grains—Hen and Chick Scratch

Oats, barley, rye, and feed wheat, particularly if you get them in bulk from a grower or processor, can be very cheap bird feed. Whole, they are acceptable to pheasants, quail, pigeons, Mourning Doves, crows, starlings, rodents of all kinds, and deer. Cracked or crushed, they are acceptable to the foregoing, with added appeal to blackbirds, starlings, House Sparrows, several species of native sparrows, and finches and buntings if no sunflowers or millet are offered.

"Hen scratch" is a mixture of cracked corn and whole grains used as a feed supplement for poultry. "Chick scratch," the "baby food" version of hen scratch, is usually a mix of cracked wheat and crushed corn. Both are readily obtainable at feed stores. Hen or chick scratch is great stuff to scatter on the ground for pheasants, quail, and pigeons. But its limited appeal to most songbirds makes it most useful as cheap lure fodder for uninvited guests. It can be scattered on the ground, away from the feeders, to divert crows, starlings, and House Sparrows.

It is also useful if you find yourself host to some heavy eaters. For example, hard winters may drive deer into yards to browse on ornamentals or paw into compost heaps. They quickly learn to rear up to reach elevated bird feeders, and will bash at them with their front hooves to liberate more food. Hunger overcomes fear; frightened off, they return when vigilance lapses. Whether you are moved by sympathy or self-preservation to feed them, you will find that once you begin, the word spreads and others arrive. Shoveling bird seed at them can get very expensive. Some state game management agencies, and occasional sportsmen's clubs, supply free alfalfa pellet deer chow to people willing to dispense it. Otherwise, the cheapest whole grain you can get, or alfalfa hay, is the best alternative.

There are other hearty eaters you might wish, or be forced, to cater to. These include porcupines and rabbits or hares, in which case a protective collar of wire or sheet metal around the bottoms of your favorite trees and shrubs is a wise precaution, even as you lay on the oats. In fall and early spring, raccoons can become prime nuisances, cleaning you out of sunflower seeds and suet in one raid. Improved security measures for these goodies, combined with a diversionary offering of grain, could be the answer.

Canola (Rapeseed)

Recently in Canada varieties of rapeseed were developed that process more easily into edible oil. To distinguish these new varieties, and at the same time dispense with an unattractive name, they were given the name "canola" (Canadian oil).

All the books say that nothing, except partridges scratching for it in a field, will eat it. Bird-feeding friends of long experience have hooted at the idea of offering birds canola.

The little black seeds of *Brassica napus* look as if they *should* be good bird feed; they are rich in oil and otherwise nutritious. But in the Pacific Northwest, as elsewhere, black oilseed sunflower has become the most-used feed. Thus, many birds are accustomed to sunflowers, have never seen canola, and, offered the two together, ignore it. This dismal showing has been reflected in various controlled tests, to the end that most of the current books on feeding birds dismiss what they still refer to as rapeseed as a feed accepted only by pheasants, quail, and pigeons.

This may be about to change. Bird feeders, myself included, who have persisted in offering canola have discovered that even finicky, sunflower-habituated species will switch. Redpolls at my own feeders in Manitoba seem the most willing to give it a try and, once familiar with it, will feed on it even when the alternative is sunflowers. Here and there in the Pacific Northwest, I find feed stores where canola is a steady seller. Who can argue with that? It's all in what the birds learn to like.

The major reason for this transition may be that rapeseed itself has changed. The level of bitter-tasting erucic acid in the old varieties of rape required extra refining to make the oil palatable for human use. Perhaps the milder-flavored canola is also more palatable to the birds.

Corn

Zea mays can be offered on the dry cob, as whole kernels, or cracked and ground to various consistencies. Whole, it is attractive to birds such as grouse, pheasants, crows, and pigeons, and it is reportedly acceptable to Steller's Jays and grackles. Cracked, it is much more widely accepted by the smaller species, including blackbirds, starlings, and House Sparrows. It is easily obtainable throughout the Pacific Northwest.

However, in a damp climate, cracked corn cakes up and spoils quickly. Birds feeding on any musty grains inhale the spores of *Aspergillis* mold and contract aspergillosis, a lethal avian respiratory disease. An alternate, less risky use of crushed or cracked corn is as an addition to suet and/or peanut butter to make them more palatable.

Corn is also the grain most prone in storage to heavy insect infestations. There is nothing the matter with a bag of weevily corn from the birds' point of view; the grubs are a tasty, high-protein supplement. But unfortunately a wormy bag of feed has the same market appeal as a wormy apple.

Milo (Sorghum)

Sorghum vulgare originated in Africa and is a major crop in the United States for both fodder and grain for livestock. Two to three times the size of millet, the round, reddish seeds are tough-coated and can be handled readily by pigeons, grouse, and partridge. Otherwise it isn't popular with the usual feeder clientele, and is regarded by many bird feeders as a filler. In times when millet or other palatable seeds are high-priced, the proportion of sorghum in commercial mixes goes up. Watch for the telltale reddish hue to the mix; if it isn't small red proso millet seeds, and you're not a milo enthusiast, skip it.

Peanuts

It would be surprising indeed if peanuts were not high on the palatability list of birds and mammals, because we humans relish them so. *Arachis hypogaea* are tasty, rich, and, as bird feed, expensive.

When you split a peanut, one half has a little knuckle on one end. This is discarded during the manufacture of peanut butter and sold as "peanut hearts." One finds them advertised in bird magazines and in bins in pet and nature shops. At one time they were readily available for bird feed, even at reasonable prices. But now high cost relegates them to use in pinch-penny feeders for small species, as a treat, or added to mixed concoctions.

Peanuts

Nowadays, most of us buy a few in the shell, string them on a wire or cord, and hang them where the jays and chickadees can get at them. Once they have discovered what they are, and if the squirrels don't get there first, it's a diversion to watch the antics of the birds trying to shell them out.

Safflower

Safflowers are an agricultural oilseed. As bird feed, they are in some locales referred to as "cardinal bait," in spite of the fact that cardinals subjected to controlled choice tests preferred sunflowers three to one. *Carthamus tinctorius* is also accepted by pigeons, House and Purple Finches, Evening Grosbeaks, and House Sparrows. Some station operators consider it an advantage that it is not readily eaten by Gray Squirrels.

Niger or "Thistle"

Guizotia abyssinica is a small tropical African sunflower called either "niger" or "thistle seed," although it appears on some wholesalers' lists as "inga." It is not related to our roadside thistles, although these produce seeds in abundance that are very important to small birds, notably goldfinches.

Niger is a small, black seed that has long been a mainstay of cage birds, and is a highly desirable item with the smaller finches. Niger is imported from Africa, which helps explain the price; it is usually considered too expensive to be served from large, generous hopper feeders or on tables. Most people use tube feeders; some designs are even called "thistle" feeders. You can also purchase a "thistle bag" with mesh tight enough to hold the seeds but large enough to permit their being pulled through by small, probing bills. Being an unrepentant sunflower advocate, I have never felt the need to own a thistle bag, but read they don't always work and can be leaky and wasteful.

FEEDS

If reasonably priced seeds are available to you without too much bother and you are happy with the birds they attract, don't worry about extras. Birds happily live, day after day, week after week, on what humans would consider a deadly boring and deficient diet. It probably is not as monotonous as their fixation on one type of seed would appear. Between sessions at your feeders, birds forage for their natural foods, which compensates for deficiencies in their one-item feeder menu.

Extra feeds, novelty items, and treats are useful for expanding your clientele to include a greater variety of species. I supplement my sunflower seeds (no reflection on them), with suet, partly because it may provide a critical extra boost of energy during especially cold periods, and partly because it is especially tempting to nuthatches and jays, and the main item for woodpeckers, including the magnificent Pileated. It may also draw in a normally feeder-shy bird such as the creepers.

In suburbia, bird-feeding neighbors often get into competitive "power feeding" to attract the most birds. This demands that the contenders lay on as many tempting goodies as they can buy or invent, and dish them up in a dazzling array of dispensers. This is a usually harmless rivalry in which the real beneficiaries are the birds and the local bird feed retailers.

Peanut Butter

A jar of peanut butter that has been too long at the back of the fridge is my only source of it for feed or bait. Otherwise, I find it too expensive, especially when the squirrels catch on. However, many bird feeders look for bargains and buy it for their birds. It is rich nourishment, and can be handled like suet, smeared into open pine cones and holes in suet logs.

Some writers claim that it can be dangerous because it may clog up birds' mouths and throats and suffocate them. I doubt very much if a healthy bird would have much of a problem getting peanut butter "off the woof of its mouf." It *is* gooey, and accumulates around the base of the bill as the bird feeds, which may reinforce the "choking" myth.

A much more likely problem is that the oil might in time saturate the facial feathers and cause acute irritation and loss of the feathers. You can cut the gooeyness of peanut butter by mixing it with softened suet or cooking grease. Adding corn meal, oatmeal, or flour will absorb the oiliness.

Suet

Suet is the fat deposited around the kidneys and loin in the body cavity of cattle and sheep. It comes from the carcass as rounded white globs held together with light sheets of clear connective tissue. It doesn't freeze solid, so birds can feed on it without too much effort even at very low temperatures.

Many people have difficulty getting suet; it is usually trimmed off before it gets to the local meat counters. If they carry it at all, it is ground up and prepackaged for use in cooking, and is extremely expensive for bird feed. Many feed, pet food, and nature shops sell it in one form or another. If the local butcher can't (or won't) get you any, and there is no specialty bird shop within reach, try to find an abattoir or packing house, and phone them. The price is usually very reasonable, and you can get all you need for the winter in one trip. It is a good idea to take your own containers.

Suet can be put out "as is." Pure, raw suet won't rot, although it will get rancid and very stale-smelling in warm weather. Any pieces of meat in the suet will rot, so it is a good idea to pull the globs apart, while everything is still fresh, and trim them out. Dispensing it is simple: Plastic mesh onion bags, wire screen baskets, or similar dispensers give birds something to cling to while pecking through for small bits, but prevent their carting everything off wholesale.

"Suet logs" are made by boring holes into a stick of firewood with a half- or three-quarter-inch drill bit, filling them with suet, and hanging the stick up by one end. Making suet logs is a time-honored way of giving youngsters, and their grandfathers, a way of occupying themselves constructively and, for the most part, harmlessly.

Some writers worry that birds' feet, eyes, or tongues will stick to the frozen

Pouring melted suet on a branch and letting it harden is a "feeder" for birds such as this chickadee. (Note: This could result in harm to the tree when birds and other animals dig into cracks in the bark after the last remnants; consider wrapping the branch with sheet metal first, or selecting a dead branch without bark.)

metal of wire suet baskets. Having in childhood stuck my own tongue to the pump handle, I can sympathize. But I know of no direct account of this having happened to birds; their feet are dry, and their reflexes so quick I doubt very much if their eyes or tongues are at hazard. A panicked bird, or one that is ill, might be vulnerable. If it worries you, buy liquid latex and coat the wire or metal parts of your suet baskets. Liquid latex is pricey.

If you are not sufficiently fulfilled by hanging raw suet out in an onion bag, it can be refined by "rendering" (melting) it. Chop it into small pieces first. Rendering should be done with care, because hot fat inflicts a severe burn if splattered on skin, and can burst into a very stubborn fire if mishandled. A double boiler is safe, but takes forever. A slow fry is my way, gently pressing the chunks to get all the oil out as the meltdown proceeds. Fished out, the crunchy brown "cracklings" are themselves a tasty bird treat. I just scatter a few on the feeder among the seeds every now and then, breaking them up so the jays can't immediately cart everything off in big chunks.

The oil is poured into molds for cooling. These can be any container of convenient shape and size, preferably of destructible material. Used aluminum foil bowls, waxed paper cups, melon shells, and grapefruit rinds have all been pressed into service. For variety, peanut butter, corn meal, or dried fruit can be added and stirred in as the mixture cools.

There are two advantages to rendering. One is that if suet is to be fed in warm weather, melting it down, letting it harden, and remelting it will make it harder when it's cooled the second time. The other is that liquefying the suet makes it easy to fish out nonfat fragments that would rot quickly at warm temperatures. For any bits that you miss, the heat of rendering has a sterilizing effect that slows down decay.

Suet will continue to be eaten by some species well after the arrival of warm weather. I suggest withdrawing it once spring has truly set in. This high-energy feed becomes less crucial in warm weather because natural foods like insects become available then.

Suet and seeds are best not mixed together. Grease-soaked seed hulls are harder to husk. Also, birds not interested in suet will dig into it looking for seeds, with the increased likelihood of their getting their facial and breast feathers saturated with grease, particularly if the mix is left out as spring weather warms. Softened and rancid, it more readily saturates facial feathers and may cause infected follicles and feather loss around the beak and eyes.

Not long ago I was solemnly assured by a butcher that suet should *not* be fed to birds at all because "the fat plugs their nostrils and they fly away and suffocate!" Aside from the fact that birds can breathe through their mouths as easily as we can, they can also snort or sneeze blockages out of their nostrils. This is more of the silly alarmism that "experts" let loose into popular lore, and which a little common sense easily exposes as the nonsense it is.

Suet is, of course, attractive to scavengers such as raccoons, weasels, coyotes, opossums, and, the worst nuisances of all, roaming dogs. Hanging it at least six feet up on a long cord or wire will keep it out of reach of these pillagers.

One final word on this excellent bird food. If you buy a prepared ball of frozen, ready-to-serve suet mixed with what-have-you, keep an eye, and your nose, on it as weather warms. I once got one of these for Christmas, molded into a cute bell, and parked it on the woodshed roof. Around about Mother's Day I discovered that it had transformed itself into a putrid blob.

Slab Fat

In the trimming process, butchers slice slabs of fat off the outside surface of sides of beef. It is tougher and much stringier, and lacks the flakiness of suet. It can be rendered, or you can simply tie a chunk to a tree. Slabs of pork fat, with or without the rind, can be similarly used. "Slab" fat (my name) can be useful in keeping heavy users such as crows or ravens diverted from the higher-quality stuff in the fragile onion bags where the chickadees feed.

"Cod" Fat

You might encounter this term when asking for fat from your butcher. This has nothing to do with fish, being instead fat trimmed from beef carcasses. What part, I've been unable to find out, and am left guessing if there's some connection with the "cod" in "codpiece."

Cooking Grease

Leftover cooking fat is nutritious, and as palatable as suet, providing it isn't heavily charged with hot spices. The higher the percentage of pork fat and/or vegetable oils, the softer and greasier it will be. Soft fats should be offered only during really cold weather, and in wire cages or other rigid containers that the birds can cling to or approach without having to press directly against the fat, as they tend to when it's in a net bag. Grease-saturated breast feathers lose their insulating properties, which could inflict severe stress on a bird in particularly cold conditions. Rendering suet with soft fats stiffens them, and adding absorbent fillers like bran, dry cereal, or corn meal cuts down the greasiness.

Bones

The birds that take suet seem to be strongly attracted to large, raw bones and will work at them diligently for what seem like slim pickings compared to what they could get at a suet bag. Such scavenging probably evolved at predator kills. Thus, banging and pulling away at bones may answer a deep-seated urge that can't be completely satisfied by hanging on a plastic onion bag. If I come by a fresh beef, horse, or deer hip, or a large leg bone, I park it in the snow on top of the back shed. By the time it has turned from its original startling red to a sombre brown, the birds will have pulled all but the toughest shreds of sinew from it.

Meat/Carrion

If you live near the coast of the Pacific Northwest, especially where a salmon stream debouches, the sight of a Bald Eagle isn't something to get excited about. But in less favored settings, spotting one of these great birds is an event. Away from their oceanside haunts, Bald Eagles migrate. But some may now and then stay over at inland locations, especially near open water, living off crippled waterfowl left behind from the goose and duck hunting seasons, the plentiful supply of carrion in gut piles, and dead and dying animals from the deer, elk, and moose seasons.

Unless you live well up in the mountains, a confirmed Golden Eagle sighting is worth a note in the diary. Goldens drift down from their nesting ramparts in the high country and the far north, cruising the southern forests and farmlands for snowshoe hares, cottontail rabbits, and game birds.

Several years ago, noting the presence of both of these great raptors near my country place in southern Manitoba, I erected a stout shelf on a post, high enough off the ground so the coyotes couldn't reach a chunk of road-killed deer that I lashed onto the deck. Magpies were the most numerous visitors, until one morning a dark, hulking bird had banished them. It was a Golden Eagle, and it came only two or three times that winter.

On two succeeding winters I have attracted Bald Eagles, one adult and one immature. Between visits from these big raptors, my "eagle feeder" out in the meadow gives the magpies something to do besides ganging up at the suet feeders in the yard.

Baked Goods

A restaurant, bakery, or doughnut shop can be an inexhaustible source of stale stock and leftovers. Doughnuts, cakes, and pastries are tasty-rich in carbohydrates and fats—just the ticket for winter calories. Unlike these, straight white bread, hotdog and burger buns, et cetera, have limited nutritional value. I can't recommend their use except as a filler for a recipe containing other, more nutritious, fare.

Take care not to be overwhelmed by the generosity of donors; some outlets create leftovers in awesome quantities and are only too happy to give them to anyone who will cart them off.

Before you start strewing these goodies about the yard, and making regular runs to the garbage dump with the stuff the yard won't hold, go to the dump ahead of time and survey the clientele there. In the bird department we're talking starlings, House Sparrows, pigeons, crows, swarms of gulls, and ravens—lots of ravens if we're in their range. Amongst the ground crew are rats, mice, raccoons, errant mutts, and cats of no fixed address.

The point is that dispensing leftover baked goodies could turn your yard into a satellite garbage dump, unless it is done with discretion. Some of your regular clients will learn to relish it, if they haven't already developed the taste. Keep it well up off the ground; the local dogs will smell it out quickly and, if they can reach it, will become repeat nuisances.

Fruit

Dried fruit, especially raisins because of their small size and easy availability, has been frequently used as a specialty or "treat" food. Waxwings, if they stick around long enough for you to get their attention, will take raisins with enthusiasm. Wintering robins and their kindred Varied Thrushes are said to sustain themselves mainly on tree-dried berries. I have seen a backyard crabapple in early spring surrounded by dozens of robins gathered to feed on the fallen fruit. The interesting bit was that neighboring trees, of different varieties but having dropped just as abundantly, were totally ignored. If you discover such a tree, gather a basket or two of its fruit the next fall. Keep them frozen in case you happen to be host to a robin, thrush, flicker, or some waxwings that winter.

The literature regularly mentions bananas, oranges, apples, strawberries, raspberries, and other fruits as being good for tempting birds that are not interested in the traditional seeds or suet. A half orange, for example, impaled on a nail or a stout twig in a tree, is said to be irresistible to orioles. If no birds show up to claim these goodies, you can recover your investment by eating the unused ones yourself.

In the gentler climes of the coastal Pacific Northwest, there is an abundance of natural and ornamental shrubbery, much of it berry-bearing and used by birds as winter feed. However, the farther inland, the higher up, and the farther north you get, the less of this bounty one finds. A provident bird feeder in these regions could watch for a good summer crop of wild fruit and gather a few buckets. Held in the freezer, they would be ready for the appearance of a flock of waxwings or a thrush.

Sweets

Sugar solutions and hummingbirds go together. But other birds are very attracted to sugar water once they discover it. Chickadees, House Sparrows, and Purple Finches are among these, but the real "sweet tooth" belongs to House Finches. Sweet solutions should not be dispensed in a bowl or bath where unsuspecting birds might bathe in it. Rather, it could be offered in the kind of hummingbird feeders that have a simple bent glass tube hanging down from the stopper on an inverted bottle or jug, placed where the non-hummingbirds can perch and feed from it. An alternative is a waterer for poultry chicks that is readily available at feed stores or rural hardware stores.

For hummingbirds, popular wisdom advocates a solution of one part sugar to four parts water. However, as a result of work done on hummingbirds wintering in cooler climates, a solution of 60 percent sugar is advocated for winter feeding. Honey, in spite of being a "natural" food, can harbor a mold that can be fatal to hummers, and should not be offered as a steady diet.

Frequently in the literature one reads of woodpeckers, chickadees, creepers, hummingbirds, squirrels, and others feeding at the neat rows of holes sapsuckers drill in trees. They lap up the oozing sap and pick up the insects stuck in it. As a modification of the suet log, a "sugar log" could be made by drilling rows of small, shallow holes in a length of smooth-barked tree trunk and filling these with crystallized honey, thick syrup, jelly, jam, or any of these mixed with peanut butter. Hung in a tree, such a lure might not only divert sapsuckers from your smooth-barked ornamentals in summer, it might bring otherwise reclusive creepers, possibly even kinglets, into view in winter.

Grit

Most birds require grit of some kind in their gizzards to grind up their food; it is particularly important to seed eaters. I have never supplied it for my birds, assuming the adjacent gravel roads to be a more-than-adequate source. So is the grit that washes out of the asphalt shingles on my roof.

However, if you live in what you believe to be a grit-deficient neighborhood, you can do your part for avian digestion by putting a shovelful of gravel or coarse sand out where the birds can get it. Feed companies sell poultry grit in three or more sizes; "chick" grade would be most suitable for the small-caliber plumbing of most feeder species. Crushed oyster shell, even the "pullet" size, would likely be too coarse except for grouse, pheasants, and pigeons.

Salt

Crossbills are frequently seen picking at the ashes around barbecues and fire pits, presumably to satisfy a craving for the minerals they contain. Many crossbills, Evening Grosbeaks, siskins, and Common Redpolls are killed by traffic when they flock onto roads for the salt scattered there in winter. A small pan of coarse salt mixed with ashes, grit, or soil might prove to be a highly tempting treat to a flock of crossbills or grosbeaks. By offering it, you might save the lives of birds that would otherwise seek this attractive supplement in traffic.

Water

There is nothing, including feeders, that attracts birds in summer better than an inviting pool of water, particularly one where a trickle or spray splashes invitingly into it. This reflects the importance of water to the well-being of birds.

However, I don't agree with writers who worry at length about providing water for birds where one must take heroic measures to keep it from freezing. In the winter, birds get moisture by eating snow, a long-established adaptation.

In Winnipeg, where I fed birds for many years, water mains occasionally burst in midwinter, creating ponds and rivulets on the street. If the birds nearby had craved water, they would have flocked to it. But I never saw a single one come to drink at these breaks.

The combination of circumstances where birds could be stressed would be during a protracted freeze when there was no snow and natural sources of open water would be iced over. In this situation there might be a case for providing a birdbath, or pan of warmed water. The heat source could be a light bulb, a heat lamp, a battery warmer, or a submersible heating coil. Just be certain the water is kept warm, not scalding hot!

There is some evidence that having access to warmed water in extremely cold weather can be fatal to some birds. One of my references noted that starlings bathed in the warmed water he supplied, and then promptly froze to death! Other references suggest that wintering birds can bathe in water and suffer no overchill, but I suspect these observations come from places where winter is rather more "cool" than "cold."

CHAPTER 3

Feeders and Shelters

There are two beneficiaries to consider in setting up a feeding station: Birds, and people, in that order. This basic priority suggests a sequence of things to ponder. Of primary importance are (1) accessibility to the birds; (2) shelter from the wind, snow, and rain; (3) vulnerability to window strikes; and (4) safety from predators, especially cats.

Secondary considerations are (1) ready visibility from a window; (2) ease of filling and maintaining; and (3) capacity, which determines refill frequency.

Site (yard) assessment (see Chapter 1, Principles of Feeding Birds) will suggest the kinds of feeders you should use, i.e., table, window shelf, post-mounted, or hanging. If you have a big window facing into an alcove on the southeast side of the house, with ample shelter from the prevailing northwesterlies, there are no priorities to sort out, because this is a setup in which everybody wins.

Suppose, however, that your best window faces west or north, and there is no shelter worth the name between it and Siberia. In this case, you have some adjustments to make.

Your best option would be to put up two feeders, in effect one for you and one for the birds. For yourself, where the view is best, fix a large shelf on the ledge at the big window, fitting raised sides on the edges so the seeds will not be scattered with every passing gust. On calm days, or when the wind is brewing up a storm against the opposite side of the house, the birds can feed comfortably at the big window, in full view.

For the birds, put up another feeder, a table or pole, in the place most sheltered from the prevailing winds. Whether there is a window view of this alternate site would be a secondary consideration.

This combination, with perhaps a couple of hanging seed feeders and a suet bag at various selected spots, would make a yard an all-weather feeding haven, with birds more likely to congregate, and remain, there in all kinds of weather.

The big window might be deserted on days when our continental westerlies whistled against it, but the feeders out back would keep everybody around until things calmed down.

VARIETIES OF FEEDERS

The Ground

The most basic feeder of all is the ground itself. Virtually all birds that use feeders, with the exception of hummingbirds, will ground feed. Many, such as House Sparrows, juncos, pigeons, grouse, starlings, and the blackbirds, much prefer to feed on the ground. Others—redpolls, chickadees, goldfinches, Evening Grosbeaks, Purple Finches—also feed there but are just as happy with something higher up.

Throwing feed on the ground is not as uncomplicated as it first appears. It can be wasteful. In rainy conditions, seeds become one with the soggy ground, are frozen in, or are washed away. In colder conditions, they get mixed in with snow and disappear. In spots close to shrubbery or other hiding places, birds on the ground are most vulnerable to ambush by cats. And from the bird feeder's perspective, from a high window, it may be awkward to see birds on the ground close below.

If you are feeding on snow-covered ground, or wish to minimize wastage of seeds spilled from an overhead feeder, pack the snow first by patting it down with a shovel or rolling it flat with a large plastic pail.

A piece of plywood, an old door, or something of the sort can be used as a modest improvement on bare ground or snow. It cuts wastage somewhat, and cleaning it off is merely a matter of upending it and giving it a kick, or flopping it over.

Tables

If you take your slab of plywood or old door and nail legs under the corners, you have yourself a table feeder. Putting a low rim around the edges stiffens it and helps keep seeds in place. You can make a neater job of sweeping it off if you leave gaps in the rim at the corners. A further modification that lets rain or meltwater run off better is to give the table top a slight tilt by cutting two of the legs on a long side a bit shorter. The water will drain off through the gaps you have providently left in the edging.

The height of the table is a matter of taste and/or convenience, as is its size, or both may be determined by the scrap lumber at hand. A general rule is that the bigger your feeder(s), the more birds you will attract, particularly the sociable species like finches. In years of high bird abundance, especially if yours

The wire screen around this low table prevents cats from turning it into an ambush for these Evening Grosbeaks and Common Redpolls.

is the only feeder in the vicinity, a modest shelf no more than one by two feet can attract an astonishing crowd of visitors. A full four-by-eight-foot sheet of plywood can accommodate an awesome mob of redpolls, Purple Finches, and/or Evening Grosbeaks.

At this point in the setting-up stage, one might as well face the fact that in any location where there are neighbors, there are going to be cats, sometimes a whole parade of them. It will be better for the birds, and your state of mind, to take preventive action now to minimize the cat problem. Recommended measures are to be found in Chapter 5, The Downside.

The space under a low table feeder is a custom-made ambush for lurking cats. The birds are baited right to the place of concealment, and spilled seeds bait the birds to the ground right in front of the cats' noses. Cats also quickly master another lethal trick. They pinpoint the location of birds on the platform overhead from the sounds of their feet and, when one is near the edge, pounce over and grab it. A simple way of preventing your table from becoming a cat-treats bar is to tack wire screen or wooden slats to the legs all the way around so they can't get underneath.

Window Shelves

Shelter and serviceability permitting, a window-shelf feeder offers the ultimate in closeup viewing and photography. I say "shelf," but several makes of commercial window feeders exploit windows to the ultimate in other ways.

Some commercial models mount directly onto window glass with suction cups. In very cold conditions, some cups are unreliable fasteners, prone to pop off when you're refilling the feeders or cleaning the glass around them. Proper installation helps: Heat the cups in hot water, dry them off, apply a slight oily film by rubbing the inner surface with your fingers, and push them onto the glass while they're still warm. If the cups hold, and the birds grow accustomed to being so close to you, the eye-to-eye proximity is captivating indeed.

Another idea, the ultimate attempt at cozy intimacy, is a Plexiglas box that is installed, like an air conditioner, into the window frame. The outside end is open, the rest of it, in effect, extends a bit of the outdoors into your home. The room-side surface is coated with reflecting film to dim the birds' view of the occupants. A neat hinged door opens on the inside for easy access.

This alcove-in-a-window is the ultimate in bird–birdwatcher intimacy, but where winters bring really cold temperatures, I would recommend a heat-conserving modification. If a door for the outside end doesn't come with the feeder, make a snug-fitting panel of plywood-backed rigid foam to close the open side at night, a measure that would also exclude coons and possums if you live in their territory. This would also cut down on problems with condensation, excessive frost accumulation, and dripping. The measures suggested in the Window Management section of Chapter 4, Enjoying Your Birds, could also be helpful.

Shelf Control

For most of us, attaching a simple shelf to the outside of the windowsill is quite sufficient. For a small shelf, bracing and bracketing are easy problems because seeds and birds don't weigh much. The bigger the shelf gets, the sturdier the supports have to be. And any shelf should be anchored solidly enough to allow for vigorous action when you have to scrape or chop away ice and crusted snow. Whatever the size, leave one inch of space between the glass and the near side of the shelf so that snow and seeds won't collect there and form an icy crust that is messy-looking and awkward to chip away.

If the platform is close enough to the ground for cats to leap up to it, that is, six feet or less, staple a fringe of woven wire around the three outside edges before you install it. If stucco or chicken wire is aesthetically displeasing to you, buy the decorative wire border trim that garden shops sell.

The shelf must have a rim at least one inch high around all the edges; otherwise the wind and the birds will waste most of the seeds. As already mentioned for tables, it is much easier to sweep snow and seed leftovers off the shelf if you leave the outside corners open by a couple of inches or more. And when you make your plans, allow for a moderate slope to the outward edge so that rainwater and melting snow will run off through the corner openings.

Add-on Protection

If the spot you really want for a window—or table—feeder isn't adequately sheltered, it can be made partially self-protecting with a roof and sides. You want protection but you don't want to go overboard and create a deep, enclosed box. Birds feel trapped in constricted spaces where vision and escape are restricted.

The window shelf, ideal for closeness, with cat guard

Roofs on feeders are a great idea. In wet weather, they keep seeds dry and give birds a place to feed in comfort. They save work, and they save waste. Hard rains wash unroofed seeds away; snow on shelves and tables needs clearing, and in the process seeds get dumped. Soaked seeds are not as palatable as nice dry ones.

A roof can also be a decorative addition to your yard. Shingles, shakes, thatch, and other novel materials have been used to add that quaint touch. Recalling that birds are rather claustrophobic creatures, don't build a roof too low. For adequate weather protection, therefore, compensate for a high roof by giving it lots of overhang.

Almost all small birds have problems dealing with even an inch or so of snow over the top of seeds. Burrowing simply is not part of their evolved behavior, even for seeds right beneath their feet. If someone doesn't sweep the snow off and uncover the seeds, they will just perch and peer in expectant befuddlement. Jays are good at digging, redpolls will poke little holes in the snow, and Fox Sparrows will scratch their way down. The best burrowers are the squirrels. They will dig in and scatter enough seeds around to see everyone else through if you haven't had the time to clear away. All this becomes academic, of course, with a good roof overhead.

I've built a feeder at a corner of the second-story deck at the back of my house where I have a great view from either the French doors leading to the deck, or from the kitchen window. The basic table is two feet by four feet, covered with a generous shed roof, completely closed off on two adjacent sides. The third side has a low six-inch wall; the edge facing the house is completely open. To make the seeds less skitterish in the swirling back-eddies on especially windy days, I covered the floor of the feeder with indoor-outdoor carpet, thumb-tacked in place.

As I write this, it is raining and breezy. The deck feeder is invitingly dry, and there is barely standing room as juncos, siskins, Purple Finches, and House Finches jostle for space. When the rush is off, Chestnut-backed Chickadees, a couple of Rufous-sided Towhees, a couple of Fox Sparrows, and several Song Sparrows will come in for their share.

One benefit that I hoped the enclosure would confer has in fact materialized: Only rarely does a crow venture in. Before I installed the roof and walls they mobbed the feeder; first thing every morning I could hear their beaks drumming away on the plywood. Now they fly by, sit, and stare, but are obviously very uneasy about committing themselves to the restricting space inside the feeder.

Finish and Color

When the heavy matters of placement and design have been pondered through to a conclusion, and the sawing and nailing are done, you might want to paint your creation. I favor a finish rather than leaving the wood bare, even though this is less "natural." My choice is more practical than decorative; the smooth surface of good quality paint is easy to clean, water runs off it more readily, and ice doesn't bond to a slick paint finish nearly as tenaciously as to the exposed fibers of bare wood.

For the feeding surface of the shelf, pick light colors that absorb less of the sun's radiation, and hence are slower to melt accumulated snow into what will later freeze into a thick crust of ice. Dark seeds also show up better on a light base.

While you're thinking paint, you might consider what tones would complement color photography, particularly if there are raised sides on the edges of your feeder. Bright ones will reflect light and have to be allowed for on your exposure meter readings. Depending on the angle of sunlight, they will provide fill-in lighting to soften the hard shadows. They will also enter into the composition of your photographs, adding or detracting from them with their shape, texture, and color.

These are things you might not notice in the excitement of fiddling with your camera to get that super closeup of a beautiful bird before it takes off. But there is nothing more annoying, when you get your slides back, than discovering that a scrappy-looking or off-color slab of plywood sticks out like a sore thumb in every one of them.

Pole Feeders

One of the more pleasing arrangements, from both the birds' and their observers' points of view, is the pole feeder. This is basically a shelf-on-a-stick, with infinite variations. It can be made or bought.

Many manufactured pole feeders come with metal tubes that fit cleverly together in sections. The bottom end of the lowest section is crimped to a rough point, and to set the device up you simply tap it into the ground, straight the first time, if possible. Don't beat on the top of the tube with a hammer or some other metal bludgeon; you'll crimp or bend the rim and it won't take the small end of the next section. Put a piece of soft wood on the top of the tube and thump on that.

The sectional rod idea is doubly convenient, because the feeders bolted to the top section are usually of the hopper variety and stretching up to fill them *in situ* can be awkward. You simply rotate and pull off the feeder, plus the attached top section of pipe, recharge it at convenient working height, then replace it. To make sure that mine detaches at the first section below the feeder, I apply a lubricant to that joint so that it comes apart easiest. If that doesn't work, I wrap a little electrician's tape around the other joints to hold them in place.

Increasingly, most store-bought pole feeders come with a squirrel baffle, a cone- or frisbee-shaped metal disc loosely fixed to the pole just below the feeder. If not, the merchant will happily sell you an add-on one.

There are a number of ingenious "squirrel-proof" feeders on the market now. If you have a real squirrel problem, first of all avoid any feeder not made of metal. Then at least you have the satisfaction of knowing that when they've finished the "squirrel-proof" seeds, they won't chew apart the feeder.

Amongst the squirrel-resistant (a safer term) gimmicks on the market is a perch that closes the feeding tray under a squirrel's weight, but not under a bird's weight. Another features a loose metal sleeve over the pole that is held up under the feeder by a pulley-and-counterweight arrangement. A squirrel on its way up the pole gets a ride back down as soon as it grabs the sleeve and hangs its weight on it. All this takes place, presumably, to the intense frustration of the squirrel and the huge amusement of the guy who bought the contraption.

It no doubt works, at least once, whereupon the squirrel realizes that if it just keeps right on climbing the sleeve during the ride down it will reach the main pole above the sleeve again and, perhaps with no more than a couple of gentle bumps on the heels as it shinnies on up, it will gain its objective: the seeds. This is called the frustration/entertainment reversal factor.

If you are making your own, the pole can be anything sturdy enough to hold whatever you intend to fix to the top: metal or polyvinyl chloride (PVC) pipe, posts, two-by-fours or other dimensional lumber, or even a slender tree trunk. A PVC or metal pole can be quite squirrel-resistant if it is more than five inches in diameter, too big for the squirrels to get their front legs around the slippery material. It can be kept nice and slick with an occasional wipe or spray with light oil.

My own largest feeder is mounted on a ten-foot section of cedar telephone pole. The seven-plus feet above ground are clad top to bottom in sheet metal, as is the rugged shelf at the top. The hopper on the platform is made of a thirty-inch section of eighteen-inch culvert. It looks like a small water tower designed by Pa Kettle, and has been described somewhat uncharitably as an eyesore. But it stands out behind the cottage in the country where few, save myself, the critic, and the birds can see it.

I have to fill it from a stepladder, but because it holds upwards of ninety pounds of seeds, this isn't too frequent a chore, and I can go away for a fort-

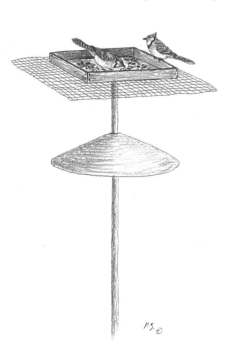

This simple pole feeder has both a cat guard and a squirrel guard.

night or more and not have to worry about my birds running short. Among its other sturdy virtues, my tower is raccoon-, deer-, and squirrel-proof except for the flying squirrels and one big male Gray Squirrel that does a magnificent Flying Wallenda leap from a maple almost ten feet away.

Ingenious Variations

The variations that can be worked into the basic pole-and-shelf pattern are infinite. The most primitive can be large berry-baskets, one-dozen beer cartons, or small cardboard boxes nailed on their sides to the tops of fenceposts. For the carton, use a small scrap of plywood as a washer so the nail won't rip through the cardboard in the wind. It's crude, but the birds don't care, and the materials

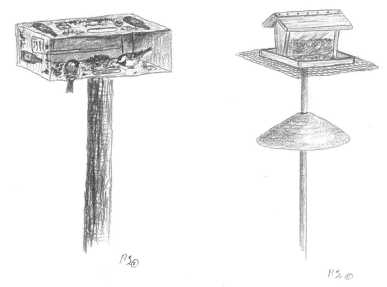

Left: *a recycled beer-box feeder;* right: *a hopper feeder suitable for a cold, dry winter without much rain.*

can be gleaned out of any roadside ditch. At this level of the technology, you are thus not only benefitting the birds, but are helping to keep roadscapes litter-free.

Opposite to crude can be a finely crafted, multistory platform with several hoppers, one or two sides made of Plexiglas, little balconies for baked scraps and other treats, eye screws on little booms for suet bags and thistle feeders, all tucked under a trimly shingled roof. Such a feeder doesn't have to be very big to accommodate a large number of birds at once.

With rustic natural finish, or tastefully selected paint, a station like this can be a quaint and attractive centerpiece to the yardscape. If you're just starting out, begin near the primitive end of the technology and give experience time to shape your decorative enthusiasm.

How High?

Your pole feeder may be a lesson in simplicity or the architectural pride of the neighborhood. Either way, squirrels and your attitude toward them may dictate basic features of construction.

The platform of any pole-mounted feeder must be high enough to prevent squirrels from jumping directly up to it. For Red and Douglas Squirrels, this means a *minimum* of four feet. Depending on snowfall in your area, allow extra height for snowpack under the feeder. It must also be set far enough away from trees or other launch points to prevent squirrels' jumping across to, or down onto, the roof. Horizontally, that means a span of at least six feet, more for a launch point higher than the top of the feeder. For Gray or Fox Squirrels, vertical clearance should be a minimum of five feet, and horizontal distances should be at least eight feet.

Low-rise Ladder

If a pole feeder is high enough to keep squirrels from jumping up onto it, top-loading hoppers will be awkward to fill, unless you happen to be seven feet tall. If the pole is fitted with telescoping joints, there is no problem. But for a solid pole one should have a sturdy wooden box or something solid to stand on. An old chair or stool is most untrustworthy on packed snow or rain-soaked turf; the legs have a tendency to suddenly poke through when you're teetering aloft.

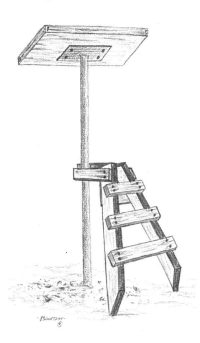

My own answer is a three-foot ladder. The sides are set very wide apart at the bottom and very close together at the top; it looks like an isosceles triangle with the odd side left off. The idea is that the close-set ends at the top rest loosely against the sides of the pole while the splayed bottom affords a very secure base. You can augment this simple design with an extension set at an angle to the top. With this resting against the pole, you are set back more comfortably from your work. (See the accompanying diagram.)

My squatty ladder is very light and also comes in handy for filling or cleaning high window-shelf feeders, servicing bluebird houses, cleaning windows, and doing other odd jobs at modest elevations where a full-sized ladder is awkward.

Light, solid, and handy—the three-step ladder

Hanging Feeders

Hanging feeders can be as large as the support will allow. But their best use is as small satellites to larger feeders. Compact and self-enclosed, they make it easy to diversify with special feeds, and to cater to smaller species. They can also be the cheapest and easiest to construct.

The commercial manufacture of hanging feeders lends itself to the whims of the plastic molder's craft. They are marketed in globe, hemisphere, toad-stool, space station, and animal shapes. Some no doubt appeal to the birds. Many, however, seem to have been crafted to catch the eye of buyers who know nothing of feeding birds but know "cute" when they see it. Some of the resulting baubles are fit only for Christmas trees.

Classic Clorox

Consider the homemade end of tacky, the classic bleach bottle. Numberless backyard *improvisarios* have rescued them in the nick of time from the garbage, hacked holes in their sides, skewered them with chopsticks for perches, charged them with seeds, and hung them by the neck from a tree limb for the winter. Children cart them off to school science fairs as proud evidence of their ingenuity.

Of equal utility are empty cardboard milk cartons.

Deserving of their historic place as the bleach bottle and milk carton are, I have nevertheless abandoned both in favor of the larger and more conveniently squared-off shape of the four-quart windshield washer fluid jug. The accompanying diagram shows how to use the flap of plastic as a little roof over the cut-out hole, and to attach the cord through a hole in the cap. The handle (not shown) is ever-so-convenient to hang onto when you pour the seeds in through the holes.

Some writers recommend putting in little perches just below the holes. But for this kind where the birds go inside to pick up seeds, I found that the only ones seeming to appreciate perches were House Sparrows. If the holes are around 2½ by 3 inches, the small birds have no difficulty getting in. I made it a bit easier by putting a strip of fabric hockey tape on the rim.

It wasn't surprising to see that the acrobatic chickadees took only a pass or two to get the knack of managing the relatively small hole. With a bit more practice they could fly right in. What did surprise me was that nuthatches, redpolls, Purple Finches, and goldfinches also quickly mastered the trick.

So did the squirrels, by sliding down the string. To satisfy their gnawing urge for improvements they enlarged my neat little doors to gaping, ragged holes, chewed away the clever little flaps, and cut the string holding them up. Then somebody cut the main cord and collected the seeds on the ground. When I substituted a length of wire, they cut the branch.

A neighbor foiled the slide-down-the-string trick by putting an old twelve-inch long-playing record on a stop knot a few inches above the cap of the bottle. I haven't applied this yet because replacement bottles are so cheap and easy to make, and I'm just not yet ready to hang my old Beatles classics out to warp.

Tube Feeders

There are a number of commercial hanging feeders that are basically a cylinder with a number of small feeding ports in the side. Inside baffles over each one allow the birds to pick out seeds, but control flow. The birds don't go inside, and since the slippery plastic sides don't allow them to cling, there are little perches below each hole. The cap at the top functions as both a roof and a filler hole.

Some of them come in sets of tubes joined by three or four long dowels that double as perches. With a good crowd on hand, there will often be a bird on every perch, a beguilingly busy sight indeed.

As a group, these are often referred to as "thistle" feeders because that's the feed they are often used for. Thistle, or niger, seed is much prized by some birds but rather too expensive for the average station operator to shovel out in bulk on a come-one-come-all basis. Since the small, smooth seeds dispense well in tube feeders, and can be extracted only one or two at a time from each hole, thistle seed and feeder are a nice combination for the person wanting to cater to the smaller birds on a somewhat selective basis. While the siskins and goldfinches are on the perches, daintily extracting the costly imports from their little hideaways, the heavy eaters like Evening Grosbeaks, Steller's Jays, and Mourning Doves are elbowing each other over less expensive fodder at the communal table or window shelf.

Canary seed and millet work equally well in these tube feeders. Depending on the length and diameter of the cylinder, they can hold quite a lot of seed and don't need constant filling. In some, the top ports run out first, but in others a clever arrangement of baffles gives each pair of ports its own feed bin. Many of the commercial varieties are made of clear plastic so the level of seeds can be easily seen.

Keep in mind that squirrels, if they can reach hanging feeders, won't be content with licking up little seeds one at a time through the dinky little holes. If the material is gnawable, and the ports aren't reinforced with metal, they'll chew holes in it to suit themselves and ruin a feeder that is expensive to buy or time-consuming to make. Retrofitting holes with metal is a fussy and awkward bit of frustration.

Laying on an easily accessible alternate supply of seeds is the simplest way of trying to beguile squirrels into leaving the hanging feeders alone. But if you have no faith in this ploy, make your tube feeders out of galvanized drain pipe. In one important respect they are much easier to make, because the baffles and the holes can be made by making horizontal cuts with a hacksaw in the side of the cylinder and pushing the top flaps inward.

If you are looking for the ultimate in quick and cheap tube feeders, the plastic container comes to the rescue again. This time it's pop bottles; any size will suffice, but the thirty-ounce size is best. Make a one-port feeder by slicing a 2½-inch cut through the side of the bottle along the ridge just above the bottom, or along the top of the plastic base if there is one. If you push in the wall of the bottle just above the cut, it will pop back out again. You can make it stay in if you just pinch the plastic between thumb and finger at each corner just above the cut, making permanent creases. The material is more workable if you warm it under hot water. Punch or burn a hole through the cap, run a piece of string through with a stop-knot, and ... voila! ... a neat hanging feeder.

For birds new to this clever device, just fill it and set it on the ground or a feeder shelf until they discover it, then hang it up. A strip of fabric tape stuck to the lip of the port gives the birds a bit better grip. You can make a multi-port feeder by slicing more holes, as illustrated below.

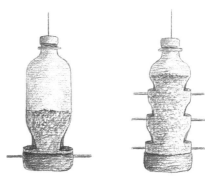

Left: *a square plastic jug holds plenty of seeds and is partially waterproof;* above: *free-swinging pop-bottle feeders are favorites with smaller birds.*

This type of feeder is the ultimate in free-swinging, gyrating instability, even in a light breeze. It's enlightening to watch how quickly the more acrobatic birds like chickadees master an offhand precision at grabbing the moving lip. By comparison, House Sparrows are rather ponderous on the wing, and many bird-feeding books reassure their readers that House Sparrows won't use swinging, unstable feeders. My sparrows might not like them, but they damn well seem to enjoy the challenge of getting their docking technique down pat, even lining up to take turns! I have no explanation for this behavior, because the same sunflower seeds were more easily available at nearby pole and shelf feeders.

Suet Dispensers

Suet can be dispensed in any way, including leaving chunks of it on a table or a window shelf. There are several good reasons for not doing this, the law

This Red-breasted Nuthatch appreciates the simplest of suet feeders, a net onion bag.

of supply and demand being one. If there are crows, ravens, gulls, opossums, or raccoons around, your place could become a bulk station supplying suet for miles around. In the interests of economy and of fair sharing, you are better off putting your suet into a dispenser that limits withdrawals to beak-sized nibbles.

What could be handier and cheaper than the plastic net bags that onions or peanuts are sold in? The chunks of suet are tucked in, the neck tied to a hank of cord, and the lot looped onto a tree branch or a hook on some overhead structure. Remember that roving dogs love suet, so hang it high. The birds that love suet—all the woodpeckers, chickadees, nuthatches, and jays and their relatives—have no trouble clinging to the bag while they peck fragments of suet from between the strands of netting.

The netting is strong enough to prevent the jays from chopping off big junks and carting it off wholesale. As the suet is eaten, the bag collapses around it and the remnants remain available until there is nothing left but strands of stringy tissue.

A supposed hazard of the onion-bag feeder is that birds can entangle their claws in the netting and die struggling to free themselves. I have never seen this, nor have any of my contacts. There is a verified account of a kinglet getting entangled in broken and frayed netting. The answer may be to replace bags before they become tattered and torn.

A shortcoming of the onion bag is that there is a limit to the amount of bulk you can cram into it, and if you have crows or ravens to contend with, they will rip it apart and clean you out in no time. In that case, the answer is wire mesh or coarse screen. As with most kinds of feeders, you can buy commercial suet cages, generally made of wire, often coated with latex.

If you wish to make your own, the raw material that I have found most useful is "hardware cloth" with either ¼-inch or ½-inch mesh. Respectively, it is called

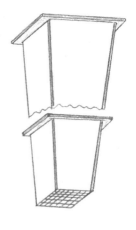

This suet feeder is virtually crow-proof.

"four-by-four" and "two-by-two" in the trade, which means four squares or two squares per inch. In spite of the name, the "cloth" is actually made of good stiff wire soldered together at the joints. It can be bought off a roll at building supply or hardware stores.

Match Size to Demand

With a pair of tinsnips you can cut your hardware cloth to conform to an imaginative array of dispensers. Size depends on the anticipated use. In the city, I feed at most only two to four pounds of suet during most winters, but in the country that amount would last only a few days.

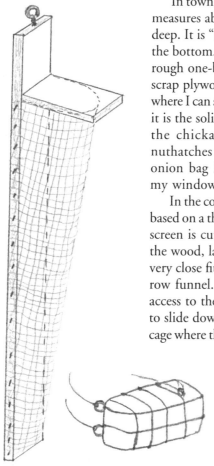

In town, therefore, I have a neat little cage that measures about six inches square by three inches deep. It is "two-by-two" mesh on three sides and the bottom. The back is a solid one-foot piece of rough one-by-six board, and the lid is a piece of scrap plywood. It is tacked to the trunk of a tree where I can see it from my office window. Whether it is the solid feel of the cage or the bigger mesh, the chickadees, Downy Woodpeckers, and nuthatches use the cage much more than the onion bag hanging from the lean-to roof over my window-shelf feeder.

In the country I have built a much larger feeder based on a three-foot slab of two-by-six plank. The screen is cut to form a semicircular cage against the wood, large at the top, narrowing down to a very close fit at the bottom, like a very long, narrow funnel. This is to give the birds continued access to the suet. As they peck it away, it tends to slide down into the constricted bottom of the cage where they can still reach it through the mesh.

This feeder holds about ten pounds of suet, and it is gone in two weeks thanks to the magpies, a family of jays, a large clan of chickadees, several Hairy and Downy Woodpeckers, and at least one pair of White-breasted Nuthatches. I can't use onion bags any more because the magpies tear them apart, a task that Northwestern Crows would be pleased to take over along the coastal Pacific Northwest.

Wire-cage suet feeders keep crows and ravens from taking everything. The yard-long suet holder, left, ensures a supply over long period of time.

The next time the handyman urge comes over me, I plan a box or tube suet feeder with access through wire mesh only at the bottom. This will be no inconvenience to the woodpeckers, nuthatches, and chickadees, because they are just as happy clinging upside down as rightside up when they eat. But it will put a crimp in the jays' access, and shut out the magpies entirely.

If you want to coat cage wire, use liquid latex. It comes in ordinary, and aerosol, cans. It would make snaggly wire, or any metal, more comfortable to handle in cold weather. As a safety factor for birds, it is unnecessary in my view. Northern birds have to deal with superchilled ice in various forms, which will also do an instant freeze-on if touched with something damp.

Hoppers

Hoppers can be an integral part of any of the above-mentioned varieties of feeders. It is to our poultry-raising forebears that we owe the invention of the hopper, or "self-feeder." This is a storage bin mounted over a trough, with a slot at the bottom just large enough to let feed trickle out as fast as it is eaten. The hopper protects the reserve of feed from the weather, and from the animals themselves, and saves the bother of having to attend them at every feeding time. Clever, those ancestors!

What the hopper does for those who feed wild birds is ensure a reserve of feed if they can't be on hand to dish it out every day. Most commercially built feeders, and the plans for homemade ones, incorporate a hopper of some kind. Most give the capacity of the hopper in volume. Given a choice between two models with similar features, pick the bigger.

In a rainy climate, or one that delivers lots of snow, look for roofs with generous eaves. When water seeps into the hopper bottom, the wet seeds plug the slot and, if not cleared out, soak upward in the bin, turning whatever gets wet into a sour, sprouting mess.

Buckets and Bottles

The simplest hopper, and one that can be very useful in combination with a table or a good-sized window shelf, is merely a container filled with seeds and inverted over boards set nicely so the rim seats snugly on them. Spaces are left between the boards where the seeds can run out only as fast as they are eaten.

With a larger container it takes a bit of nerve and practice to whap the open container upside down over the boards in just the right place, and not spill seeds all over. One can, of course, build a lid that doubles as a base when the whole contraption is turned upside down.

Once that has been done, it's a good idea to put a rock or some other weight on the container to hold it in place when the contents run low and no longer anchor it against the wind, or pushy squirrels.

You can make another version of this by taping or tying a bottle upside down to an upright so that the rim of the neck is just far enough clear of the feeder floor for the seeds to trickle out as fast as they are cleared away.

The advantage of these simple arrangements is that the bottom of the inverted container provides a totally waterproof cap and will keep the store of seeds dry no matter how bad the rain, snow, or wind get.

The size of the container can vary according to the area of the feeder; a big table could take a five-gallon bucket, a small shelf a quart- or liter-sized juice can or plastic pop bottle.

For filling bottles and other small-port receptacles, homemade funnels can be easily made by cutting plastic pop bottles in half and using the top as a funnel. You can also buy scoops in the form of funnels with a gizmo that closes off the spout until you've got it into the hole.

Prevention being superior to cure, it is best to avoid the curse of the itty-bitty filler hole when either buying or building feeders. Not all designers appreciate the joy of playing thread-the-needle with a can of seeds, a funnel, and an awkward filler hole after dark, with a whistling gale driving snow or rain into your face.

For scooping seeds you can make a very good scoop/funnel, complete with convenient handle, out of the top two-thirds of a one-gallon plastic jug simply by cutting off the bottom.

The Basic Bin

The standard hopper bin viewed from the end is a *V* shape, with the sides tapering to the runout slot at the bottom. This design ensures that even the last of the seeds are within reach as the supply runs out. The roof, or part of it, comes off or is fitted with a hinge for filling. It is important that the roof be waterproof, and big enough to keep rain or snow out of the feeding tray at the bottom.

A bin can be an integral part of a feeder, or added to a table or a window shelf. If you have a big table catering to a large number of birds, a large hopper will keep them supplied without too much waste and without

A simple hopper made from a bottle keeps a continuous supply of seeds on this window shelf feeder.

your having to keep running out to replenish the supply. It will also allow you to leave for a period of time without breaking the "once started, never stop" rule.

A final word about squirrels. If they are going to be feeding from any hopper, the edges of the runout hole or slot should be reinforced with sheet metal.

MAINTENANCE

I have a permanent shade over my main window feeder. It doubles nicely as a passive solar control in the summer when the sun is high. But my shade doesn't keep wind-driven snow off the window shelf, so I am faced with the occasional task of sweeping it off. Being cheap, I hate to whisk the sunflower seeds onto the ground where most of them are trampled into the snow and wasted. Therefore, as well as a stiff-bristled little hand brush for whisking off the feeder and a putty knife for chipping away crusty snow, droppings, and (occasionally) frozen squirrel urine (remembering to keep my mouth shut), I have a screen sieve, the largest I can find. All three hang in a neat row on the wall of the carport.

Come a snow problem, I take my tools, mount my stubby ladder, and sweep the snow and the seeds off the feeder through the open corners and into the waiting sieve. With a bit of vigorous shaking and winnowing, the snow and smaller fragments are gone, and the seeds are replaced on the feeder. Voila!

I repeat the process until all the seeds are separated from their admixture of snow. Then I hang my tools back up in their neat row and retire, enormously satisfied that this little ritual would be the best-organized part of my daily routine, if I had one.

Neatness Counts

Good storage of your bird feed is very important; seeds must be kept dry and out of reach of rodents or raccoons. It is also nice to have them convenient to the feeder(s). The container that does this best for me is a new metal garbage can with a tight-fitting lid. For seeds on reserve, I stack extra bags in a rodent-proof metal shed.

This may seem to be a bit over-cautious, except to someone who has caught a bad dose of mice, rats, squirrels, or that nocturnal burglar, the pack rat. No garage, back porch, workshop, or attic is sacred to these bite-and-enter rodents. Once they discover a source of good food, it is extremely difficult to keep them out of it. They can dig or gnaw their way into wooden sheds with ease and even bite holes through plastic siding. Once in, they chew holes in bags or boxes and shred nesting materials from whatever valuables are stored there. Pack rats add insult to injury by fouling everything with pungent urine. Mice, for their part, will immediately set up housekeeping, and begin demonstrating their awesome reproductive capacity.

Birds and mammals are not the only animals that exploit the nutritious bounty of seeds; thousands of species of insects do so as well, some adapted to take special advantage of stored grain. Almost any sample of bulk seeds will have its share of these, plus a few accidental ride-alongs. In a warm environment they can multiply at a rate that makes even mice seem chaste. Keeping your seeds outside in winter cools the reproductive capacity of these stowaways.

The answer to undesirable preemption of your bird feed is found in the ounce-of-prevention homily: Keep the seeds out of reach, outside. Sweep up any spills, put lids back on. I keep my trusty garbage can conveniently under my windowshelf feeder. Anything that spills is picked up by the birds or other foragers that stay where they belong ... out! For more suggestions on how to keep control of the situation and still be a generous host, see Chapter 5, The Downside.

Sanitation

Diseases and parasites are natural hazards for birds. But the unnatural crowding at feeders is not a part of life for many species, and we should take precautions to minimize the possibility of our feeders being a source for the spread of communicable diseases. For the serious bird feeder, a bottle of household disinfectant should be next in importance to a good supply of seeds. Regular sanitation ensures that the benefits feeders confer are not compromised by the possibility of their becoming a source of infection.

Contrary to what we might assume, crisp, dry cold is not necessarily lethal to pathogens or spores lodged on feeders. Indeed, deep-frozen salmonella bacteria remain viable longer than they would in damp, above-freezing conditions.

Salmonella bacteria are normally present in the intestinal tracts of wild birds, and spread from one to the other in droppings. As long as the birds stay healthy and vigorous, the salmonella inflict no significant ill effects. But if the birds suffer abnormal stress, such as a prolonged spell of particularly bad weather or a food shortage, the bacteria may gain the upper hand in weaker birds. Critically infected birds appear listless, droopy-eyed, and in generally poor condition. In severe outbreaks, dead birds may turn up around feeders.

Another disease that shows up at feeders is bird (or avian) pox, a virus infection. It is usually first spotted as lumpy, funguslike crusts on the birds' feet and legs, although the head and the bend of the wing are also affected. Severe infection cripples the feet and wings, and may impede vision if the growths form heavily around the eyes. Most songbirds are susceptible, but Evening Grosbeaks, Purple Finches, and House Finches seem to be most vulnerable.

Feeders should be disinfected at least once a month, preferably every fortnight. During spells of particularly bad weather, once a week is not too often. An effective solution consists of one part chlorine bleach in nine parts tepid water, mixed immediately before use.

The equipment is simple: a whisk brush, a basin or a bucket, and rubber gloves. Shelves, railings, and perches should be brushed off, then given a good slosh and a scrub. The whisk can double as the scrub brush. Birdbaths and waterers should be emptied and given the same treatment.

From time to time, epidemics break out amongst wild birds and alarmed people begin asking whether feeding is the culprit. In almost all cases, such outbreaks coincide with prolonged spells of bad weather. This is more probably the main causative effect, not feeders. Feeders stocked with plenty of good, nutritious seeds in fact are far more likely to keep birds in good condition and thus better able to survive the stress of bad weather.

SHELTERS

A shelter, as meant here, is basically a winter birdhouse, except that it is not used for nesting. Many of our birds, notably chickadees, titmice, nuthatches, woodpeckers, House Sparrows, and starlings, use cavities of one sort or another for both nesting and as nighttime roosts. These are so important that some tree-hole nesters that do not excavate their own remain paired over the winter in order to maintain property rights to a territory that has the all-important, second-hand nesting/roosting hole.

Every winter I am told by puzzled bird feeders that when they first put out feed they attracted a nice clientele of chickadees, nuthatches, and sparrows. But as soon as the first cold weather and/or snow arrived, the chickadees vanished. Why?

I have no pat answers to this problem, except to speculate that the reason may be that there were no suitable winter quarters close at hand, and that the chickadees moved to another feeder that had a den tree close by.

If this notion is true, then it might be worthwhile to provide several artificial tree holes in the form roosting boxes, or even a length of hollow tree trunk. Chickadees are particular; almost invariably they insist on a hole they have excavated themselves. This they do by pecking the soft, punky wood from decayed branch sockets in dead or aging trees. Nuthatches may either do this or take over a vacated woodpecker hole. I have even had a Downy Woodpecker, a bird quite able to excavate a tree cavity, take up winter quarters in a bluebird house.

If you already have bluebird houses at hand, shelters can be made quickly by taking the fronts off, turning them upside-down so the holes are near the bottom, and tacking the fronts on again. It would be helpful to put several pegs, or some twigs, inside for roosts, and to plug all holes and cracks other than the entrance. They should then be set up in trees, preferably conifers, dense hedges, or some other natural growth that offers the best shelter from the wind.

Since chickadees really feel better about clearing out their own quarters, fill one or two birdhouses with wood shavings (not sawdust) that they can empty out. Titmice are apparently not so fussy.

Lacking a store of disused birdhouses, you can of course go to work and construct custom-made shelters. Refer to Appendix 2, Feeders and Shelters, for specifics. Nest boxes intended for winter use by any bird should be snugly constructed of thick material, or fitted with extra insulation. A flimsy, drafty box could be a death trap during a period of severe cold.

It is important that a shelter like this be on the side of the tree away from the prevailing winds.

CHAPTER 4

Enjoying Your Birds

Part of the excitement of feeding birds is that once you have the basic needs in place, and the birds are coming regularly, you develop an itch to learn more about them. This chapter deals with some of the things you can do to enhance your pleasure and broaden your knowledge.

Field Guides and References

Obviously, it is very useful to have one of the major continental field guides parked on the coffee table. These deal with the 600-odd species occurring in North America north of the Mexican border, plus likely strays from Europe and Asia. Bear in mind that the Peterson and Audubon guides are published in two editions, one for the west, the other for the east. The dividing line in both is roughly the eastern foothills of the Rockies.

Field guides are sturdily bound in durable covers, and for good reason. Sooner or later you will spot a new bird at the feeder, and that will send you flicking hurriedly from page to page, trying to match it up with one of the illustrations before it takes off. As you gain experience, you learn to guess better, and hence flick less. But in the meantime, the old field guide grows dog-eared and scuffed earlier in life than most books.

For a beginner, a good choice is to get a book where all the information is on the same, or facing, pages. It can be a drag if the range maps are in the back of the book or the write-ups and illustrations aren't together, as is the case with the Peterson and Audubon guides, respectively. Your first field guide would best be either the Golden or the National Geographic.

Recognizing the importance of the major field guides to your feeder-watching pleasure, with each species write-up in Chapter 8, Knowing Your Winged Visitors, I have listed the page numbers where that bird is found in each of the four major field guides. All refer to the most recent editions, as of 1994.

Regional References

If your interest is growing, look for books focused more on your region. Depending on how active the birders in your area have been, you may have a whole range of them dealing with the birds of your region, state, county, district, or town. They range from checklists, which can be encompassed in small brochures, to full-blown, exhaustively researched breeding bird atlases filling one or more fat volumes. There are even booklets that deal with individual marshes or sewage lagoons!

Books that deal with the common species of this or that region can be useful, depending on just how intelligently the author has made his/her judgments on what is "common." If the choices are too few, or not made astutely, such a book quickly lives out its usefulness. Better to spend a little more and go for a more comprehensive reference.

The Bibliography in the back of this book lists some of the publications available on the Pacific Northwest.

Software and Oldware

Computer-owning birders wishing to keep in step with the Information Age can shop around for a range of birding software that stores, cross-references, retrieves, and transmits their accumulated observations with dazzling speed. For some, the humble notebook and pencil are almost relics of the past, replaced by electronic "notebooks" in which data can be entered afield. In the right hands, they are very useful tools. In certain others, the gadgetry takes over and birding becomes a way of keeping a new toy in play.

The mindset that goes with computer technology and the information explosion fosters the attitude that any reference published before 1980 is not worth space on the shelf. Such an assumption robs one of the opportunity to acquire knowledge, and along with it the chance to gain a historical perspective on the traditions of birdwatching. Nature study, birding, and bird feeding have their own well-established body of literature, much of it written by talented amateurs whose dedication and scholarship have added enormously to our understanding of the life sciences.

The Compleat Birder should therefore pop into a good used-book shop on the way home from the computer center. For example, the contributors to Arthur Bent's encyclopedic *Life Histories* delivered scientific fact in lyric prose; some of them unashamedly rhapsodized. Today, however, even in popular publications, writers anxious to be taken seriously grind out copy purged of any taint of fervor. Dulled as we are by such dry fare, old-style writers seem at first to be grandiloquent, emotional, even pompous. But considered in sympathetic perspective, the lyric style of the best of them is a refreshing antidote to the sterile research-paper prose of many of today's writers.

The Notebook

If I were asked to recommend a gift of something essential to a young naturalist, it would not be a camera, computer program, or set of binoculars. It would be a pencil and notepad.

Strange as it may seem, in this age when technology seems to need no justification other than to keep advancing, the most valuable aid to the nature watcher is still the humble notebook. Keeping daily notes of weather, species, numbers, behavior, and anything else of interest gives you an accurate and balanced record of your observations.

If you trust to memory alone, you forget routine details and remember only the unusual or the dramatic. This explains why anecdotal evidence is treated with such scepticism by scientists, and why folklore is full of bizarre and misleading tales of animal behavior. If everyone kept notes and glanced back through them from time to time, to restore the balance of recall between the normal and the sensational, our natural history folklore would be much richer, better balanced, and more reliable.

As time goes by, the possessor of a growing pile of notebooks finds the ones on the bottom becoming increasingly valuable. They give you a look back into the history of your observations, and of your life. What was the weather like this time last year? Ten years ago? Was it in 1976 or 1977 that all those Varied Thrushes descended? When did they arrive, when did they depart?

Without notes, a lifetime of observations by even the most gifted observers is buried when they die. Those of the organized observer have a chance of making a permanent contribution to the body of knowledge we call "science."

Binoculars and Other Magnifiers

To the untrained, naked eye, most songbirds are just little brown things flitting around in the bushes, too far away to be of much interest.

But clap a set of binoculars on them, and suddenly they are at breathtaking arm's length. Wearing their own unique colors, some "little brown things" reveal almost tropical beauty. The immediate response, particularly from children, is "Wow!" It's easy to get hooked.

The pleasure of having feeders in your yard can be enormously enhanced with binoculars. But what kind to buy? What's wrong with Grandpa's venerable World War II set in the leather case? The answer is, nothing—until you compare them with modern models. Until after World War II, binoculars of the sort the average person could afford were bulky and heavy, and all but the most expensive were optically low-performance. Birders of earlier generations used opera glasses—handier but, from samples I have seen, of toy-shop optical quality.

Today's binoculars are sophisticated, lightweight, versatile optical instruments.

Without them, birding could not have grown to the level of popularity it enjoys today. They are as essential as the trusted field guide.

Power

The capacity of binoculars is indicated by a formula, "7x35" for example, in this case referred to as "seven-power." The "7" indicates the degree of magnification; an object seen through it will appear to be six to seven times closer than with the unaided eye. The "35" indicates the diameter in millimeters of the objective lenses, the big ones on the front end of the tubes.

At one time the 7x35 was the birder's standard. It is still very popular, and for most of us is the size with which others are compared; that is, the farther you get from 7x35, the more you depart from "normal."

It is easy to depart from "normal" these days. The vast popularity of birding has turned the binocular market into a designers' free-for-all; the competitors woo customers with an array of choices that bedazzle the first-time buyer. There are lightweight, compact, armored, and waterproof models, Porro prism and roof-prism designs, and a host of other features.

Magnification, or "power," isn't everything. Quality, and resulting clarity, must be considered; you will see far better with good seven-power binoculars than with poor ten-power. In binoculars, power range begins at 6x and ends at 10x—anything lower is rather unexciting, anything higher is difficult to hold steadily enough to be useful. Even your heartbeat registers as a rhythmic shake with high-power, hand-held scopes. Prices range from $50 to well over $1,000.

In 1991 Carl Zeiss Optics abruptly rendered the foregoing obsolete for those to whom cost is no obstacle. In that year the company introduced to the European market 20x60 binoculars. A built-in stabilization system, activated with the touch of a button, eliminates most of the shakes. They are large—ten inches long, six inches wide, weighing about 3½ pounds. The suggested retail price of $4,725 (as of 1994) could be justified to some degree if owning a pair meant you wouldn't need to buy a spotting scope and tripod. As of 1992 these "super-binoculars" were available on the North American market.

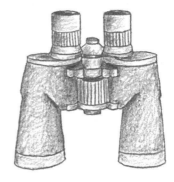

Large or small, good binoculars aid thorough appreciation of birds.

Quality

How to know good quality? Try them! Step out of the shop with a couple of sets. Focus down the street on signs and license plates. You should be able to see at least as clearly through binoculars as you can without them in good light conditions. And since color is important in identifying and enjoying birds, make sure this comes through without distortion. If elements of the image are edged with rainbow borders, forget them; this is a sign of really cheap optics. Is the image clear right to the edges? Are there streaks of stray light or flashes inside the image that are bothersome? How wide is the field of view?

On even casual birding trips you spend a lot of time looking through your binoculars; it is therefore important that they feel comfortable. How heavy are they? Do they fit your eyes easily? Is the focusing rotor stiff, or is it so loose the binoculars will be turned off-focus with every nudge?

You may run into the term "exit pupil." This is a number obtained by dividing the objective lens diameter by the magnification. The larger the objective lens, the more light it gathers. Thus, you will see better under dim light with 7x50s, exit pupil seven-plus, than with equal quality 7x35s, exit pupil five.

"Eye relief" is the measure (in millimeters) of how far from the eyepiece your eyes can be and still see the whole field of view in the ocular lenses. As critical as this feature is to eyeglass wearers, it is often not mentioned in descriptive blurbs.

If you hold binoculars several inches away from your eyes, you see two bright spots in the center of each ocular lens. As you bring the glass closer, the spots enlarge until the image fills the lenses, or the eyepieces bump your glasses and you are still looking through a peephole. Short eye relief can be a curse to the birder with spectacles; you are either constantly juggling the two sets of eyeware, or must resign yourself to forever squinting through that peephole.

Eye relief is something you had better get right when you buy new binoculars; it is built in and cannot be adjusted. It ranges from one-quarter to five-eighths inch (six to sixteen millimeters), with most falling between three-eighths and one-half inch (ten and twelve millimeters). Some models with mid-range eye relief have rubber eye cups that fold back, supposedly allowing you to use glasses. For some, these may not compensate for short eye relief.

As convenient as long eye relief is for spectacle-wearers, a disadvantage of not having the eyepieces pushed close to your eyes is the extraneous light that shines into the space. Especially in bright glare—snow, bright sand, water—the stray, distracting light dims the image. This can be partially offset by wearing a long-peaked hat with a dark underside, and blocking off the space between eye socket and eyepiece with your fingers.

In cold weather, eyepiece lenses fog over when you hold them close to your eyes, a problem that is aggravated by the tendency of your eyes to water in the cold. Your glasses will help prevent fogging due to the greater distance between your eyes and the cold eyepiece lens, and the barrier of the eyeglass lenses.

The adjustment range of most binoculars compensates for quite a range of short- and long-sightedness. Since the focusing mechanism moves both barrels simultaneously, one eyepiece (usually the right) can be independently adjusted to allow for differences between your eyes. When you buy binoculars, get the shop owner to show you how to "balance" them.

If it is too late for that and you must balance your binoculars yourself, go outdoors and select an object—a dead tree, a billboard, or a high-rise building—with good, sharp lines to focus on. Shut the right eye and, using the central focusing wheel, focus the left until you have the sharpest possible image of your distant object. Then shut the left eye, and focus the right on the same object using only the eyepiece focusing ring. Once you can see the distant object as clearly with the right as with the left, your binoculars are balanced and you will get equal sharpness at all distances.

When you have done your "balancing act," it's a good idea to note the position of the focusing ring on the "plus" and "minus" scale on the right eyepiece so that you can quickly reset it if it is nudged off-focus, or if a friend has a look and fiddles with the adjustments.

We associate binoculars with distance, hence "near focus" is usually ignored by beginning shoppers. But if you are buying binoculars in part at least for through-the-window viewing of feeders, a set that won't focus down to ten feet (three meters) will be less useful. Try for the shortest focus you can get; eight feet (2.4 meters) or less is great. These binoculars will come in handy for museums, art galleries, conservatories, and other exhibits where close-up study, or reading labels, may be otherwise difficult. As an item of interest, the near focus distance of the Zeiss 20-power binoculars discussed above is fifty feet (fifteen meters).

Zoom is the ability to change magnification and is essential on video cameras. On binoculars, zoom is a nonessential. Cheap is bad luck. As for good-quality zoom, the extra money you have to lay out for it would be better spent on going to better quality on standard features.

Monoculars

Monoculars are the modern miniature of the old sea captain's telescope. They are incredibly compact and very lightweight, and some have great optical qualities, including very close focus. Several of my acquaintance focused down to a matter of a foot or so, permitting examination of the interiors of flowers and the surface features of insects! Price, of course, since you are paying for only half a binocular, is very reasonable.

Spotting Scopes

In any well-frequented birding spot you will see people with spotting scopes mounted on tripods. These are the trademark of the serious birder. They are essential for work on shorebirds, waterfowl, and hawks, where distant flocks or individuals cannot be approached closely enough to be accurately identified with even the best of binoculars. The tripods are no affectation; at powers ranging from 20x to 60x, scopes can be used only on a very secure base. A good scope is a significant investment, one that should be made only after it has become evident that birding is, for you, a serious pastime.

Window Management

The charm of a window feeder—the closeness of the birds—can turn into its chief disadvantage under some circumstances. If there is a lot of activity inside the room, the birds may be constantly startled away. Some species are more flighty than others, and some individuals seem to quickly grow accustomed to the activity inside and ignore it altogether.

If there are drapes or venetian blinds on the window, leaving them closed, or partially so, for the first few days that a feeder is in use, and then gradually opening them, will enable the birds to get used to the sight of movement inside. It helps, as you move about or draw closer for a better look, if you are wearing neutral or dark clothing.

For my own feeder window in the city, I installed a temporary curtain of dark netting across the lower half. White netting is difficult to see through, impossible if the sun is shining on it. Camouflage netting, unless you enjoy the paramilitary association, is only slightly better than white. Black is best. It obstructs the birds' view of the room, especially if it is relatively darker than the outdoors, and allows you a somewhat hazy view of them. For photographs from a concealed position, cut several strategically placed vertical slits in the netting big enough to poke the camera lens through.

Solar Films

A partially mirrored or tinted layer can be added to window glass with a thin sheet of reflective or tinted plastic film, the same stuff used for office building and vehicle windows. Accordingly, it is available from glass specialty dealers or auto accessory shops. In the event that you are willing to follow directions, it can be applied by the do-it-yourself method. It goes on the inside.

The silvered variety, which imparts a semimirrored effect, could precipitate window collisions in some locations. Try it, and if this is a problem, see Window Pain, in Chapter 5, The Downside. The only reaction from my birds that a newly installed solar film prompted was in a chickadee that challenged its own reflection a few times before dismissing it as no threat. Other than this minor reaction, there have been no complications, and I find that during full daylight, with my study lights on, I can move about on my side of the window without alarming those on the other side.

Both the tint and mirroring will cut down on the amount of light passing through the glass, and the tint will slightly affect the color values of photos taken through it. There is also some loss of clarity, but this is not a critical handicap for the superclose-ups you can get with good telephoto lenses and the extreme closeness of subjects at window feeders.

Frost and Ice

In those regions of the Pacific Northwest where winters are cold, frost, or persistent vapor on the inside of the glass can be a problem, particularly in kitchens or rooms close to the bathroom. Scraping at frost or wiping away vapor is a waste of time and frightens the birds.

One alternative is a fan. It can be quite small, and it needn't be a heater; all it has to do is move enough warm room air past the glass and the frost will disappear very rapidly. On severely cold days it will begin to re-form soon after you turn the fan off. At full speed the whirling blades are invisible to the birds, but if you turn the fan off so you won't stick your elbow into it while preoccupied with a camera, remember that in the last couple of revolutions the flash of the slowing blades might scare your subjects. My fan has pliable plastic blades that won't harm straying fingers—or elbows.

Photography

Taking pictures—prints, slides, or videos—of the birds at a feeder can be an absorbing way of recording their presence and behavior and of sharing your interests with others. Behind your window, you can set your camera on a tripod, pre-focus it on the feeder, and leave it there, ready for action. You enjoy shirt-sleeve comfort no matter how rough conditions are outside. Photography, although it can be a fascinating adjunct, is not one of birdwatching's essentials. Refer to a photography guide for additional information.

CHAPTER 5

The Downside

Feeding birds and other drop-ins should be a happily benevolent pastime. But anyone who elects to live close to wild animals of any kind invites possible aggravation. They do not come to our feeders to be cute and entertaining, they are there to help themselves survive. Therefore, they deal with us, our dwellings, and our handouts on *their* terms.

Knowing ahead of time what some of the pitfalls are can prevent your pleasant hobby from turning into a disappointment. This is important, not just for your own peace of mind, but for the well-being of the animals. If you abruptly quit feeding, or try to get rid of your erstwhile guests, you will be adding another burden to their fight for survival.

"Animals," by the way, includes birds. When people refer to "birds and animals" they usually mean "birds and mammals."

Some parts of this chapter deal with clearly sensitive questions. What about the highly emotional issue of cats? To some they are beloved pets, to others intolerable nuisances because they trespass and eat birds. What should be done if you are faced with a clearly undesirable animal? Are there ethical challenges to bird feeding that one should think about? In addressing these and other questions, I adopt the "ounce of prevention is worth a pound of cure" philosophy. Unpleasant cures are mentioned only to provide humane alternatives if the precautions don't work.

"Problem" animals are not uniquely a bird feeders' headache. People who would not dream of throwing a seed to a bird still have to confront raccoons, squirrels, rats, and cats. But those of us who feed birds adopt a special relationship to wildlife and in good conscience must deal with animal problems humanely and with the animals' interests in mind as well as our own.

BIRD PROBLEMS

No-Limit Demands

One downside of feeding arises from the fact that all animals, the desirable just as much as the undesirable, must survive by taking maximum advantage of resources when they have the chance. Therefore they have no built-in limits to their demands on your hospitality. In human terms, they may seem plain greedy.

This is actually an easily managed appetite. The demands of the vast majority of species are easily met by simply ensuring that there is a continuing supply of the right kinds of feed, accessible in the right places. No matter how insatiable their appetites, a half dozen chickadees, a few juncos, and a family of jays are not going to strain your patience or your budget.

That state of tranquil stability can change quickly if you are abruptly blessed with a big flock of winter finches, a clearly desirable class of visitors. Birds like Evening Grosbeaks have big appetites and love to gang up on your feeder in noisy mobs. If you have a small feeder and elect to leave it at that, these cheerful nomads will likely move on, possibly to someone who has a bigger table. From time to time a few may drop in as they make the rounds of neighborhood feeders.

But if you choose to play the major host by setting up a big table, be ready to serve up a lot of seeds. It would be thoughtful as well to put up several hanging feeders or pole feeders to give your faithful little chickadees and juncos a chance if they are crowded off the main feeder by the jostling finches.

What you will have is more of everything: more feeders to fill and keep clear of husks and droppings, more window washing if you have a window shelf, more cats. None of this is a problem if you feel you are still in control and that the rewards of having more birds to entertain you compensate for the extra effort.

Window Pain

A sound that many bird lovers learn to dread is the thump of a bird colliding with glass.

Their heartache is amply justified. In the 1989–1990 feeding season, the Cornell University Lab of Ornithology, through its Project FeederWatch, asked participants to tally window kills. Although the sample was small, it pointed to a problem of massive proportions, indicating at least 95 million window fatalities a year throughout North America.

This distressing figure backed up studies done by Daniel Klem of Muhlenberg College in Pennsylvania. Alarmed at what he perceived to be a serious problem, and irked by the birding establishment's indifference to it, he began in the mid-1970s to conduct surveys and tests to quantify the damage. A major objective was to make window kills a public conservation issue.

Klem found that there are some 98 million housing units, commercial complexes, and public institutions in the United States and Canada. If each kills an average of one bird per year, the loss is a major one. However, since this is based on only one building per company or school, when in fact most consist of more than one, and many office buildings are literally sheathed in glass, Klem suggests that his estimate may be ten times too low; 980 million kills per year is a horrific loss, the more so because it is in large part preventable.

Several factors cause window collisions.

If birds can see through a building, or a corner of it, they may attempt to fly through the transparent passage. Closing one set of drapes will correct this situation. In my view, however, the main cause of collisions is the mirror effect of glass. Birds see their world reflected in it and attempt to fly through. Pulling the drapes in this case will merely muffle the sound of each collision.

The Panic Zone

The number of birds, and the proximity of the feed source to the window, affect the number and severity of strikes. A large feeder four to eight feet from a window is within what I call the "panic zone."

Depending on the level of alarm, birds flaring in commotion off a feeder go some distance in whichever direction reflex panic sends them before control takes over from fright. The more birds there are (mob hysteria being what it is), the more severe the panic is, the more distracting the commotion, the wider the panic zone.

If a window is in the panic zone, frightened birds will flare into it. An obvious mitigating provision would be to place a large feeder ten feet or more from the nearest large window.

An exception to this guideline are feeders that are either very close to the glass, or actually fixed to it. They hold fewer birds as a rule, and in such close proximity the birds bump or touch the glass during their normal activity, and learn to avoid it, even in a panic.

Some windows, even large ones, rarely cause collisions; others, even small ones, are real killers. If you have one of these, and feed birds, you are conscience-bound to immediately do what you can to minimize the casualties. The hastiest fix is to cut the reflecting effect of the glass by smearing or spraying the outside of it with something to create a visible film. This may look messy, but will give you time to devise something more satisfactory.

Prevention: Paper Hawks and Nets

Among the touted deterrents are silhouettes or cut-outs of hawks or owls that can be mounted on the glass. I have never tried these; some who have say they work, others say they are useless. Remember that a black silhouette with a darkened room behind it will be virtually invisible. I have also heard that sticking a round piece of bright red paper in the middle of the window will work. If one doesn't, maybe a scattering of them would. They will be *much* more effective on the outside; anything on the inside will be largely obscured behind the reflective surface.

This falcon silhouette might help prevent window hits.

Effective solutions devised by two readers of *Bird Watcher's Digest* were reported in the May/June 1994 issue. One sprayed the inside of her picture window with a light scattering of artificial snow, which "solved the problem entirely." The other cut one-inch strips out of black garbage bags and tacked them over her big "killer" window. The first spring she used three, but later found that just one provided enough movement to keep birds wary. I have heard of one case where strips of fluorescent orange survey tape, hung three feet apart and hanging down to the bottom of the window, completely prevented window strikes in a cottage where, along with many previous songbird fatalities, a Ruffed Grouse had once crashed right through.

The only method that I have thus far found to be completely effective is nylon netting sold in garden supply stores to protect strawberries and soft fruits from birds. It comes in packets, six feet wide in varying lengths, and is not expensive. It is easily stapled or taped on, and is a minor intrusion on the viewscape if stretched on neatly. It also has the advantage of not flailing about in the wind, as the plastic tapes do, and thus doesn't alarm birds on breezy days.

Rescue and Recovery

Contrary to their floppy-headed condition when you pick them up, collision-stunned birds suffer concussion, not broken necks.

Birds that stun themselves against windows should be picked up immediately; many cats have learned to come on the run when they hear the thump of bird on glass. If you get there first, put the bird into a small box or paper bag. Make sure there is a hole for fresh air, and put the bird in a quiet place. In a few moments you may hear it scrabbling about. Leave the container closed, take it outside, and give the convalescent a chance to fly. If nightfall comes while the bird is recovering, leave it alone until morning, then liberate it.

Injured birds unable to fly after a decent period of recovery might be nursed back to health if they can be persuaded to eat. Fruit- and seed-eaters are easy to provide for; a generous cage, water, and patience could have the desired effect.

If, sadly, you do end up with a dead bird, don't just chuck it into the garbage. Museums, universities, government wildlife agencies, wildlife artists, and some serious birders maintain study collections and appreciate getting specimens in good condition. Wrap the bird in a plastic bag and put it into the freezer, labeled with date and location of death. Remember that unless you have a collector's permit, it is against the law to maintain a collection of wild specimens.

Woodpeckers

Now and then woodpeckers take it into their heads to hammer on buildings at dawn. It may help the afflicted householders to know that this is in the interest of romance, not public disturbance. Most woodpeckers drum, although the most enthusiastic seem to be Downy and Hairy Woodpeckers, and Northern Flickers.

The drumming is a super-fast rapping on surfaces that resonate well. It is a courting ritual that begins in early spring. You can deny the drummers access to their instrument by draping it loosely with netting or some heavy fabric. Or you might muffle it with scraps of carpet. Putting up hardware cloth with spacers to keep it an inch or so clear of the surface may be a sufficient foil. These deterrents can be tacked temporarily in place until the birds find other drums, or the silly season ends.

Sufferers who have simply persisted in scaring off the birds when they begin their drumming report that this works. As a diversion, one might put up a piece

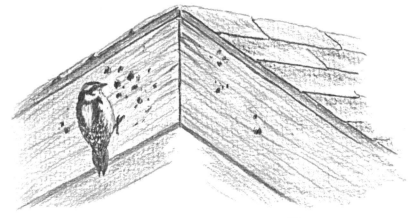

This Downy Woodpecker is drilling for insects in small spaces in the wood.

of thin plywood some distance from the house. This may give the birds an alternative drum, and the neighbors a new perspective on nature. People who have tried to frighten off woodpeckers with a plastic owl have found that it works only until the bird realizes it's a dummy, which usually doesn't take very long.

Another form of woodpecker damage is drilling, in some cases a full-sized hole obviously intended as a nest. In an old shed this may be acceptable, but it is not usually tolerable when done on a house. Again, scaring off the birds or covering the hole with metal or screen will eventually discourage them.

What they really need is a nest tree, a dead-hearted trunk, still fairly sound on the surface, ten to fifteen feet long, six inches or more in diameter at the top. Here, you might repeat an experiment conducted by Lawrence Kilham, medical scientist and amateur ornithologist of note.

Unable to get to the woods to pursue woodpeckers one busy autumn, he decided to try to lure them to his yard instead. He collected a number of fallen tree trunks of various degrees of unsoundness and wired them upright to the posts in his backyard. To his delight, four Downy Woodpeckers soon called and began tapping up and down and around the new snags. All eventually made roost holes.

It was apparently important that Dr. Kilham gave the Downies a choice, so if you decide to repeat the experiment, don't be stingy with the imported "trees." And don't trim the branches off closely; some woodpeckers show a definite preference for locating holes under good-sized limbs.

Among a number of biologists who have recently taken to the clear-cuts to assess their effects on wildlife, Ken Bevis of Ellensburg, Washington has conducted studies on, among other things, woodpeckers. He reports that they are very specific about where they do their nest-hole drilling. They seek out trees or snags where the heartwood is at just the proper stage of decay—not really rotten, but mellow enough to provide relatively easy excavating once the harder sapwood has been penetrated.

Selecting a location for, and excavating, a nest cavity is an essential part of woodpecker courting ritual and mate bonding. That is why they rarely use nest boxes. Mr. Bevis relates that at one time a pair of flickers were damaging the siding of his house. His attempt to divert them with a nest box failed. Instead he got starlings, which, when they had settled in, drove away the flickers!

Woodpecker drilling often has nothing to do with either courting or nesting, but consists of rows of punctures in plywood, cedar, or other wood siding. The birds are insect-hunting, probing into natural cavities or pre-existing insect tunnels in boards, or into gaps between the inner plies of plywood. They may actually be digging out flies, wasps, or tunneling insects that got in at the edges of the plywood.

The trick is to keep the bugs out. A good coat of paint or a filler material can be applied to any exposed ends of board or ply siding. This will effectively block the insects' access points and, hence, the woodpeckers' reasons for poking holes.

MAMMAL PROBLEMS

Rodents: A Gnawing Problem

Rodents of all kinds are enthusiastic about seeds, as any squirrel will be glad to demonstrate. But inadvertently attracting rats and mice is another matter. Hence, prevention—*strict* prevention—can save a great deal of aggravation and possible expense.

The first line of defense is good seed storage. The best containers for me are metal garbage cans with sturdy, tight-fitting lids. They hold a lot of seeds and are rain- and raccoon-proof, so can be left outside, handy to the feeders. Anything made of plastic can easily be chewed into by a determined rodent, and raccoons can pry off the lids of the flimsier models.

The second perimeter of defense is the buildings. In advance of each winter I do a patrol of the premises to check for burrows, holes, and gnawings. Tunnels under ground-level footings or slabs can be doctored with a few mothballs and then filled with coarse crushed rock. Above-ground breaks or holes can be sheeted over with metal, which can be a flattened tin can if the patch is out of sight or you're not proud—or both.

Having taken all reasonable measures to keep rodents from getting in where they don't belong, I can enjoy the prospect of a season's feeding with reasonable assurance that I can play host to pretty well anything without suffering damage, or creating a nuisance for my neighbors.

I'm pleased to record that my own system of preventive maintenance works; it has been several seasons since I have had problems with squirrels, and longer ago than I can easily recall when a mouse breached security long enough to make its presence felt, or to reproduce. Rats, however, have posed some problems.

There Goes the Neighborhood

The northwestern coast of North America enjoys the distinction of being the only place on the continent still blessed with two species of nonnative rat. Notorious stowaways, they found their way to seaports around the world. The first to jump ship from the earliest vessels to drop anchor in the New World was the Roof Rat, *Rattus rattus,* also called the Black Rat. Once abundant in Europe, it was almost totally displaced by another Asian invader, inappropriately called the Norway Rat, *Rattus norvegicus.* It too stowed away for North America, where it again routed the Roof Rat. The conquest was incomplete, however; the Roof Rat has been able to hang on in coastal locales in the Pacific Northwest and in British Columbia.

I became personally acquainted with the Roof Rat because, for awhile, its territory happened to include my compost heap and bird feeders. I first noticed one of these animals sitting on the top rail of the picket fence near a hanging feeder that dangled amidst the stems of a mock orange growing against the kitchen wall. The rat, a rounded ball of glossy black fur with beady eyes, big ears, and a long, slim tail, looked like a giant mouse, cute in a way. It, and others, quickly demonstrated their climbing ability by whisking up and down the thin stems of the mock orange to grab seeds from the feeder, nimble as any squirrel. I noticed that they came in two colors, the other shade being more your basic rat gray.

Rats aren't usually as visible as the Mock Orange Scrambler and its friends were. Most of the time the signs are more subtle: bean-sized droppings left overnight on or around your bird feeders, tunnels, and scufflings around the woodpile, compost heap, or the foundations of nearby buildings.

Depending on where you live, peaceful co-existence might be an option, given a measure of tolerance on your part, and a house made secure against invasion. But where there are neighbors, which was certainly my case, harboring rats is socially unacceptable and is, indeed, an offense against civic regulations. Long before things get to the point where you, and perhaps your hobby of bird feeding, can be fingered as contributing to the deterioration of the nieghborhood, you should take action.

If direct intervention is distasteful to you, summon outside help. Pest-control techniques have been improved to respond to heightened public sensitivity to environmental and humane concerns. Check with animal control agencies and animal care societies for recommendations on whom to contact to deal with rats—or any animals—that become an intolerable nuisance.

Relying on a cat to keep rats at bay is a forlorn hope. Very few cats will ever lay a paw on one of these pugnacious fighters.

Squirrels

Squirrels are the most likely members of the walk-in crew to use your feeders as a platform from which to evaluate the possibilities of your house as a den site. The most likely to be doing this in the Pacific Northwest are the imported Eastern Gray Squirrels. They can be at least as much of a challenge as rats because they can chew their way in at roof level as well as burrow in around the foundations.

It takes a round of personal experience to appreciate what large rodents can do to the interior of a dwelling. Once inside, they keep their teeth busy and can be very destructive, especially of things stored in attics where they present the added, nagging fear that they could chew through the wiring and start a fire.

Before you start feeding birds, or before resuming it in the autumn if you are already feeding, it is prudent to make sure the house is as squirrel-proof as you know how to make it. In addition to the measures already suggested for keeping your house rat- and mouse-free, put a heavy screen guard over the chimney. This will not only deter squirrels, but will keep other climbers such as opossums and raccoons outside where they belong.

If you've left it until too late, and squirrels have already moved in, it rarely does any good to try shutting them out by boarding up entrance holes, or stuffing them with steel wool laced with mothballs. In most cases this will simply result in more damage when the squirrel chews its way around them. Sooner or later most people have to face the conclusion that removing the intruder is the only satisfactory conclusion.

Cage Traps

Long ago I equipped myself with two cage traps, one squirrel-sized, one raccoon-sized. If you bait a cage trap with everything the squirrels seem to be eating, plus some peanut butter, and place it where they do most of their scurrying, you might make a catch. Be sure, of course, to check the trap at least a couple of times a day.

Then what? If you have caught a squirrel it will be battling frantically to get out. You owe it to the animal to make up your mind in advance what to do, and to act promptly.

Whatever your plans, first check the captive from underneath, particularly any time between March and the end of July. If it has a double row of swollen nipples, it is a nursing mother and you had better apologize and turn her loose again to finish her maternal duties. Trying to relocate an entire family would simply result in death by starvation of the pups when the traumatized mother abandoned them.

There is one slim hope of early solution to this particular dilemma. One spring some years ago I had a Red Squirrel nesting in a new workshop, and resolved to put up with it until I was sure there were no innocent dependents around. One afternoon I hammered something into the wall of the shop near the nest. Within a half hour the mother squirrel was busy moving her brood. Gripping each pup by the skin of its belly, its body curled around her chin like a pink shrimp, she carried them one by one to a hole in a nearby maple.

The lesson is that the right kind of threatening din could cause a mother squirrel to relocate her brood to a quieter neighborhood.

Back to our captive in the trap: If immediate release is not possible, cover the trap with something or put it into a box. This calms down the occupant.

Non-returnables

If exile is an option, it should be timed with sensitivity. Assuming no maternal complications, conscionable release time is between spring and the end of September. This allows the deportee some chance of establishing itself and laying in a store of winter food. Later than this, its chances greatly diminish; dumping a squirrel into strange territory in late fall or winter is almost certainly condemning it to death by starvation and stress.

To ensure that your exile is non-returnable, drive it well out into the country and liberate it near an extensive patch of likely-looking wooded habitat. Taking squirrels a few blocks away, or even a couple of miles, means they will be back in your yard in a few hours.

If relocation is unconscionable or impractical, you may have to have the animal destroyed. The options here include the local veterinary clinic, humane society, or pest-control firm. There is a fee, usually less if you take the carcass back and dispose of it yourself.

Rat Traps

The standard mouse or "snap" trap is available in an oversized version for rats. When a mouse or rat is caught in a snap trap, it is usually stunned instantly and killed by the blow of the stiff wire bail. Theoretically, a rat trap should be big enough to kill a Red or Douglas Squirrel, since they are about the same size and conformation as rats.

However, they rarely work; one finds the trap sprung. The reason is that these squirrels, given enough maneuvering room, are too quick for the trap. They may get smashed on the head or the nose, but at the instant of contact are already recoiling and end up with an injury. For this reason, rat traps should not be used in an effort to trap Red or Douglas Squirrels. As for Gray or Fox Squirrels, they are so much larger that I have doubts that unless it caught one right behind the ears, or the animal was a very young one, a rat trap would do no more than deliver a painful injury.

Once rid of a problem squirrel, immediately remove accessible nests and close off all the access holes. If you delay, you'll very likely find a replacement has moved in within a few days of the former resident's departure. As well as closing, sheeting, or screening over all holes, try to mask the scent of the previous squirrel. Put mothballs into the holes before closing them off, spray or wipe the area around the holes, and the patch, with something strong-smelling, like household ammonia, or apply a fresh coat of paint.

Domestic Cats

The scene through my study window is cheery and heart-warming. Before a backdrop of brilliant sunshine on fresh snow, chickadees and nuthatches come and go to the feeding tray at the windowsill, sorting out sunflower seeds and darting away with them.

Abruptly there is a heavy thump, a shower of seeds, and an instant of frantic scrambling. On the feeder is a neighbor's tomcat with a chickadee jammed in his jaws. He fixes me with a momentary stare and is gone. He leaves behind some drifting feathers and two converging downstrokes smeared on the glass where his flailing paws trapped the bird.

Had my chickadee fallen prey to a full-time, wild predator I would have viewed the little casualty at my window with fascinated excitement quite untinged by resentment. But the cat is a subsidized predator that does not really live by any ecological rule. He does not need what he kills, but his depredations diminish harmless, desirable wildlife, and deplete the prey base of wild predators, such as owls, that must survive by the rules.

Having licked his chops and smoothed his fur, this on-again, off-again predator would have meowed for readmission to his keeper's cozy house and its unlimited supply of nutritionally fine-tuned kitty-dins. Another mild day and the urge for some excitement, and he would be back, as would my resentment at seeing my birds turned into cat treats.

I should point out that since this event I have evolved passive deterrents to cat depredation. One of these is a protruding fringe of wire mesh around the feeder shelf that foils the jump-and-grab trick.

Tooth-and-Claw Genetics

Cats' nonprofessional status as predators is no reflection at all on their efficiency as killers. Cats, at least the "Brand X" variety that constitute the overwhelming majority that prowl through our yards, have retained their physical and instinctual integrity despite generations of dependency on humans. They have done so because house cats are freelance breeders, legacies of the "free kittens" appeals one sees scrawled on signs tacked to roadside fences. Not for them a succession of those arranged marriages that have made such oddities of some breeds of dogs. However pampered the average suburban tom might be, he must still win his reproductive rights in tooth-and-claw brawls out behind the garage. He is thus prevented from passing on to his descendants anything but physical prowess of the winning kind.

Dazzling athletic ability goes with this heritage. The chickadee-hunter beneath my window pinpointed the location of his unseen victim by the sound of its feet on the wooden tray. From five feet below he launched up, blasted over the edge of the platform, and nailed the bird. His control and balance had to allow him an accurate, lightning-fast grab in whichever direction the bird's own split-second reflexes launched it.

At one time the keeping of cats was judged to be a matter of good domestic and barnyard management, to prevent the premises from being overrun with mice and rats. Little mice and baby birds are one thing, rats are another. Tough and strong, they will fight to the death with frenzied desperation. The average cat has no stomach for such a scuffle. In fact, a study of feral cats in Sweden disclosed that they ate weasels more frequently than they did rats! Alley cats and rats in dumps and back alleys in New York City have been photographed rummaging through garbage virtually nose-to-nose, ignoring each other.

But today's cat need claim no practical justification to be cherished; sentiment and affection rule the day. Good citizens aware of the effect of rain-forest burning on our migrant birds think nothing amiss of the routine of putting the cat out every summer evening. If it tucks away an occasional bird, that's "nature's way." Puss returns from the nightly forays, soft-furred and purring, its adventures cloaked in mystery.

Feline mystery did not deter a couple of scientists in Britain, however. Peter Churcher and John Lawford turned an analytical eye on just what impact pet cats have on animal life. In a study begun in 1981 they monitored cat predation in a small Bedfordshire village by having owners tally all prey their pets brought home or were seen eating.

Their discoveries included some interesting insights into cat behavior: It appears to make no difference if a pet cat is well fed; hunger is not the main hunting motivator. The younger the cat, the more animals it catches. Older cats get lazy, and neutering of males brings on earlier retirement, otherwise there was little gender difference in hunting success. Cats are fair-weather hunters, disinclined to go afield on cold, wet, or windy days.

Nevertheless, in the course of a year, from one-third to one-half of all House Sparrow mortality in the study village was attributable to cats, even though this species accounted for only 16 percent of the total prey tallied. Cats living in the center of the village caught less prey, but the percentage of birds increased. The heaviest months were June and July, due to the large proportion of easily caught baby birds, followed by September, the month of migration.

Massive Impact

Figures tallied by the study disclose massive impact. Although the seventy-seven village cats were actually tallied with an average of four birds per year, Churcher and Lawford note that this is a minimum figure. An American study demonstrated that cats bring home only half of what they catch, either eating the rest on the spot or leaving them behind. This raises the annual average to a more credible eight birds per cat/year.

On the basis of personal observation, I believe even this estimate to be low. I regularly find feathers, wing-ends, flying-squirrel tails, and other remains around the yard. I once watched a friend's pet cat, evading my efforts to intervene, catch and eat five fledgling juncos from a nest alongside his lawn. On the record is one cat in Michigan that brought in 1,660 small mammals and birds in an eighteen-month period.

A simple proportional estimate of the toll by cats in the United States is appalling. Creditable estimates put the number of pet cats at 62 million. If they catch birds at the same rate as their British counterparts, they kill 496 million birds a year. Given that the mild climate over much of the United States encourages year-round hunting, this estimate could well be very conservative. In addition to the pets, there are from 8 to 16 million feral cats in the United States, plus uncensused millions of strays.

Outright kills are only a part of the picture; large numbers of wild animals are injured by cats. A pamphlet published by the Progressive Animal Welfare

Society (PAWS) of Lynnwood, Washington cites a survey of Washington state wildlife rehabilitators. Seventeen percent of the animals in their care were injured by cats, compared to 2 percent hit by cars and 1 percent poisoned. The pamphlet points out that this accounts only for those cat-attacked animals taken to rehab centers.

Coastal areas of the Pacific Northwest have populations of feral cats. "Feral" animals are domestics that have gone wild, breeding and sustaining themselves without direct aid from humankind, although they may rely partly on garbage. In some areas, feral cats have become a real threat to wild bird and small mammal life, and major nuisances around hobby-farm poultry.

You are unlikely to see or hear one of these animals. They are full-time, wild predators, nocturnal, and with all the evasive skills that cats employ.

Strays are a different matter. These are animals that have taken up the wild life after having been in contact with people. Whether lost, abandoned, or just "on the lam," they subsist on a combination of easier pickings from the wild—mice, fledgling birds, baby rabbits—and whatever food they can scrounge from humans. Back-step pets' dishes, open garbage cans, dumps where garbage is left unburned and/or uncovered are important sources.

How to tell a stray from a roving house pet? About a month after cold weather has set in, its behavior and appearance are the giveaways. It can be seen aprowl on miserable days, when house cats are comfortably indoors. Unlike a sleek pet, it will be rough-coated and humped-up. A real stray will also tear into garbage bags and strew the contents around. It will pull down larger game, like rabbits. If you observe it carefully, you will discover that it is living under or in a shed, a brush pile, or a heap of scrap lumber.

Some strays are half-wild and cannot be approached, even though they will yowl at your door if you have been feeding them. Feeding strays simply sustains their impact on wildlife, but ignoring them may be difficult. Aside from their constant hanging about and preying on your birds, their deteriorating condition might be a sorry sight to watch. You may decide that removal is the most humane alternative. Again, there are options, the most likely being your closest animal control firm.

Contrary to what many people assume, animal shelters are not in the business of capturing stray cats. If you want to commit a local stray to a shelter, you are expected to bring it in. If you don't have a suitable-sized cage trap and don't want to buy one, some shelters and agencies will loan or rent you one.

Capturing such a cat is usually very easy. A bit of bacon fat or fish oil on a couple of paper towels will do for bait. Put the trap up off the ground. This eliminates two possible accidental catches: small dogs and skunks. Turning the neighbor's beagle loose is no problem; liberating a skunk is something else again. Two other snoopy prowlers, opossums and raccoons, might also end up behind bars, but with suitable finesse can be released with no loss of blood or dignity.

Pets and Politics

Many devoted cat owners who are also dedicated bird feeders manage their pets to minimize these conflicting interests. Their solution is as obvious as it is effective: Keep cats confined.

Advancing this method as a way of saving the lives of several hundred million songbirds a year may sound reasonable to non-cat owners. But major protests have errupted around issues involving quite reasonable cat-control proposals.

When the city ©of Calgary, Alberta, recently proposed a cat control bylaw, militant cat lovers collected more than 20,000 signatures opposing it. The new law was not harsh; it authorized animal-control officers to capture roving felines and charge their owners before returning the cats to them.

The May/June 1992 issue of *The Bird Watcher's Digest* related a controversy over burrowing owls on the Atlantic University campus in Boca Raton, Florida. The campus had been declared a breeding sanctuary for the owls, threatened or extirpated over most of their traditional range. But they were so heavily preyed upon by roving cats that in the 1991 nesting season only four out of forty young owls survived, and cats were seen with baby owls in their mouths. A proposal to remove or capture the cats was so vehemently opposed by cat lovers that the measure was stalled, and at the time of publication advocates for the survival of the owls had been compelled to launch an appeal for public support to counter the blocking tactics of the pro-cat lobby.

At the heart of the rhetoric mustered in opposition to any civic proposal for cat regulation is the claim that confining a cat is cruel.

This is rubbish, as cats by the millions prove every winter by not only tolerating confinement indoors, but insisting on it. The owners of purebred cats, who must keep their valuable bluebloods inside all their lives, scoff at the notion that doing so is inhumane. Cats raised in confinement are healthier, generate fewer vet bills, and have a life expectancy three times that of their roving counterparts.

Behind the defensive rhetoric of the cat lovers lies the basic fact that it is much less bother to just let a cat out whenever it wants rather than make the extra effort needed to keep it happy indoors. Let it yowl by night under somebody else's window, let it bury revolting surprises in the neighbor's kids' sandbox.

If you have a feeder, you bear the brunt of this abdication of responsibility. The minute they are let out, neighborhood cats head straight for it. Whilst there, they do their territorial marking; my yard and carport constantly reek of cat urine, an irritating and unsanitary reminder of the other side of the "open door" school of cat management.

This imposition is all the more annoying because it runs counter to another tradition. Everywhere, except for cattle on open rangeland, the law requires the owners of pets and livestock to keep their animals *in*, not everyone else to keep them *out*. Why must cats be the only exception?

However ecologically supportable the arguments for confining cats might be, the likelihood of effective civic control is very remote. Public education is having its effect, and you might further this on the local level by explaining to your neighbors the damage that cats do to bird life, and appealing to them to keep their pet indoors for at least part of the day, especially when baby birds are in evidence. In my experience this has had little effect, because most cats that you see in your yard are from anonymous owners. A diplomatic initiative, however, can backfire, triggering the countercharge that your feeders attract cats, and that it is you who is being irresponsible!

Whether you like it or not, the problem is yours, to manage as best you can. It is particularly important that you deal with the problem if you feed birds. Ignoring cat predation might be a way of keeping peace with the neighbors, but it's a betrayal of the birds' interests.

Because the vast majority of nuisance cats are not strays or ferals, but cherished household pets, there is a definite limit to the kind of countermeasures you can take. Forget about setting out booby traps of the Tweety-Bird-and Sylvester kind; they work only in the imagination. And, irony of ironies, any overt signs of hostility toward cats, no matter what the provocation, can leave you open to a charge of harassing an animal.

Aside from the fact that dashing outside, yelling, throwing things, or brandishing the garden hose could get you charged with an offense, they are a waste of energy and dignity. Cats quickly learn contempt for such futile spluttering, and respond by simply becoming more evasive. They remain habitual lurkabouts, adding insult to injury by leaving little piles of bloodied feathers and wing-ends for you to find.

Ownership of a spirited dog is one way of keeping the environs cat-free. But a dog doesn't fit in with everyone's life-style, mine included. At one time I enlisted the help of a friend's dog, an explosively energetic fox terrier that responded with impressive zeal when the word "cats!" was spoken. "Zip" was a stayover guest several times, to the chagrin of the cats. Once she had put several persistent ones up a tree, minus some fluff from their back ends, they got the message.

Some well-meaning owners put a bell on their cat in the belief it will warn birds. Some creditable observations indicate this works, but in other instances it is a failure. Cats kill by slow stalking and motionless waiting. A bell gives no warning tinkle until the final spring, by which time it is too late. The only really effective bell, as a friend wryly observed, would be one weighing about forty pounds.

Bells, dogs, and other deterrents aside, my own strategy centers on doing what I can to make it as awkward as possible for cats to ambush my birds. I do this by removing or altering potential ambush points, and fencing off any that can't be neutralized. Based on passive obstruction, it is nonviolent, calls for a minimum of time and cash, and needs little tending. Done with sufficient ingenuity it can create a safe haven for birds in which all but the suicidally foolhardy can safely alight and feed even as the cats look on.

Thinking Like a Cat

The first step is reconnoitering the territory and, from a cat's point of view, looking for potential ambush points. The ideal place of concealment is close under a feeder where birds habitually go to the ground, and are preoccupied in their search for spilled seeds. Ornamental bushes, scrap piles, and items of yard furniture are all good hides. If there's a clear space in front of the hiding place it makes it easier for a hidden cat to make a quick, unobstructed rush.

In such a setting, a cat has only to hide and wait. Eventually, pinpointing a target that is close by, preoccupied with feeding, and has its back turned, the cat springs. Everything explodes as the birds burst away—all except one.

For ambush points that cannot be removed, the trick is to screen them off, using the same principle that governs the use of barbed-wire entanglements by the military, which is to impede movement at key points. This simply means putting a low fence around places of concealment.

Let the cat lash its tail and drool under the junipers all it wants; a low perimeter of stucco wire or poultry screen (chicken wire) between the bush and the feeding place robs it of a clear rush. The birds can clearly see through the screen, and if the cat has to break cover first by jumping over the wire at the start of its rush, they will have that split-second of warning they need to get away.

Construction requirements are simple. The wire barrier need be only eighteen to twenty-four inches high, and it can be tacked or stapled at the ends to

This yard has really been wired for cats.

This little scene says it all.

a couple of stakes driven into the ground or pushed into packed snow. Curving the wire around the hideout gives it more stability and minimizes the need for props.

For post feeders or shelves close to a hideaway that you can't eliminate for some reason (like not wanting to dynamite the garage), you can frustrate the grab-over-the-edge trick by installing a fringe of wire that sticks out horizontally around the sides of the shelf for eight to ten inches.

The most suitable and least expensive screen for my purposes has proven to be stucco wire. It comes in 4- and 4½-foot widths, with a 2-inch-square mesh, and you can buy it off the roll from building supply retailers. It can be snipped to the desired shape with wire cutters or sturdy tinsnips. It stands up more stiffly than poultry screen, and thus doesn't need to be put in a frame or propped up except at the ends. It is also much neater; deployed around the ornamentals at the front of your house, it tends less to give the place the look of an unfinished rabbit run.

A further advantage of stucco wire is that small birds can flit through it easily, larger ones like Steller's Jays and doves can squeeze through it, but crows and pigeons are excluded.

Although I resent having to fuss with controlling other people's pets in my own yard, the passive fences are the only humane, socially acceptable, low-cost, and reasonably effective response I can come up with.

CHAPTER 6

Those Fascinating Birds

Birds have wings and can fly. As if this wasn't enough of a miracle, when we land-bound pedestrians study these creatures, we discover that they possess a suite of other physical gifts that goes far beyond the humble capacities of ourselves and indeed of most other mammals of our acquaintance.

Take survival. From the centrally heated side of our windows, we see tiny birds that can feed and fly and move about on their side of the glass no matter that it could be forty below. And they do it in their little bare feet! We hear of pilots spotting geese, vultures, and other large birds cruising or soaring along at altitudes three times higher than the point where humans require supplementary oxygen.

And yet, when you pick up a bird or one hits the windshield of your car, it seems vulnerably delicate, light, and fragile. Obviously, this is a very special kind of body. And since we are dealing with its ability to withstand our winters, it is appropriate to do a brief review of how it accomplishes this.

Physiology

Free, powered flight is the ultimate form of transportation. On wings you float in the cushion of air, free of the rough, entangling path and the pounding burden of gravity.

But there is a catch—indeed, several of them. The laws of physics limit your weight to a maximum of around forty-four pounds, found in the Great Bustard of Europe and Asia. On this continent, the flying heavyweight is the Trumpeter Swan. Any heavier than these and you walk, like the ostrich.

Flying also involves energy trade-offs. It is expensive to fly, since you burn energy three to four times faster than you would if you walked. But in terms of distance covered, flight is very efficient because it takes only one-quarter as much energy to cover a given distance. Managing this trade-off demands a high intake of both food and oxygen.

To minimize the penalties of flight, birds evolved aeons ago for a combination of strength and lightness, beginning with the skeleton. The bird airframe is rigid, the backbone fused along most of its length into one member, the ribs braced against each other, the sternum a huge keel set in a supporting hull of light bone. The wing and leg bones are hollow, light, and supported inside by a latticework of supporting struts. They are part of the bird's respiratory system.

Supercharger Lungs and Heart

A bird's lungs are small, relative to those of comparably sized mammals. But they have phenomenal throughput, being connected to a system of air sacs and the hollow limb bones that permit a flow of air that is largely one-way. In 1758, to demonstrate the whole-body nature of bird respiration, British naturalist John Hunter cut through the humerus (the main wing bone) of a bird, then tied off its windpipe. He found it could still breathe, after a fashion, through the hollow bone. He then repeated the experiment on another unfortunate subject and discovered that it could breathe through its femur, the main leg bone.

When a bird breathes under effort, each puff clears almost all the stale air out of the lungs. When a mammal gasps for breath, a certain percentage of each exhalation is left behind. In terms of performance, this means that birds can exert the considerable effort of flight and maintain it for long periods at high altitudes, as they do in migration.

A vivid demonstration of the relative respiratory ability of mammals and birds is cited in an account in *Birds of Britain and Europe* in which sparrows and mice were placed in a chamber where the air pressure was equivalent to that atop Mount Everest. The birds went on with their usual activity, unperturbed, while the mice were severely distressed and could only grope and stagger about.

To complement the capacity of the lungs, birds' hearts are relatively much larger than are those of mammals of similar size. And they operate at high-performance levels; even at rest a chickadee's heart beats 400 times a minute, and double that when it is active.

High Body Temperature

Metabolic processes work faster at higher temperatures, and birds have higher normal body temperatures than mammals. As a farm lad, when farms were still a menagerie of various animals, I observed that hens could survive deep wounds that would have killed other animals from infection. The reason was that mammal-adapted bacteria can't survive in the birds' high body temperature, which hovers around 104° Fahrenheit for a bird at rest. This is very close to the critical upper limit; above this, protein enzymes become unstable and begin to break down, and essential body functions go awry.

Very obviously, feathers are critical to the maintenance of stable body temperatures in our wintering birds. They are a double defense; the smooth, slick contour feathers, arranged shingle-fashion, are an efficient wind and water barrier. Beneath them lies a layer of insulating down, one of nature's most efficient ways of enclosing a small body in an envelope of warm air.

High-performance Foraging

Gathering the food to fuel this high-temperature, high-speed body is made possible by the very equipment that burns most of it: the wings. Birds have access to insects, their eggs, and their pupae in places few mammals can reach. This includes the outermost twigs of trees as well as their woody hearts; chickadees forage among the smallest branches of trees, woodpeckers drill beneath the bark. In the chickadees' case the pressure to be productive is intense; it is estimated that in winter they must find a food item on the average of every two or three seconds in order to survive.

Winter Survival

A few winters ago in mid-February I was watching a Whitethroated Sparrow on my window feeder. At that time I was living and feeding birds in Winnipeg, where Whitethroats are very unusual winter holdovers, so I had been paying particular attention to him during the several weeks since his first appearance.

On this particular morning he seemed to be dizzy; whenever he attempted to lift one foot into the warmth of his belly feathers, he teetered sideways drunkenly. It would have been a mildly comical performance, except on that bitterly cold day he was in the last throes of starvation. Too weak to feed, he finally fluttered away. I never saw him again.

Every winter a few individuals from species that normally migrate either choose, or are forced, to stick around. In a very severe climate, of the kind Winnipeggers enjoy, it takes a lot of luck to survive—a mild winter, very good shelter, a source of plentiful food. But considering the behavioral and physiological adaptations that allow nonmigrants to live through the rigors of a subarctic winter, my unfortunate Whitethroat was undoubtedly more the rule than the exception.

Cold Tolerance

Low temperature of itself is a secondary problem because birds are already equipped to fly about in frigid air, as they must do for extended stretches at high altitudes during migration. When at rest and not generating surplus heat, they fluff up their feathers and stay out of the wind if they can.

To test just how well adapted birds are, winter-acclimatized goldfinches, Pine Siskins, and Purple Finches were experimentally subjected to sustained temperatures of –94 degrees Fahrenheit. They went on with their usual activities apparently little stressed by the numbing cold. They maintained normal temperature and mobility as long as they had sufficient food to maintain a critical level of body fat.

Feathers explain how the body can stay warm, but all of us who feed birds have marveled at why the wire-thin little legs and toes are able to function no matter how cold it gets, unlike human fingers, which become uselessly numb when chilled. It helps that the oily tissues of the fleshless feet and lower legs retain little residual moisture and resist freezing. Unlike human fingers, which are rendered uselessly numb when the nerves cannot function at even slightly depressed temperatures, the nerves in birds' feet retain their function at near-freezing temperatures.

Behavior also plays a part; in severe conditions birds often momentarily stand on one leg, pulling the other up into the belly feathers. Ground feeders like juncos and redpolls crouch low, from time to time squatting down to cover their legs and feet.

There is a further adaptation in the circulatory system feeding the lower legs. In the upper, feathered leg, the arteries and veins pass close to each other in a heat-exchange network of capillaries where incoming veinous blood is warmed and outgoing arterial blood is cooled. Blood flow to the lower legs and feet can thus be controlled in response to the need to either conserve or radiate heat.

Hoarding

For most birds, the supply of winter food and, even more crucially, the amount of daylight in which to search for it are severely restricted compared to summer conditions. To use an extreme example, in arctic Fairbanks, Alaska midwinter daylight can be as short as three and a quarter hours, and temperatures during the long nights regularly drop to forty below or lower. And yet Boreal Chickadees survive these conditions, with or without the help of Fairbanks bird feeders. In these conditions, hoarding could be a crucial factor.

Feeding stations provide a marvelous opportunity for hoarders, and for the people who enjoy watching them. Chickadees, jays, and nuthatches will hurriedly feed at dawn, then spend the rest of every day diligently stashing sunflower seeds, to the end that by springtime each probably has enough hidden away to feed at least twenty of its kind. Complementing the hoarding impulse is a good memory; chickadees have shown an accurate recall interval of up to eight months.

Given unrestricted access to suet, crows, jays, and magpies usually start hauling away chunks of it, in great haste, before eating. They will keep at it until the supply is exhausted, a habit that has taught bird benefactors to offer suet in protective cages that limit the take to peck-sized pieces.

Gray Jays have raised hoarding to a fine art. Like most jays, they "scatter hoard," hiding each bit in its own niche—the dense twigs at the tips of a conifer branch, a hole in bark, or a crack in a snag. Unlike other jays, they avoid storing food in the ground, instinctively selecting hideaways high enough to not be buried under the snow the following winter.

These jays have hugely oversized salivary glands. They use the copious, gooey saliva to form fragments of food into a sticky glob and to help hold it in its hiding place. An essential property of the saliva is that it dries into a water-resistant glaze that helps preserve the food. Not the least of the birds' skills is remembering where hundreds and hundreds of tidbits are concealed. Gray Jays begin nesting in winter and rely on this stored food to raise their young.

Cuddling Up

Further behavioral adaptations help solve the problem of the long, cold, foodless nights. Woodpeckers roost in tree holes excavated for the purpose. Chickadees habitually sleep together in holes. Twenty-nine White-breasted Nuthatches have been found in one tree cavity, and twenty or more Brown Creepers in close huddles beneath slabs of loose bark. Redpolls may avail themselves of mouse holes in the snow, or dig their own.

Among House Sparrows, the more fortunate get into buildings, signs, and light fixtures with a built-in source of heat. The less privileged wedge themselves into holes and crannies, perhaps utilizing last summer's nest for additional insulation. Ravens, sometimes in large numbers, roost in dense conifers.

Hibernation, which turns winter into one long night of deep torpor, was unconfirmed in birds until a Poorwill (*Phalaenoptilus nuttalli*) was found dormant in a rock crevice in the Colorado Desert of California in 1946. Others have since been discovered dormant, with body temperatures down from normal 106° Fahrenheit to 64° Fahrenheit. Less pronounced torpor occurs in swifts, swallows, and hummingbirds, enabling them to cut energy expenditure during periods of food shortage.

The point of this example is that it is not surprising to discover that during cold winter nights, roosting chickadees become torporous. Their body temperature drops by 13 Fahrenheit degrees, and their respiration falls from ninety-five to sixty-five breaths per minute.

Big Is Better

The smaller a creature is, the greater is its surface area relative to body mass, and the greater its problem of retaining heat. We demonstrate this ourselves when slim appendages like ears and fingers chill, even freeze, although the rest of the body is comfortably warm. Within warm-blooded species, northern animals tend to be larger-bodied and have smaller appendages than their southern counterparts, a principle known as Bergmann's Rule. Accordingly, Hairy Woodpeckers of Alaska weigh more than 4⅓ ounces, while those of the subtropics weigh 1⅓ ounces.

Over a minimum body size, and given adequate reserves of fat, sitting still may be more efficient than foraging. When a domestic hen simply stands up from resting, its energy consumption increases by 40 percent to 50 percent. In his *Watching Birds*, Roger Pasquier relates an extreme example of the sit-and-save strategy short of outright hibernation: In Finland, Ringneck Pheasants are reported to roost in trees, immobile and insensitive to disturbance, for forty or more days at a stretch.

This may not be as farfetched as it appears; captive Golden Pheasants routinely brood their eggs for twenty-two days, taking no food or water and moving very little. Chickadees, too, may opt for the sit-and-save strategy, waiting out storms and extreme cold in their roosts rather than fighting a losing battle in which the energy costs of foraging exceed the returns.

All-Important Fat

The key to cutting losses by minimizing energy expenditure is having a reserve of fuel: body fat. The high-performance metabolism of birds enables them to alternately lay on, and burn off, significant percentages of their body weight in fat with each twenty-four-hour cycle. A House Sparrow going to roost may weigh ⁹/₁₀ ounce (25 grams), two of these fat that it can metabolize overnight to maintain itself.

Chickadees will raise their daily fat deposits by from 4 percent to 7 percent of their body weight of ⅓ to ⁴/₁₀ ounce (10 to 12 grams) on a natural diet of dormant insects and weed seeds, and up to 11.8 percent on black sunflower seeds. Under severe winter conditions most of this store of fat will be depleted by morning, and the birds must quickly replenish it upon awakening. This accounts for the flurry of intense dawn feeding familiar to bird feeders. There is a similar last-minute stoking-up at dusk.

The Midnight Snack

Our seed-eating winter finches have a supplementary method of surviving the night's long fast in the form of an esophageal diverticulum. This, like the analogous chicken's crop, is used to store hastily gathered seeds. Redpolls will collect a load of alder seeds, then retire to a sheltered hideaway to regurgitate and husk them. These and other finches go to roost with what amounts to a packed lunch, supplementing their fat reserves by arousing from time to time for a nighttime snack.

A Meal of Ticks

A quite unusual source of winter food for Gray Jays was noted by Bill Walley of Dauphin, Manitoba, while doing work on these birds in Canada's Riding Mountain National Park. He observed several of them intently pursuing a moose, picking blood-engorged ticks from around the tail.

These moose, or winter, ticks (not at all the same as "wood" ticks) can be present in numbers of more than 100,000 on severely infested moose. Every one of them takes at least three blood meals. The torment the moose endure can be judged by the fact that some scratch and rub themselves so much that most of their hair is worn off by late winter. Small wonder many die from exposure as well as blood loss and stress.

Blood-engorged ticks would be a rich source of food for birds, and one might wonder if ravens, magpies, and others could be among those also taking advantage of the moose's misfortune.

Midwinter Nesting

A book on wintering birds may seem a strange place to find mention of nests at all. Actually, for those interested in feeding birds, an appreciation of nests is a helpful avenue to understanding an important aspect of their adaptive strategies. And winter is a good time to take inventory of all those constructed above the snow line. Bare-stemmed weeds, bushes, and trees reveal nests otherwise concealed in summer by foliage. In snow country, the nests themselves often carry tell-tale caps of white that show up starkly against the backdrop of frozen vegetation.

Although one might clip and collect these abandoned lodgings with a clear conscience on the grounds that the builders have no further use for them, the law has other ideas. Almost all birds, and their nests, are protected, the migratory species by federal law, the nonmigratory by state laws. The only exception are "nuisance" species such as the common pigeon, House Sparrow, and starling.

Logically, cavity-nesters turn their secure nurseries to good use by roosting in them in winter. Hairy and Downy Woodpeckers even excavate new holes for use as winter bedrooms. Tracking them, as well as chickadees and nuthatches, to their nighttime bivouacs solves the small mystery about where they go at night. As a winter project it also amply justifies postponing some tedious domestic chore in the interests of enlightenment.

One of the marvels of winter bird survival is the ability of some to nest in the harshest conditions. Some, like Great Horned, Boreal, and Saw-whet Owls, even use their nests as food warmers, thawing out frozen prey by incubating it as they would an egg.

Crossbills have been found nesting every month of the year, the determinant being a supply of conifer seeds. Their winter nests are noticeably more bulky and well insulated than those they make in summer, the chinks between the fibers of the lining filled with punky powdered wood. Thus, the temperature under a brooding female can be as much as 100 Fahrenheit degrees warmer than the air temperature.

For the first week the female broods the young and the male supplies food, a creamy soup of regurgitated seeds. Thereafter, both parents do the feeding. Unbrooded young, exposed to the cold, become chilled and grow torporous but revive quickly when the female warms them up again.

Gray Jays commence nesting in late February or early March. Preparations begin early; the tidbits they cadged from natural sources and from campers the previous summer are crucial to their strategy. It is thought that they even store nesting material. When the time to build comes, the nest is invariably in a dense conifer of middling size located in a site exposed to the southeast. Most nests are precisely oriented in the tree itself where the strongest rays of the winter sun will warm them.

"Double brooding" took on a new meaning some years ago when *The Canadian Field Naturalist* ran a photo showing a male Gray Jay sitting on top of his mate in their nest, presumably to help her keep warm in a spell of extremely low temperature.

By the time other birds have begun nesting, juvenile Gray Jays will be on the wing, learning from their parents the art of snitching morsels from wolf kills and cadging handouts from backcountry picnickers.

This Gray Jay could be incubating at –20° or lower.

CHAPTER 7

Census-Taking

Feeding birds, and enjoying their proximity and trust during the course of the long winter, is usually considered an individual, if not even a rather solitary, pleasure. This does not preclude joining a local naturalists club, the place where, in fact, many of us first heard about the pleasures of bird feeding while finger-feeding ourselves and socializing at some club function.

Whatever the process, nature clubs foster a broader sharing of values on subjects such as conservation and the environment. While most people share concerns over the environment, very few have the time, the resources, or the nerve to speak out individually. Joining forces with a group of like-minded folks can give direction and impact to those concerns when they are voiced in concert.

Christmas Bird Count

It was an issue dealing with environmental abuse that led to the organization, in 1900, of the Christmas Bird Count. Naturalists of the day were disgusted over the annual Christmas "side hunt" conducted by the hunting crowd. "Sportsmen" would assemble on Christmas Day, choose sides, then fan out in teams over the countryside. According to Frank Chapman, the American Museum of Natural History's ornithologist, they shot "practically everything in fur or feathers that crossed their path." The team that killed the most, including piles of songbirds, hawks, and owls, was the winner and given the routine hero's treatment in the sporting press.

To give positive vent to the outrage this bloodthirsty ritual generated, Chapman organized a humane alternative. He summoned members of the Audubon Society to spend a portion of their Christmas Day "with the birds." The objective, which acknowledged the ingrained competitive bent in human nature, was to correctly identify, and count, as many species as possible. The time spent, weather conditions, locality searched, and names of participants were recorded and handed in. In February 1901 the results were published in *Bird Lore*, the then journal of the Audubon Society, which was edited by Chapman.

In the "CBC" of 1900, twenty-seven counters censused twenty-six localities. It was a small beginning, but the canny Chapman had started something
that was to have lasting appeal and enduring value. Today's CBC draws around
40,000 counters and covers all of the United States, most of Canada, and localities in Central and South America and the Caribbean. Some guidelines for
the count have changed: Area boundaries are more specific, and the counts are
no longer limited to Christmas Day but can be done on any day within a two-
week period around Christmas. But the methods remain essentially those laid
down by Chapman, and this element of consistency means that there is a
continuum of comparable statistics going back to 1900.

The CBC is still run by the Audubon Society, and the results, with the
names of all the counters, are published in *Audubon Field Notes* (formerly
American Birds), published by Audubon. Each counter pays a small fee ($5 as
of 1994), which helps cover part of the cost of compiling and distributing the
results.

Today's CBCs are coordinated by local naturalist clubs or individuals. To
get involved, contact your nearest naturalist club, state wildlife agency, the nature
columnist in your local paper, or a natural history museum. Or you can contact
the Audubon Society directly (see Appendix 3, Naturalist Organizations). You
should, by the way, begin your enquiry no later than mid-September; do not
leave it until a few weeks before Christmas.

Important Statistics

One of the most interesting results of CBCs is the variety of species that
turn up, particularly after the counters have a few seasons under their belts and
gain experience. Songbirds, hawks, owls, meadowlarks, and various waterfowl,
some far out of their winter range, are tallied, along with hordes of House
Sparrows and Rock Doves (pigeons).

At first acquaintance, a local CBC may seem a rather scattered and insig-
nificant effort. How, after all, can the birds counted over eight hours (the required time period) in one day, by scattered groups of people, mostly amateurs,
have any value? They cannot possibly count all the birds!

Of course they can't. The value of what they find out is twofold: First, each
count is only a small part of a much larger effort that has been going on for
decades; second, each set of findings, rated for each species on a birds-per-person-
hour-scale, can be compared with results elsewhere, for that species, for that
year, and over many years previously. There is a rule of statistics that says the
longer you accumulate data, and the more you gather, the less effect small errors
will have if your methods remain consistent.

For example, it was the records compiled in the CBCs that revealed steady,
inexplicable declines in raptor populations. This triggered the investigations that
disclosed the impact of pesticides on the reproductive biology of birds of prey.

Project FeederWatch

Project FeederWatch was founded by Dr. Erica H. (Ricky) Dunn, its present coordinator. In 1976 she organized the Ontario Bird Feeder Survey and ran it through the Long Point Bird Observatory on Lake Erie. Encouraged by the response, and realizing the value of expanding the survey to cover the continent, Dr. Dunn enlisted the cooperation of the Cornell University Laboratory of Ornithology in Ithaca, New York. It is now run by the Cornell Laboratory, and managed in Canada by the Long Point Observatory.

To participate, all that is required is the ability to identify the species that visit your feeders, to count them, and to record the results on computer-readable forms supplied by Project FeederWatch.

The survey lasts from November to April, with observation times spaced two weeks apart during that period. On any two consecutive days in each fortnight, you take note of weather conditions for those days, and record the greatest number of birds of each species you see at one time at your feeder(s) during the two days of observation.

Project FeederWatch painlessly channels the fun of feeding birds into the service of a greater scientific purpose, assembling increasingly useful population and distribution data from some 10,000 participants. By involving people in an organized way, Project FeederWatch gets its participants into the habit of taking notes, which not only gives them a personal record of what they observe, but sharpens their powers of observation.

The fee for joining Project FeederWatch for one season is $12, which includes the biannual *FeederWatch News*. See Appendix 3, Naturalist Organizations, for the address.

CHAPTER 8

Knowing Your Winged Visitors

This chapter describes the individual species of birds likely to visit feeders in the Pacific Northwest, and the families to which they belong.

Family Write-ups

There turned out to be much more of interest about most birds and mammals than could be encompassed in the confining structure of the individual species accounts. Therefore I incorporated the more interesting of the leftover gems into family write-ups. Where the subject and available material warranted it, I also wrote on subgroups, such as the crossbills, and even about individual species like the juncos.

Species Accounts

In this chapter each species is discussed under a standard set of subsections: common and scientific names, descriptions, behavior, range, food, and nesting habits. The "Comment" subsection provides space for interesting miscellany not suitable to the spare format of the preceding subsections. The final entry gives page references in the major bird field guides.

What's in a Name?

Each species account begins with a thumbnail summary of the sources of both the common and the scientific names.

British author R. D. Macleod advocated separating common names into "popular" and "book" names. "Popular" names are those that develop with a language, like "hawk" or "sparrow." "Book" names are more specific labels bestowed by biologists, or committees of them, like "Red-tailed Hawk," "Song Sparrow," et cetera.

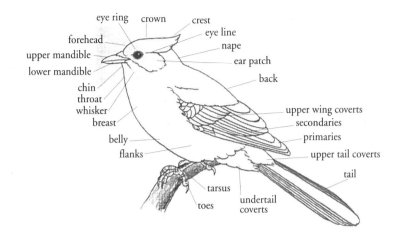

I don't approach scientific names as a necessary evil, but as an opportunity to learn something. Occasionally one can even have a little fun with them. For both purposes I have drawn on Ernest A. Choate's *The Dictionary of American Bird Names*, revised edition, 1985, and on Edward S. Gruson's *Words for Birds*, 1972, with some help from *Webster's New World Dictionary*, second college edition.

Descriptions

For each species account where a comparison to another familiar bird could readily be made, I have given relative sizes.

The surface anatomy, or "topography," of birds has long since been mapped in detail. The appendages and each contour and pattern of the body and flight feathers have been accorded names. The accompanying diagrams identify the major parts of a typical bird. Knowing these will aid in the enjoyment of this, and other, reference books and will also sharpen your ability to spot key field marks on birds at your feeders.

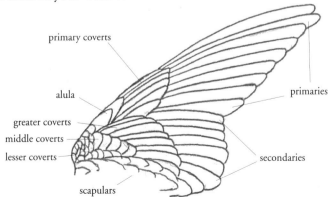

Behavior

This subsection discusses the social and foraging habits of each species, including its calls, and its songs, if any.

Range

Although this is a book about birds of the Pacific Northwest, it is more useful to deal with breeding ranges on a continental basis and, where appropriate, to be more regionally specific about wintering ranges.

Food

Both the natural foods and feeder preferences are given.

Nest

In Chapter 6, Those Fascinating Birds, I discussed winter-nesting birds. Some incredibly well-adapted birds build nests, brood eggs, and feed and warm their fragile young through our worst winter weather. Most people would agree that such heroic care-giving deserves more than passing mention. The less heroic summer breeders also deserve mention because their works remain in the frozen landscape the following winter as potential objects of interest. Therefore, each write-up features a brief description of that species' nest and preferred location. For those birds that actually nest in winter, I describe the eggs.

Comment

This subsection allows me some space to fill out each brief sketch with interesting detail.

References

Each species account concludes with a list of page references in four of the major field guides. All are the latest editions, as of mid-1994. The color illustrations (photos in the Audubon guide) will provide a complementary reference to Peter Sawatzky's black-and-white interpretations in this book. In the Audubon guide, the species accounts are separate from the photos; the page references are for the write-ups. Following is the key to the reference abbreviations:

A(W)—*The Audubon Society Field Guide to North American Birds, Western Region*

GO—*Golden Guide Birds of North America*

NG—*National Geographic Field Guide to the Birds of North America*

P(W)—*Peterson: A Field Guide to Western Birds*

Grouse, Partridges, Pheasants

Family Phasianidae

This family is a member of the larger order, the Galliformes, which includes the chickenlike, scratching, ground-living birds found the world over. Collectively they are often referred to as "game" birds due to their most commonly being regarded as objects of sport hunting, or "upland game" birds as distinct from hunted waterfowl. Galliformes is from the Latin *gallina*, "a hen," and Phasianidae is from the Greek *phasianos*, "a pheasant."

Some 5,000 years ago the Red Jungle Fowl of India was domesticated and became the farmyard, and latterly factory, chicken in its many varieties. The qualities that made it valuable then were its high reproductive rate, its flocking habit, and the tastiness of its meat. Obligingly nonmigratory, it was easily kept happy around the dooryard scratching through manure and litter for waste grain, picking shoots and leaves, and chasing insects.

The high reproductive rate meant large clutches of eggs, a trait that could be exploited with a little management. If you systematically stole the hen's eggs as she laid them, preventing her from accumulating a clutch large enough to trigger her brooding mode, the confused bird just kept on producing. Wild Gray Partridges will occasionally fill nests with more than twenty eggs and, if captives are subjected to nestbox larceny, will overproduce heroically. If you know where to shop, you can buy tins of diminutive quail eggs.

Would Rather Walk

Given a choice, most members of this group prefer to keep their feet on the ground. Their wings have, in fact, been described as getaway devices held in reserve to escape predators that can't be hidden from or outrun. Our native grouse, however, do routinely use their wings as feeding aids when they flap a few feet up to browse on tree buds.

The grouse-type wing is short, broad, and rounded, and has to be flailed at a high speed to achieve flight. Liftoff, particularly for heavier species like turkeys and pheasants, is straight up in a burst of thrashing wings that gets the bird from zero to flat-out in a couple of seconds. The buffeting of this blastoff is often augmented by a simultaneous cackling or other vocal racket. The object is to startle the unsuspecting, to get out of reach, fast, before a predator can collect its shattered composure and pounce. Or shoot.

Once airborne and at cruising speed, the bird sets its wings stiffly and glides, usually settling a short distance away.

"White" or "Dark"

The huge breast muscles that power this explosive burst of energy are the "white meat" of the dinner table. Powerful as they are, they can be exerted for only short periods because they contain fewer blood vessels and less oxygen-storing myoglobin and are made up of coarser fiber bundles than "dark" meat. The breast muscles of migratory birds give evidence of different priorities. Compelled to work over long periods, they are richly supplied with blood vessels and myoglobin, and made of finer fibers. You can see, from the contrasting color of the muscle groups, where evolution has put the emphasis: on a duck the breast meat is "dark," on a chicken or grouse, it's the leg.

According to popular woods lore, if you were able to pursue a pheasant or grouse closely enough to force it to fly repeatedly, after four or five takeoffs the bird's flight muscles would be so tired you could simply pick it up. Between footrace and frying pan another factor could intervene, however. Even a wing-weary grouse or partridge can still turn on some brisk footwork, and they invariably head for the thickest cover to do it. If you could match a pheasant's top speed of eighteen miles per hour in thick brush, you indeed might be able to pick it up.

Snowshoe or Shovel?

A clue to the adaptive background of some members of this family can be seen in their footwear. Native grouse have furlike leggings down to their toes, and in winter the toes grow combs of stiff bristles along each side. Neither pheasants nor partridges have these accessories.

The toe bristles are assumed to be an adaptive "snowshoe" giving the wearers better "float" on soft snow. It has also been observed that the toenails grow longer, probably for the same reason. This is no doubt true. But there is another possibility that I haven't seen suggested yet, and that is increased digging facility in soft snow.

As most readers of nature lore know, grouse and ptarmigan sleep under the snow in winter, often plunging in from flight. They burrow along horizontally for a foot or more, plugging the entrance hole and creating a snug, insulated pocket for the night. In the morning they usually burst through the roof into flight.

How they actually dig through the soft, yielding snow is an interesting question. It is probably with a combination of beak and footwork. But scooping the loose stuff back behind them would have to be done with the feet. For this, those toe fringes would help a lot because, without them, moving loose snow would be a bit like trying to shovel sand with a fork.

An important factor in native grouses' winter survival is their ability to switch to tree buds or conifer needles as food. Seton mentions that Sharp-tailed Grouse he shot toward the end of the winter had a large gap in their beaks behind the tip where both mandibles had been worn down, presumably from "budding"—plucking aspen and willow buds.

The Spruce Grouse has adapted to survive in winter on what constitutes most of the scenery in its vast range: evergreen needles! To handle such tough, dry fare its digestive tract increases markedly in size with the onset of winter. The constant ingestion of aromatic spruce, fir, and pine needles imparts to the flesh a distinctive flavor of turpentine.

The Spruce Grouse's plumage pattern blends so well with the dead leaves and duff of the forest floor that to vanish from view it may merely have to sit stock still. But it frequently does the same thing when sitting in plain view in a tree, a behavioral error that makes the poor "fool hen" the first and easiest target for trigger-happy plinkers. The camouflage, plus the fact that both "plinking" and bird surveying are done near roads and settlements, may in part account for the fact that the bird is routinely listed as rare or scarce, even where there is plenty of apparently suitable habitat.

This grouse is found throughout the dense coniferous forests of Idaho, northern Washington, and the northeastern corner of Oregon. It remains in these regions in winter where, even if there were many feeders, it would very rarely visit them. It has not been included in the species accounts in this book.

The Imports

Trying to do nature one better by introducing exotic species has fallen into rightful disrepute. Those matched scourges, the House Sparrow and starling, and the nuisance pigeon, serve as constant reminders of previous folly.

Thankfully, relatively few of the hundreds of attempted introductions have become successful in North America. Among those few birds that made it in the Pacific Northwest are three that were brought in to provide sporting targets in place of native species wiped out by a combination of the gun, axe, plough, and cow. These are the Ring-necked Pheasant, the Gray Partridge, and the Chukar.

Whether or not their overall contribution to the environment is beneficial, it is difficult now to criticize the presence of these hardy and beautiful imports.

Some introductions were wildly successful; Gray Partridges from Hungarian stock planted in southern Alberta around 1908 multiplied abundantly, inspiring a rush on "Hun" introductions in many other places on the continent. After a few years of heady success, however, all the population explosions fizzled, most to oblivion, some to small but stable present-day levels.

Three other game birds—the California Quail, Mountain Quail, and Gambel's Quail—are represented in a mix of indigenous and introduced populations in the Pacific Northwest. But all Northern Bobwhites and Wild Turkeys are introduced. These are all native to North America, so their presence should be considered as assisted range extensions.

Assuming they are hardy enough to brave climatic hardship, introduced game birds' ability to thrive is directly related to land-use practices. Earlier introductees often started out well because the limitations of old farming methods left brushy gullies, weedy fence rows, overgrown ditches, woodlots, straw stacks, and scrubby pastures for shelter and food. But modern agricultural technology has no tolerance for "waste" land and the outlaw plant life it encourages. So the bulldozer has taken care of the shelter, the sprayer the weeds and scrubland. Even ditches are cultivated right to the shoulders of the roads.

In areas where some exotic or another is still plentiful enough to be a significant game bird, they are winter wards of the public. Wildlife management agencies, sympathetic farmers, and sportsmen's clubs shovel grain out to keep them alive until forgiving spring comes around again. Very often they also become guests of rural and small-town bird feeders.

Magnificent as it is, and indisputably indigenous, the Sage Grouse is so rare a visitor to feeders that it has not been included in the species accounts in this section. Neither, because of their relative scarcity, have the Wild Turkey, the Bobwhite, and the Mountain and Gambel's Quail.

Gray Partridge
Perdix perdix

Also "Hungarian partridge" or "hun." "Partridge," says Webster, arises from Middle English *partriche*, a direct descendant of the Latin and Greek *perdix*, which in turn is probably akin to *perdesthai*, "to break wind" (whence "fart"), from the whirring sound made as birds burst into flight; the term is incorrectly but widely applied also to Ruffed Grouse; *Perdix* is from Latin and Greek, "a partridge."

Description

Chunky, squat, short-tailed, larger than quail; gray chest and neck, flanks barred in rusty brown; males have a brown, upside-down *U*-shaped patch on belly; cheeks and throat rust-brown; in flight the flared tail shows ruddy side feathers; upper parts a pattern of gray and browns, with light feather edgings and fine lines.

Behavior

Social; feeds, flushes, and flies in close flock; strictly a ground bird of open country; family covey sleeps huddled in a circle, tails inward, presumably for a fast getaway if alarmed; in snow they dig open craters in fields, ditches, and weed patches to scratch on the ground for seeds and green bits, and apparently also sleep in these; call a harsh, rasping "*krrrr-ik*," heard particularly in spring; cackle when they flush.

P.SAWATZKY ©
1990

Range

Nonmigratory; originally a Eurasian grassland bird released widely in North America; favors grain cropland; nowhere plentiful in Pacific Northwest, but occurs widely in agricultural land in the Columbia Basin and the Snake River Plain.

Food

Seeds, green leaves, shoots, rose hips; growing chicks insectivorous, and may be starved out if agricultural insecticides are widely used; attracted to feeding stations by spilled seeds and by screenings or grain offered on the ground.

Nest

Very well-hidden cup scratched in ground, lined with grasses; in crops, fencerows, tall grass, edges of low shrubbery.

Comment

After a number of failed attempts in the Atlantic coast states as far back as the late 1700s, an introduction near Calgary in 1908 really took off, and was followed by successful stockings throughout prairie Canada and adjacent plains states. The birds prospered in association with spring wheat farming, surviving in winter on straw stacks and waste grain.

Very sensitive to agricultural practices, they were once abundant in areas where they have now vanished. Populations that had spread naturally and prospered in Washington and adjacent Okanagan in British Columbia collapsed in 1926–27 and never fully recovered. The loss of field-edge habitat, clearing of weedy ditches, and early-season mowing of hay, which destroys nests, are among the factors contributing to their continuing depletion.

Winter is hard on them, especially when it brings ice storms. But they make up for losses with huge clutches—the largest in the bird world with an average of fifteen to sixteen eggs, and up to twenty. The female doesn't start brooding until the clutch is complete, so during the laying period, which may be up to three weeks, she covers the eggs-in-waiting with grass and leaves. The male takes no part in brooding, but when the chicks arrive he helps tend them, bringing up the rear of his numerous brood, ready to fight, or feign a broken wing to lead a predator away.

REF: A(W)—577; GO—92; NG—220; P(W)—164

Chukar

Alectoris chukar

Partridge and pheasant subfamily. Name possibly originates in Indo-European echoic root *kau*, "to scream," (whence "howl"); *Alectoris* from Greek *alektor*, "cock"; until recently, considered a subspecies of the Rock Partridge, the "Grecian hen," hence listed as *A. graeca* in older references.

Description

Slightly larger than California Quail; throat and face light buff outlined in black "necklace"; upper body brownish gray, flanks boldly striped in vertical black and white; bill, eye-ring, and legs red; flared tail in flight shows rust-red.

Behavior

Social; ground feeder; covey roosts on ground in a circle, tails in; normally very elusive, may evade hunters by scurrying upslope, flying back down when flushed; call described as a low, decelerating chucking, or a harsh "*chuck-arr.*"

- P. Sawatzky -
1992 ©

Range

South Asian exotic established in drier mountainous or hilly regions of American West and Southwest; described as "rock-loving," prefers grassy, arid, rocky slopes, canyons, and benchland; population center in Pacific Northwest is northern and southwestern Oregon, but found in isolated patches of suitable habitat in Washington and southern Idaho.

Food

Grass seeds, especially that of cheat grass, *Bromus tectorum*, with which it seems to have a close ecological relationship; grass, clover leaves, grasshoppers; said to be keen on the berries of Russian Olive, an introduced shrub that has gone native in sandy, river-valley land; migrates to lowland during some winters when it may flock to haystacks, feed lots, and feeders.

Nest

A shallow scrape with meager lining of nearby straws, grass, leaves; one of few species to "double clutch," female leaving male to incubate and raise first brood while she starts a second in a new nest.

Comment

There is a good argument for *not* including the chukar in a book on feeder birds, shy and of limited distribution that it is. However, for those who share sagebrush uplands with this bird, getting it to come to the yard with a generous deployment of chaff and chicken scratch is a challenge well worth taking on.

While the dictionary says the name should be pronounced "ch-car'," I notice that countryside Oregonians say "chuckers."

REF: A(W)—595; GO—92; NG—220; P(W)—164

Ring-necked Pheasant

Phasianus colchicus

Sometimes "Chinese" pheasant; "pheasant" is from Greek *phaisianos*, "a pheasant," referring to the river Phasis flowing into the Black Sea in the ancient country of Colchis, now part of Georgia, and at the mouth of which these birds were especially numerous; *colchicus*, Latinized "of Colchis"; taxonomy has thus given us a double locality name.

Description

Chicken-sized; males resplendent in brilliant copper-maroon and gold with parts of body bearing beautifully contrasting base colors and varying patterns of spots, teardrops, bars, checks; head iridescent green with small "ear" tufts; eyes set in red face patches; may have white ring around neck; very long pointed tail; spurs on lower legs; females smaller, in subdued brown camouflage pattern, tails proportionately shorter.

Behavior

Social; females and grown young may be escorted by territorial male; ranges in grainland, irrigated fields, and pastures; a swift runner; when flushed bursts straight up on thrashing wings, cackling; scratches through snow cover for seeds and green pickings in winter, may scrounge in farmyards and feedlots, sometimes in considerable numbers; male's call in spring a raucous two-note crow followed by rapid flurry of wingbeats.

Range

Widely and unevenly distributed throughout entire region, with a population center in southern Idaho and adjacent Nevada and Utah; favors open fields of grain, alfalfa, corn adjacent to good tree or scrub cover; presence often depends on local restocking and winter feeding programs.

Food

Omnivorous; seeds, grain, green leaves, shoots, and buds; insects, small vertebrates; will feed on carrion in times of scarcity; at feeders will pick up spilled seeds of all kinds and can be attracted with screenings, corn, grain, baked goods.

Nest

Depression in the ground lined with leaves or grass, in tall ground cover, fencerows, under bushes, and along woodland edges.

Comment

Pheasants were brought to Britain by the Normans not long after A.D. 1066, where they rapidly became a favorite of the sportsman and the gourmet. Many

attempted introductions into North America failed until 1881 when the U.S. Consul-General in Shanghai sent thirty birds to Oregon. The twenty-six that survived the trip were released in the Willamette Valley. Visitors to Sauvie Island can see a sign marking the spot of the exact release.

Subsequent releases across the northern United States and southern Canada were highly successful, several areas such as South Dakota becoming famous amongst hunters. Numbers are maintained by constant restocking and heavy winter feeding.

However, in many regions where it prospered for a few years, its numbers diminished for reasons not apparently due to habitat or weather changes. Even in England's mild climate, where it has been ranging free for nine centuries, its numbers dwindle very quickly and it may vanish altogether if restocking efforts lapse.

REF: A(W)—576; GO—92; NG—222; P(W)—158

Ruffed Grouse

Bonasa umbellus

Also "bush" or "birch" partridge; "Ruffed" from dark ruff of erectile feathers on sides of neck; "Grouse" from French *griais*, "gray," descriptive of several kinds of partridges; *Bonasa* from Latin *bonasum*, "aurocks" (wild ox), or "drumming," as voice of male grouse suggested bellowing bull; *umbellus* from Latin for "sunshade" (umbrella), referring to shape of ruffs when erect.

Description

Large, long-legged, chickenlike bird; large tail banded in black with especially obvious subterminal band, ends of feathers light tan; buff line through eye; hackles on crown may be raised into ragged crest; dark or coppery ruff on sides of neck, raised if bird excited; plumage a complicated pattern of flecks, bars, and edging in black, dark brown, or rust red; two color phases present in all populations, some birds being an overall rusty brown, some grayish; legs feathered; female slightly smaller than male, tail shorter with two central feathers lacking the black subterminal band, neck ruffs are less prominent; winter bird has fringe of stiff bristles on sides of toes.

Behavior

Relies on concealment and camouflage to avoid detection; if disturbed but not flushed, will step cautiously away, often to quick, high, peeping note; alternately, it might await your close approach and burst almost from underfoot, sailing swiftly away to re-alight a short distance off; male drums from low vantage points in cover, starting with hesitant, muffled "*whups*" that accelerate to staccato roll;

drumming heaviest in spring, with secondary busy time in fall, but can be heard during much of year except for coldest part of winter; in winter switches diet from ground feeding to tree feeding; in winter, roosts in tunnels under snow, locations of these marked in spring by small piles of pale, macaroni-shaped droppings.

Range

At times erratically dispersive; a woodland species, found in open deciduous and mixed deciduous–coniferous forests; not found in open, dry steppelands nor in heavily cultivated agricultural land; range in Pacific Northwest extends southward only into extreme northwestern California.

Food

Adults vegetarian, taking shoots, leaves, buds, petals, berries, and seeds; young insectivorous; at feeder takes sunflower seeds, screenings, and cracked or whole grain.

Nest

Bowl scraped at foot of tree or stump, near log or clump; lined with leaves and some feathers; hen and clutch leave as soon as last-hatched young are out and active.

Comment

"I don't think that thing'll fly even if he does get it started!" The similarity to someone's attempt to start a balky motor comes to mind when the grouse's muffled drum roll throbs out of the woods. In her charming book *Wings of the North*, Candace Savage says that if you walk softly into the woods of an early spring morning and thump your hands on the ground in a reasonable imitation of the grouse's signature drum roll, you will get a reply.

Along with other northern species, like the lemming and Snowshoe Hare, Ruffed Grouse are subject to a seven- to ten-year population cycle. During the lows one rarely hears or sees a grouse, but during the highs they seem to be everywhere.

In the autumn of years when populations are at their peak the young of the year seem to be overcome by a wild urge to disperse and under its spell fly into utility wires, fences, windows, and vehicles, often with fatal results.

REF: A(W)—635; GO—86; NG—210; P(W)—160

California Quail

Callipepla californica

Quail subfamily. "Quail" from Middle Dutch *quacken*, "to croak" (whence "quack") and *quackel*, "a quail"; entered Latin as *quaquila*, "a quail," evolving to Old French *quaille*, which made it, intact, into Middle English; *Callipepla* is from Greek *kallos*, "a beauty," and *peplos*, "a robe," hence "beautifully dressed"; former generic name *lophortyx* is from Greek *lophos*, "crest" and *ortyx*, "quail."

Description

Short-tailed, plump, chickenlike bird, smaller than street pigeon; male's comma-shaped black plume curves forward from crown of head; jet black throat and face bordered with bright white line, white headband above eye, forehead yellow; breast slate-blue, belly beautifully scaled in gold; flanks flecked with white streaks; female much more subdued pattern of browns overall, head plume smaller.

Behavior

Social; covey scoots along in "follow-the-leader" fashion;

-P. SAWATZKY-
1992 ©

nervous, alert, fast runner; feeds after dawn and before dusk, preferring to stick close to tall plant cover or low brush; unlike other quail, roosts at night in tree or thick bush; foraging call a soft clucking "*ut ut*"; assembly call is loud, three-note, usually short-long-short, usually with emphasis on long, having something of Pileated Woodpecker twang to it; "*ku-kwa'-kup*," "*shut-Jack'-up*," "*Chi-ca'-go*," et cetera.

Range

Nonmigratory; originally Southwest United States, small part of western Nevada, California, southern Oregon; plantings begun in mid-1800s, and continuing, now doing well throughout Pacific Northwest except southeastern Idaho; favors lower-lying croplands adjacent to thick scrub cover, and orchards, pastures, golf courses, gardens; at home in suburbs adjacent to natural cover.

Food

Weed seeds, especially clovers, waste grain, acorns, scratched for in leaf litter; leaves, tender grass shoots; at feeder almost any seeds, much preferring them scattered on the ground; very attracted to ground-level water during dry spells.

Nest

Shallow depression scratched out and lined with leaves, grass, rootlets, needles; concealed in ground cover, usually near log, post, tree, rock.

Comment

Quail love a good dust bath, a habit clever bird feeders can cater to by providing a suitable spot that stays dry in wet weather.

In my own limited experience with these delightful birds, I have found it takes patience, and a good supply of hen scratch, to lure them to the vicinity of a feeder. In dry weather a trickling fountain or birdbath would turn the trick much faster.

According to Starker Leopold in *The California Quail,* the early days of settlement in California saw "valley quail" shot and trapped by the hundreds of thousands to cater to the city taste for quail on toast. Hunters blocked off springs with brush, then lured the parched birds with pans of water under set nets. Because in dry times birds might have to fly many miles between springs, the takes were huge. "Ground sluicing" was shotgunning birds packed around springs; forty to sixty could be killed with one shot. The hunter got from 75 cents to $1.75 a dozen; in one good year during the height of the slaughter some shipped up to 10,000 birds.

In 1931 California officially made this quail its state bird.

REF: A(W)—594; GO—90; NG—218; P(W)—166

Raptors

Family Accipitridae, Subfamily Accipitrinae

"Raptors" includes all of the birds of prey that most of us easily recognize as hawks and eagles, and because it is a rather imprecise term, to some it also includes the owls. Ospreys belong to the family Accipitridae; kites, hawks, eagles, and harriers belong to the subfamily Accipitrinae. The word comes from the Latin *raptor*, "plunderer."

There is a further division into two groups of the birds popularly lumped together as "hawks." These are the hawk group, which includes all of the day-flying birds of prey except the falcons, which are a family (Falconidae) of their own.

Within the larger hawk group is a small subgroup with only three members in North America. These are the accipiters, short-winged, long-tailed woodland hawks. Because the two smaller species, the Sharp-shinned and the Cooper's Hawks, specialize in hunting other birds, they are the species most likely to enter the lives of bird feeders. "Accipiter" has two possible sets of roots, from Latin *accipiter*, "hawk" or "bird of prey," or from Greek *aci*, "swift," and *petrum*, "wing," a particularly apt description for these fast-flying, maneuverable hunters.

Nothing in the busy life around a feeder has a more profound or sudden effect than the appearance of a small hawk. What was noisy and busy one second changes abruptly to utter silence the next. Then there will be an eruption of panicky flight as all the birds flee in one direction. Alternately, there may be no warning at all, just the sudden racket of frightened birds all bursting away at once, perhaps a few feathers drifting in the air. If you check nearby trees or shrubbery, you may see a smallish hawk, its strongly barred tail flaring as it balances on a branch, bending over and pulling at something in its feet. The "something" will be one of your birds, playing its role in nature's food chain.

The body and feathering of accipiters is adapted to their life in pursuit of swift-flying prey in thick cover. Their short, broad wings give them fast acceleration and speed over short sprints, the long tail great agility. I once watched a Cooper's chasing a sparrow across a river, both birds straining to do their best. The fleeing sparrow dived into the tangled willows on the shore. Instead of veering off, as I expected, the hawk plunged right in after it, wings flailing noisily against the branches. The racket continued for perhaps ten seconds, and I marveled that the hawk seemed heedless of the punishment its wings and flight feathers were taking. I wondered how many of these fearless little hunters, especially the young, did themselves fatal damage when they careened into tangled cover and thrashed their way through it.

In most of the pursuits that I have been lucky enough to see, the victim simply outmaneuvers the hawk after a brief, pell-mell chase. I would think that most adult songbirds in fit condition would have a very good chance of outflying a hawk in a wing-on-wing race, and that if the hawks relied on sheer speed and agility they'd starve to death.

Obviously, they don't, relying heavily on the element of surprise to put a meal in their grasp. The hawks that have appeared around my feeders will fly in as unobtrusively as possible and sit in concealment if their presence has gone undetected. They will wait quietly in ambush until they can zero in on a bird that shows signs of inattention, weakness or some other vulnerability. When the victim seems most distracted, out and down they plunge. More often than not they miss their target, alight nearby, ruffle their feathers, think about it for a few moments, then winnow their way off to try another ambush somewhere else.

It is during these dive-bombing attacks that many hawks smash into picture windows. I have never lost one of "my" hawks in this way; most of the time, possibly because they have evolved to withstand the clouting they take when they streak through the branches, they fly off to sit, dazed but alive, in some nearby tree until their heads clear. But I do know that many hawks die of such collisions. Some learn to use a picture window to their advantage, flushing feeder birds and grabbing any that in their panic bump into the glass.

Another tactic these birds use is to fly low over, around, or through semi-open cover. Such "hedge-hopping" offers the possibility of surprising something edible.

In order of probability, the hawk most likely to show up at feeders in the Pacific Northwest is the little Sharp-shinned, which, being migratory, will likely pay its visits in the winter. Next is its larger cousin, the look-alike Cooper's, once referred to as the "chicken hawk." Like most raptors, the males are considerably smaller than the females, so a male Cooper's may be not much larger than a female Sharp-shinned. Aside from the size differences, the adults of the two species look so alike that telling them apart in the field is a frustrating challenge.

The biggest of the trio of accipiters is the majestic goshawk, a two-foot-long bird of the northern boreal forest where it kills snowshoe hares, squirrels, and Ruffed Grouse. When the cyclical populations of these animals crash, goshawks by the thousands drift southward. If one appears around a feeder it is more likely that it will be interested in the rabbits, squirrels, and quail than in the songbirds.

The other raptors that visit feeders are the two smallest falcons, the brightly plumaged little Kestrel, formerly "sparrow hawk," and the bigger Merlin, formerly "pigeon hawk." These birds bear the distinguishing conformation of their kind: the long, pointed wings for sustained swift flight in the open, and for soaring high in preparation for the spectacular dive, or "stoop," on flying prey. They also have a distinct notch on each side of the upper bill just behind the hook.

Whatever the species of native wild predator that appears at my own feeders, I bear them no grudge for hunting my birds. They live and die by the rules of natural survival, rules that the songbirds have evolved over millennia to deal with, rules that help keep the survivors strong and alert.

Sharp-shinned Hawk

Accipiter striatus

In old guides, *A. velox*, where former names, including "little blue darter" and "bullet hawk," may be given; "Sharp-shinned" because tarsus (lower leg bone) in cross section has a raised ridge in front, where in most land birds it is rounded; "hawk" is from Anglo-Saxon *hafoc*, "a hawk"; *Accipiter*, "hawk," from same word in Latin compounded from *ad*, "after," and *capita*, "take"; *striatus*, "striped," from same Latin word, descriptive of striped underside.

Description

A little hawk, jay-sized, ten to fourteen inches (twenty-five to thirty-six centimeters) long, with a long, strongly barred tail; long, thin legs; wings relatively short and rounded; adult has bluish gray back and tail, underside and leggings off-white with rusty, broken, horizontal barring; immature is dark brown above with breast boldly streaked with vertical striping; male noticeably smaller than female; told from very similar Cooper's Hawk by smaller size and by square-ended or slightly notched tail—Cooper's is slightly rounded.

Behavior

Light and quick on the wing, flying with rapid wingbeats alternating with a short glide; may soar, tail flared, usually on morning thermals, sometimes very high; hunts small birds, usually by sitting in cover, dashing out to grab or pursue prey; may chase small birds through thick cover, dodging and turning at full speed; voice a high, rapid, loud "*keek-keek-keek-keek*"; especially noisy near nest.

Range

Migratory; frequents open woodland, deciduous or mixed; breeds throughout boreal and parkland woods of northern and western Canada, including forested areas of Pacific Northwest; widely scattered winterer throughout Pacific Northwest, commonest during fall migration.

Food

Primarily birds, up to size of quail or pigeon, but may take insects, small rodents.

Nest

A large, flat platform of twigs usually well up in a conifer on horizontal branches close to trunk; nest out of proportion to size of bird, usually big enough to completely conceal brooding female from viewer on ground.

Comment

It may be difficult for bird lovers to accept a small hawk that settles in nearby and, for the season, proceeds to feed itself on the birds that come to their feeders. I have had this happen several times, the most recent when two immature males spent the winter of 1992–93 on the small island off northeastern Vancouver Island that I call home. They had a number of other feeders to choose from, and an abundant base of non-feeder birds to hunt. I saw a number of attacks, most of which were unsuccessful. But every now and then a junco or a siskin would be carried off, and every one that I saw was picked off the ground, or near it.

How did I feel about this? Far from upsetting me—after a brief absence following each alarm the birds all returned to the feeders with spirits undiminished—I found that the presence of these diminutive hawks added a great deal to my enjoyment of my feeders, and enhanced my knowledge of, and appreciation for, the natural history of raptors. If the crowded feeders increased the attendant birds' vulnerability somewhat, I felt that this was probably offset by a higher survival rate generated by the improved nutrition the feeders afforded.

REF: A(W)—696; GO—70; NG—190; P(W)—172

Pigeons
Family Columbidae

There are nine species of pigeons occurring in the United States, several barely making the list as casuals from Mexico. Mourning Doves, Band-tailed Pigeons, and feral domestic pigeons are common in the Pacific Northwest. The difference between doves and pigeons is one of semantics, the smaller by custom called doves, the larger, pigeons.

The wild Rock Dove, antecedent of all our domestic pigeons, still nests on cliffs and rimrocks from the Atlantic coasts of Europe south to North Africa and east to China. The earliest reference to domestic pigeons dates back to 4500 B.C. These were most probably birds from the gorges and sea cliffs around the Mediterranean. Since then, more than 300 breeds have been developed, some for meat, some to satisfy a fancy for the exotic or bizarre, some for racing.

Our pigeons are the street-mix blend of domestics that flew the coop or were released. Without ongoing recruitment from these, street ferals would in time revert to an ancestral type. Escapees, however, keep the gene pool stirred up.

It has therefore always struck me as a bit precious for birders to refer to street pigeons as "Rock Doves." In North America, all but a very few live close to humans in a semi-dependent relationship, quite removed in their habits, and usually in appearance, from ancestral wild stock. Are they any more Rock Doves than a stray mongrel dog is a wolf? In my view these would more accurately be called Common Pigeons.

Pigeon "Milk"

Many birds regurgitate to feed their young; pigeons, flamingos, and Emperor Penguins are unique in the production of special "milk." In pigeons the lining of both parents' crop swells and forms thick folds, tripling its bulk within a few days before the eggs hatch. The surface layer of cells sloughs off continuously to form a thick semi-fluid like cottage cheese. Hatchlings are fed exclusively on it until they are about half grown, then it is increasingly supplemented with regurgitated seeds.

They thrive mightily on this ration; a day-old nestling is twice its hatching weight, and for several days thereafter gains 38 percent every twenty-four hours.

In about a month it reaches adult weight. Pure "milk" is about 15 percent protein, 8 percent fat, 1 to 2 percent minerals, with several vitamins. Poultry chicks fed a ration supplemented with it were more than 30 percent heavier at the end of the test than comparables on regular feed.

Pigeons make up for two-egg clutches by more or less nonstop nesting. Under optimum conditions they may begin a new clutch before the previous hatch has fledged.

The flying ability and "homing" instinct of pigeons has long been exploited by humankind for practical purposes and for sport. They have been used to carry messages in times of emergency and war. In the province of Manitoba carrier pigeons played an important role in forest-fire fighting during the 1930s, displaced only by the advent of two-way radios.

In the sporting world, thousands of carefully bred birds are pampered and trained for racing every year. Champions' flight muscles constitute more than 30 percent of their body weight, compared to 20 percent for most other strong-flying birds. In July 1992 a male racer from Holland was sold for $200,000 to a British breeder. In three races from Barcelona to his home loft in Holland he covered 720 miles, averaging 40 miles per hour. He lived up to his name, "Invincible Spirit," by flying up over the Pyrenees where lesser birds veered off course to seek easier flight paths. He battled high mountain winds, was baked by the sun, and flew nonstop through the night.

Pigeons are said to be the favored prey of Peregrine Falcons, particularly for those that have taken to nesting in cities where little other good-sized prey is available. But, notwithstanding the dazzling speed it achieves in a hunting dive, considered opinion is that a Peregrine would be hard pressed to overtake and capture a healthy pigeon in level pursuit. Invincible Spirit's top speed is 60 miles per hour.

Supersenses

Explanations for the astonishing ability of pigeons to find their way home over long distances begin with the fact that the cliffs where ancestral birds nested, often along ocean coasts, could be far from inland fields and prairies where they foraged for seeds. A commuting regimen was thus demanded of the birds, which in turn developed the ability to fly accurately over long distances in all kinds of weather.

Several senses combine to affect an unusual navigating skill. They can recognize home territory by scent. An awesome hearing range allows them to detect infra-sounds as low as 0.05 hertz, about one cycle every ten seconds. These are sounds made by storms, winds flowing over mountains, and surf. Ultralow-frequency sounds travel through the atmosphere for hundreds of miles, giving the birds a sound fix on geographic features far beyond visual limits.

They have extraordinary visual memory. In experiments using several hundred color slides of landscapes, they could recall months later which ones could be responded to to provide a food reward. They can see ultraviolet light, detect changes in light polarization, and sense small differences in intensity. These together enable them to pinpoint the sun's location on overcast days. They are highly sensitive to changes in atmospheric pressure and are attuned to ground-borne vibrations.

What a rich world of signals and sensations our humble street nuisance lives in, a world far beyond the dull senses of its human critics.

Rock Dove

Columba livia

Most commonly "pigeon"; "Rock" is from wild stock's nesting on cliffs; "pigeon" from Old French *pijon*, "a young bird," derived from Latin *pipio*, "to peep" or "squab"; Latin *Columba*, "a dove"; *livia* from Latin *lividus*, "bluish."

Description

Smaller than crow; plump, with small, high-crowned head; short, pinkish legs; varicolored, but tending to gray body, wings, and tail, with darker iridescent head and neck; tail usually has dark bar at end.

P. SAWATZKY ©
1990

Behavior

Social; ground-feeding in flocks, often on roads; gait a hurried walk, head bobbing in time; steady, strong wingbeats, glides with wings raised to high angle; wings clap sharply together over body on takeoff; courting males bow, coo, strut, and turn animatedly around female; coo is a soft, throaty, chortling *"bucket-a-gooo."*

Range

Nonmigratory; found throughout Pacific Northwest where humans, deliberately or otherwise, provide food and nest sites; often plentiful around harbors, where they nest under wharfs.

Food

Seeds; buds, leaves, and shoots in season; human leftovers; at feeder takes grain, peanuts, baked scraps, popcorn.

Nest

Shallow saucer of straw and/or twigs on ledge in or on building, under bridge; casually colonial where facilities permit; two or three nestings per year, may even attempt winter nesting if shelter adequate.

Comment

For many urban bird feeders, pigeons are greedy, messy usurpers, and there is a minor growth industry based on selling "pigeon-proof" feeders. However, for an apartment balcony feeder well above access of other birds, street pigeons might be welcomed as the only clients.

In several places in the Pacific Northwest, geology and climate have allowed feral pigeons to revert to the ancestral Rock Dove life-style. There are colonies on rimrock bluffs about two miles southwest of Princeton, and in Home Creek Canyon along the Catlow Valley, both near the Malheur National Wildlife Refuge in southeastern Oregon.

REF: A(W)—584; GO—166; NG—224; P(W)—210

Band-tailed Pigeon

Columba fasciata

"Band-tailed" from field mark; *Columba* is Latin for "a dove"; *fasciata* is Latin for "a band," referring to tail markings.

Description

Darker, but closely resembles slightly smaller street pigeon; end of tail paler, separated from upper tail by dark band; feet yellow, bill yellow with dark end;

- P. Snowziki -
1991 ©

narrow white line around back of neck; in flight doesn't show white rump as street pigeon does.

Behavior

Social; feeds either on ground or in trees; more likely to perch well up in trees than street pigeon; voice a deep, owl-like "*hoo-woo*" or "*woo-hoo-woo.*"

Range

Migratory; down west coast of continent to Nicaragua; a forest bird not at home in dry, open country; populations from British Columbia winter in the more moderate slopes of the Cascades and Sierra Nevada; expanding breeding range east and north.

Food

Pine nuts, acorns; madrona and mountain ash berries; fruit of manzanita, arbutus, holly, and ornamentals; visits urban yards for berries, and feeders for seeds.

Nest

Typical pigeon "nest," a flimsy lattice of twigs at widely variable heights but usually from six to twenty feet up, often overhanging steep slope or cliff.

Comment

This bird shares some of the nomadic tendencies of the mourned Passenger Pigeon, roving widely in search of food and, on finding it, nesting. The pair broods only one egg, two nestings per year. The population seems to be on a continuing rebound from near-extinction due to hunting, and as a parallel adaptation is turning into an urban bird in cities of the Pacific Northwest.

REF: A(W)—699; GO—166; NG—224; P(W)—208

Mourning Dove

Zenaida macroura

"Mourning" from sad-sounding call; "Dove" assumed to be from Anglo-Saxon *dufon*, "to dive," from birds' swift flight; *Zenaida* after wife of Prince Charles Bonaparte who, after uncle Napoleon's setback at Waterloo, moved to the United States, where he is credited as founder of systematic ornithology; *macroura* from Greek *macros*, "long" and *oura*, "tail."

Description

Trim, small, long-tailed, somber-colored pigeon; short-legged; slight iridescence to neck feathers; central tail feathers pointed, marginal tail feathers flared in flight to show white ends; body a wash of soft beige, tan, light smoky brown with hint of blush on breast; small, dark "ear spot" on sides of head, black flecks on wings.

P. SAWATZKY
1991 ©

Behavior

Moderately social; often perches on utility wires, otherwise feeds on ground; in pairs during breeding season, otherwise in flocks up to a dozen; wings whistle in flight, especially on takeoff; flight straight and swift on steady wingbeats; voice a measured series of ventriloquistic, hollow "*coos*," the first ending in a short rise in tone, the other two or three a monotone.

Range

Migratory; breeds right across southern Canada and throughout United States; prefers open woods or scrub with access to water; plentiful winterer in mild, moist areas of Pacific Northwest, absent to rare in drier, colder regions of the interior.

Food

Weed seeds, spilled grain in fields; at feeder, or on ground beneath it, takes most seeds, cracked corn, grain; all pigeons drink by submerging bill in water and sucking it up rather than dabbling bill and raising head to let water run down, as other birds do.

Nest

A flat, flimsy, sometimes see-through arrangement of twigs, up to fifty feet up, but usually between ten to twenty-five feet; may use abandoned nest of robin, catbird, or grackle as nest base; prefers thick cover, as in heavy shrub, evergreen, vine tangle; favors open woodland; rare host of cowbird.

Comment

Doves are symbols of peace and love, the expression "billing and cooing" arising from their courting and grooming behavior. In fact, doves are very aggressive birds; mating-season fights between males are fierce, drawn-out, sometimes bloody struggles.

Most writers can't resist a go at doves' slovenly housing standards, wondering out loud how such a precarious platform can hold eggs and young long enough for brooding. Candace Savage, as she often does, says it best in *Wings of the North:* "The birds often turn lovey-dovey during nest-building as well, since every straw that the male brings to his mate may stimulate a new round of endearments. The finished nest is what you'd expect from a pair of love-blurred minds ..."

The sneers of critics to the contrary, the nests work very well for the purposes intended, which is to raise young. Doves are diligent, all-season parents, in the milder parts of the Northwest bringing off as many as four clutches. The male broods during the day, the female at night. Like pigeons, they feed their broods, usually a pair, on rich "pigeon milk."

A game bird in much of the United States, the Mourning Dove's annual kill runs around 50 million, the highest by far among all game birds.

REF: A(W)—544; GO—166; NG—226; P(W)—208

Hummingbirds

Family Trochilidae

Hummingbirds are strictly a New World avian phenomenon and one of its most successful, with 319 species thus far identified. Most of them live in the zone of tropical forest between ten degrees south and ten degrees north of the equator. One can say "thus far" because several known species are each found only in single, very small pockets of habitat. It is reasonable to predict that in this vast region, other undiscovered species exist in other pockets where the questing biologist has still to set foot. Unhappily, the biologist may lose the race to the chain saw and bulldozer.

Hidden in museum collections there are unsettling reminders, as if any more were needed, that exploitation has a way of outrunning biologists. Fashion decreed, in the late 1800s, that women's hats be adorned with stuffed hummingbirds. To answer the demand, dealers in tropical America paid natives for skins, shipping well over 1 million a year to London, Paris, and New York. Museums added new specimens to their collections by simply buying them from the importers.

Among these collections there are six species known only by trade skins. Were the birds wiped out for fashion? Did they vanish when their habitat was obliterated? Or do they still whir and dart among the orchids in places only the Indian huntsmen know?

Tropical as they are, only thirteen species breed north of the Mexican border. Of these, six nest in the Pacific Northwest; the Black-chinned, Rufous, Calliope, Anna's, Allen's, and Broad-tailed. The Rufous is listed as a summer resident and nester all the way up to Anchorage on the south coast of Alaska.

Avian Helicopter

Hummingbirds are unique for their small size, but it is their whirring flight with its amazing speed and exquisite control that distinguishes them from all other birds. From a standing start they can zoom into full flight almost instantly, and "de-zoom" just as abruptly to hang, motionless except for the blurred wings, in front of a flower or a feeder. They can fly backwards, even upside down, thanks to wing design and musculature that give them equal power on the up and the down stroke.

Like the human hand, the hummer wing can be turned "palm up" or "knuckles down" through a 180-degree rotation, except that the wing rotates at the shoulder socket, not in the forearm and wrist. On hover, the body hangs down from the shoulders at about a 45-degree angle. On the change from forward stroke to back, the wing rotates a full half-circle so that its front edge still leads on the backstroke with the top surface of the flight feathers underneath. All this goes on at a rate of from 22 to 80 beats per second. In a real hurry, some hummers can accelerate this to 200 per second. Small wonder they hum.

Hummingbirds and swifts are related, and both share the ability to go into a torpid state to conserve energy. The souped-up metabolism of the hummingbird needs copious quantities of fuel; deprived of food for even a couple of hours at the wrong time, a hummer will starve. To get through a mild night, it merely sits still to conserve energy. But if this doesn't cut heat loss sufficiently, the torpor mechanism takes over and drops the bird's temperature from 105° Fahrenheit to within several degrees of the surrounding air. The heart rate slows to 40 beats per minute, a drastic cutback from a rate of 500 per minute on idle, 1,200 at full throttle during flight. In the morning the system revs up again, but apparently doesn't achieve full recovery until the bird can take flight.

Going torpid isn't an option for brooding females because they must maintain their eggs at normal body temperature all night. Thanks to their deep, snug-fitting nests they can keep their temperature up and minimize energy loss.

A flurry of controversy has arisen recently over whether hummer feeders should have perches in front of the feeding holes. Hummers have been seen falling off perches and expiring on the ground below. A tempting explanation was that the birds were taking their first feed of the day and hadn't reached full operating temperature. It followed that if they had continued hovering, instead of perching, they would have maintained sufficient body temperature to withstand the chill of taking on a large swig of cold syrup at the feeder. Expert opinion greeted this explanation with much skepticism, to the end that for the time being at least I'm leaving the perches on my feeders.

In the Amazonian tropics many species of flowers have evolved to rely exclusively on hummingbirds for pollination, rejecting insects. Many blossoms have long, tubelike corollas with narrow openings and no landing pads for bees. Flowers are positioned well free of leaves and tendrils that would interfere with hovering hummers. They are red or orange, colors that the birds can distinguish but insects can't. They produce copious quantities of nectar that isn't as concentrated as that of the insect-pollinated blossoms, since bees are more efficient at collecting small quantities of concentrated nectar. In their turn, some hummingbird species have evolved bills that are specialized to probe or pierce flowers inaccessible to rival pollinators, including, in some cases, all other hummingbirds.

Anna's Hummingbird

Calypte anna

If there ever was any association between *calypte* and the Greek proper name Kalypte, it has been lost; *anna* is from Anna, Duchess of Rivoli, whose beauty and grace, having caught the eye of Audubon, were memorialized by one of his associates, the French naturalist Lesson, who prudently also named another bird, *Lampornis clemenciae* (the Blue-throated Hummingbird), after his own wife.

Description

The largest of coastal Pacific Northwest hummers, 3½ to 4 inches (9 to 10.2 centimeters) long; in sunlight adult male flashes purplish red iridescence on forehead, throat patch, and sides of neck—areas that may appear black in dull light; upper body and sides greenish; female similar, paler, lacking iridescent patches.

Behavior

Visits feeders, flower beds, and blossoming shrubs; like all hummers, very pugnacious in defending territory and feeders; a courting male power-dives from height, zooms back up, giving an explosive "*pop*" at bottom of each dive; song a pattern of scratchy squeaks lasting several seconds; call a sharp "*chip*" or a series of rapid "*chee-chee-chee-chees.*"

Range

Nonmigratory, but some may disperse north or east in fall; very much a coastal breeder, found from Baja California to Seattle and the Olympic Peninsula; at limits of range, associated exclusively thus far with yards, gardens, and feeders.

Food

Nectar, and a higher proportion of small insects than any other North American hummer; readily visits feeders for sugar-water which, in winter, should be increased in strength to 60 percent sugar content from the 20 to 25 percent customarily used in hot weather.

Nest

Relatively large compared to other hummingbird nests; made of fine stems, plant down, fibers bound together with spider webbing, lined with plant down and feathers; often finished on outside with flakes of lichen; saddled to slim, horizontal support in a variety of locations.

Comment

All the field guides and checklists inform me that this hardy little Californian winters as far north as Victoria on the southern end of Vancouver Island, and in very small numbers on the adjacent mainland around the Vancouver, British Columbia, area. However, from early September 1993, a male Anna's became a regular visitor at my feeder, zooming in a half dozen times a day until he was last seen on February 23, 1994, presumably because he was able to find enough natural food. My home, and his, is on the northeastern end of Vancouver Island!

The "winter of the Anna's" was an easy one for these parts, quite a bit of rain, not many nights of below-freezing temperatures, and only a couple of snow flurries. During a mild spell in late January the bird disappeared, and I wondered if northern exposure, or someone's cat, had finally got him. It turned out that during an extended mild spell a few salmonberry bushes and some cultivated shrubs had broken into bloom, and my hummer had turned to this natural food as a welcome change from straight sugar-water. As soon as a snow flurry ushered in colder temperatures again, he was back.

REF: A(W)—597; GO—186; NG—258; P(W)—216

Woodpeckers

Family Picidae

Worldwide there are 210 species of woodpeckers, 20 breeding in North America, 13 occurring in the Pacific Northwest. They represent a highly successful group, having evolved to exploit, virtually unchallenged, the rich food buried in the bark and wood of the earth's abundant forest habitat.

Other birds have made creditable attempts to imitate woodpeckers, not surprisingly two of them members of the limitlessly ingenious finch family. The Maui Parrotbill chews into branches with its stout lower mandible, seeking insects. The Akiapolaau, another Hawaiian, chips into soft wood with its heavy lower mandible while holding out of the way its curved upper mandible, which it will later bring into play as a probe for the insects its gouging exposes. But neither of these has mastered the wood-chipper's trade as thoroughly as the woodpecker.

A number of specialized adaptations combine in woodpeckers to enable them to excavate efficiently into hard wood. It isn't enough to have a straight, hard, chisel-shaped bill and strong neck muscles. In the course of a day's activity a busy bird might whack a hard surface 8,000 to 10,000 times with sufficient energy to generate ten Gs of force on the rebound from each blow. Under such a merciless hammering a mammal skull would shatter apart and the brains turn to bloody slop. But the woodpecker skull is strong, heavily reinforced, and bound about with unusually heavy muscles. The mountings of the bill are set with some components that slide enough to absorb and dissipate impact shock. The brains are padded, packed snugly into bony housing and protected with both pneumatic and hydraulic pads. The delicate eyes are similarly cushioned.

This chopping implement is mounted on a body supported solidly by two sturdy clamps—the feet—and a brace—the stiff tail quills. Thus tripodded, the woodpecker maintains a secure but relaxed stance. This is obviously an important consideration; anyone who has watched a woodpecker at work notices that its torso bobs slightly back and forth in time with its head, adding speed and force to each stroke of the bill.

A Versatile Tongue

The capabilities of the chiseling beak are admirably complemented by the extensible, probing tongue. It is mounted on a remarkable apparatus, a stiff but flexible probe of bone, muscle, and cartilage. This divides at the back of the mouth and, supported by the forked hyoid bone, lies in a sheath that curls around the back of each side of the skull and over the top of the head to its attachment point near the nostrils. In most woodpeckers this elongated organ enables the tongue to be stuck out from three to five times the length of the bill. Extended, it resembles the tongue of a garter snake, whiplike and quick. The tip is fitted with a horny point carrying rows of backward-pointing barbs—a miniature harpoon. As tongues tend to be, it is richly supplied with nerves and the ability to taste. Oversized salivary glands on the floor of the mouth coat the tongue with sticky saliva that entraps small insects.

Together the chiseling beak and the gooey, probing tongue give the woodpecker access to a menu few other insect-eaters can reach. The fact that most of our woodpeckers have no need to migrate is evidence of their ability to exploit a nourishing and abundant food source year-round.

The spectacular Pileated Woodpecker uses its bill to hatchet gaping holes through the outer walls of carpenter ants' tree-trunk fortresses and into their inner galleries. Alarmed by the breach, the ants swarm to their colony's defense, unwittingly playing into the invader's scheme. They are lapped up by the hundreds on the darting, gummy tongue. The size of the Pileated, as big as a crow, is testimony to its ability to exploit the nourishing abundance of carpenter ants in the mature forests it inhabits.

A Big Investment

Chopping holes in wood is hard work. Not surprisingly woodpeckers are known to have prodigious appetites. The stomach of a Pileated Woodpecker was found by an enquiring investigator to contain 2,500 ants.

Housing your nest in the bowels of a solid tree trunk well above ground achieves extra security for your brood. Some cavity nesters look for natural holes or secondhand ones; woodpeckers custom-build their own. This demands a high investment of energy and time. For the larger ones, some 10,000 chips have to be chopped out and dumped. Depending on the species, nest hole preparation can occupy from ten to twenty-eight days. But the new home is weather-tight and safe from most predators.

The added security allows more time to raise a brood, whereas owners of exposed open nests must rush their young through the hazardous nestling period. Young robins are off and crash-landing on the lawn two weeks after hatching, and most warblers are out in eight to ten days. But a young Downy Woodpecker takes three weeks, and a Hairy a relatively leisurely four.

There is a least one documented downside to nesting in a hole with no back exit. When a predator sticks its face in the entrance, you're trapped. Observations of titmice in England showed that 20 percent of brooding females get caught by nest predators, a significantly higher percentage than for females on open nests.

Woodpeckers may or may not reuse last year's nest hole; most in fact do not, preferring to chip out a new one. Wintering Downy, Hairy, and Pileated Woodpeckers also excavate separate roosting holes. The result is a good num-

Lewis's Woodpecker

ber of used tree cavities that, with minimum renovations, can be used over and over again. Depending on the size of the original builders, the new tenants include swallows, bluebirds, chickadees, squirrels, small owls, and Wood Ducks. Most of these cannot breed unless they have access to a suitable tree cavity.

There is another, less obvious spinoff effect; by providing nurseries and shelter for Saw-whet, Screech, and Boreal Owls, as well as dens for Pine Martens, woodpeckers indirectly affect populations of these predators' prey species, particularly small rodents.

There are subtleties that go beyond the obvious tree–woodpecker connection. Woodpeckers evolved to meet the conditions presented by natural forests, which means a mixture of tree species in all stages of growth and decline. To many birds, young or healthy mature trees are of little value. It is the old, the decaying, and the dead that furnish the key element to survival. Trees in decline become insect nurseries and their punky innards and rotted-out knotholes prime cavity nesting sites. For many woodpeckers a forest without dead snags is just not a forest. In the conifer forests of the Pacific Northwest, woodpeckers must have dead snags to survive and reproduce.

A case in point is the Lewis's Woodpecker. This species was abundant in the Pacific Northwest and adjacent British Columbia once fires and logging had begun clearing away extensive tracts of virgin coniferous forest. Here, fires and old-style logging practices left an abundance of tall snags and dead standing trunks of giant Douglas fir, Western Red Cedar, and Western Hemlock. This mix ideally suited the Lewis's unusual (for a woodpecker) foraging behavior. It eats fruit, acorns, and berries, but its main fare is flying insects that it catches on the wing, like a flycatcher. The isolated snags, overlooking cutovers, provided ideal lookouts from which to launch pursuit of winged prey.

Then a change in forestry practices required that all snags be cut as a safety measure. That wiped out this woodpecker's livelihood so completely that except for isolated localities it is now listed as "rare" or "absent" in regional checklists in the Pacific Northwest. Where Garry Oaks are still found, Lewis's Woodpeckers may congregate to feed on them in winter.

The Drummer

Singing is a proclamation of a bird's being, a claim to territory, an invitation to mate, a threat to a rival. Lacking the voice for it, at least for the kind of noises we humans arbitrarily declare to be "song," woodpeckers advertise themselves and their intentions by drumming. Hammering on a resonating hollow trunk, a dead limb, a sheet of plywood, or a piece of sheet metal is a song in the generic sense of the word, although it is anything but melodious, particularly if played on your metal chimney at daybreak, morning after morning.

Signs of this tympanic exuberance begin showing up in early February if you happen to be neighbor to a pair of courting Downy or Hairy Woodpeckers. Later, when they begin nesting, they will drum at each other in debate over potential locations. Whatever the reason, their staccato bursts enliven the frosty silence of a late winter's day, or most emphatically punctuate the chorus of birdsong of an echoing spring sunrise.

Downy Woodpecker

Picoides pubescens

Downy seems no fluffier than its larger look-alike, the Hairy, seems hairy; *Picus* is Latin for "a woodpecker," *oides* is Greek compounded from *o*, "the," and *eidos*, "similar"; *pubescens* is Latin for "downy," as in fine hairs of puberty; in older guides, the now outdated generic name is *dendrocopos*, from Greek *dendron*, "a tree," and *kopis*, "a dagger."

Description

Bold pattern of black and buffy-gray on head, back, wings, tail; white stripe on back, belly plain buff-gray; male has small red bar on back of head; told from almost identical Hairy by smaller size and proportionally smaller bill; in life often doubtful who is who until the two can be compared close together;

diagnostic black spots on white outer tail feathers of Downy (absent on Hairy) may be indistinct or not visible.

Behavior

Typical woodpecker feeding, perching posture straight up on vertical surface, clinging with the feet, propped on the stiff, pointed tail feathers; forages on tree trunks and branches, females tending to work lower trunk and large branches, male upper trunk and smaller branches; pert, inquisitive, friendly bird around feeders, sometimes beating even chickadees to newly offered foods; call a short, sharp "*kyik*" or shrill rattle descending in pitch at end.

P. SAWATZKY ©
1990

Range

Nonmigratory; in mixed, deciduous, all-aged woodlands and burns; common throughout Pacific Northwest; not common in pure conifer forests.

Food

Largely insectivorous, which it searches out in tree bark; at feeder loves suet, meat scraps, and sunflower seeds.

Nest

In winter each bird drills its own roosting cavity in dead or decay-softened trunks; entrance hole perfectly round, 1¼ inches in diameter, from three to fifty feet up; occasionally uses nest boxes for temporary shelter.

Comment

Why Downy males forage in the upper levels of trees

and their mates the lower has been explained variously. Some dismiss it as mere male dominance, others attribute it to a provident parceling out of foraging resources and point to the slightly longer tongue of the male as suggestive of division of the sexes at mealtime. Whatever; both search randomly for dormant insects and pupae in and under the bark of trees, sometimes flaking off the bark, sometimes drilling into the insect's refuge and spearing it with the pointed, barbed end of the tongue. Once condemned as injurious to trees, Downies and other woodpeckers, with the possible exception of the sapsuckers, are now tolerantly regarded as important controls on insects whose interests conflict with ours.

The mere presence of trees is no assurance that woodpeckers will be there. Downies require mixed-age woodlands, including a decent complement of the soft-hearted senior trees that forestry types sneer at and label "decadent."

REF: A(W)—641; GO—200; NG—270; P(W)—224

Hairy Woodpecker
Picoides villosus

"Hairy" is a puzzlingly undescriptive name for a bird with so many other distinguishing features; *Picus* is Latin for "a woodpecker," Greek *oides* compounded from *o*, "the," and *eidos*, "like" (similar); *villosus* is Latin for "hairy"; in older guides the now outdated generic name is *dendrocopos*, from Greek *dendron*, "a tree," and *kopis*, "a dagger."

Description
Robin-sized; oversized version of Downy; head, back, wings patterned in sharply contrasting black and gray-buff; belly, outer tail feathers plain gray-buff; adult male has small red flash on back of head; bill proportionally heavier, longer, than Downy's.

Behavior
Typical woodpecker affinity for perching and feeding on vertical surfaces, especially tree trunks, suet cages; more wary than Downy, usually not as numerous where both share feeding site; in spring, drums rapid-fire on resonant surface as part of territorial/courting ritual; call is a sharp, abrupt "*kyeek*" or "*pik*," as well as a rapid, strident rattle resembling kingfisher's; during strongly powered flight, as in takeoff or sharp turn, wings make pronounced "*whuck-whuck-whuck*" noise, possibly a controllable sound used as alarm signal.

Range
Nonmigratory but seasonally nomadic; nests throughout the continent north

P. SAWATZKI ©
1990

to the tree line; favors coniferous and mixed woodlands with some mature growth; winters through most of Pacific Northwest, when it may take up residence in parks, well-treed yards, and riparian (riverside) habitat.

Food

Insectivorous, especially on wood-boring kinds in trunks and larger limbs of mature trees; at feeder, very fond of suet and, secondarily, sunflower seeds.

Nest

Generally in dead trees, or live trees with heart rot, seeming to favor poplar/alder group; hole round or oblong, 2 to 2½ inches long by 1¼ to 1½ inches wide.

Comment

Woodpeckers tap sharply to test the resonance of wood, very likely to detect the hollow tunnels of insects. The sudden concussions might also startle hidden insects into moving and giving away their presence to the keen ears of the bird, upon which it drills in to make a capture with its probing, barb-tipped tongue.

Holes or cracks between the layers of laminate siding sometimes excite the excavating reflex in Hairies. They punch holes in the outer plies to check the hollow spaces behind them, just as they would to expose insect tunnels in a tree trunk. This habit will explain, if not justify, what may seem to exasperated householders to be willful property damage.

REF: A(W)—702; GO—200; NG—270; P(W)—224

White-headed Woodpecker
Picoides albolarvatus

Picoides from Latin *picus*, "a woodpecker," and Greek *oides*, "similar"; *albo* from Latin "white," *larvatus* "masked"; recent generic change from *dendrocopos*, from Greek *dendron*, "a tree," and *kopis*, "a dagger."

Description

Robin-sized; unmistakable; black all over except for pure white head, and wing primaries frosted at edges to form white patch in flight, white streak when folded; male has horizontal red patch on back of head.

Behavior

Pries off loose bark in search of insects; more often seen at watering places than other woodpeckers; comes readily to feeders in winter, occasionally in company of young of the year; call is a sharp "*chik*," or rapid "*chik-ik-ik-ik-ik*."

Range

Elevationally and erratically migratory; limited to intermountain valleys and plateaus in the Cascades and Sierra Nevada south almost to Mexico; strongly associated with Ponderosa Pine, incidentally with other conifers; threatened by the disappearance of old-growth Ponderosa Pine forests.

Food

Insects, seeds of Ponderosa Pine, and Common Mullein, an abundant introduced roadside weed; at feeders, readily takes suet and sunflower seeds; observed affinity for water would bring it to backyard ponds and fountains.

Nest

Excavates in dead or punky-hearted tree trunks of large diameter, at widely varying heights; entrance 1½ to 1¾ inches in diameter.

Comment

Keen birders visiting the Pacific Northwest relish the chance to add this striking bird to their lists on trips to the eastern slopes of the Cascades. And although it

is so thinly distributed throughout its territory, it is nevertheless occasionally seen wintering in the yards and orchards of lower altitudes, where, no doubt, it is a treasured visitor at feeders.

REF: A(W)—706; GO—198; NG—266; P(W)—224

Acorn Woodpecker
Melanerpes formicivorus

Also formerly "California woodpecker"; *Melanerpes* from Greek *melas,* "black," and *herpes,* "a creeper"; *formicivorus* from Latin *formica,* "an ant," and *voro,* "devour"; since all woodpeckers eat ants, "acorn eater" would be more descriptive.

Description
Smaller than robin; "clown-face" from bright pattern of black, white, and yellow, with red crown; back, wings, and tail black, wings with small white patch especially noticeable in flight; rump white; chin black, throat yellow, breast black, belly white.

Behavior
Intensely social; cooperative nester and forager; stores nuts, mainly acorns, in close-spaced pockets cut in "granary" trees; occasionally hawks for insects like flycatcher; noisy, voice harsh and loud, raising and/or moving wings during vocalization; calls include raucous "*wake'-up, wake'-up, wake'-up*" or "*jay'-cob, jay'-cob.*"

Range
Nonmigratory; southwestern United States and Mexico in pine–oak habitat; in the Pacific Northwest associated with range of white oak from north-central Oregon south and westward through the Cascades and Sierra Nevada.

Food
In summer, insects, sometimes caught on the wing, fruit, green corn; in winter, acorns, other nuts; noted for storing huge numbers of nuts in "granary" trees.

Nest
Drilled in large dead or dead-hearted tree or limb, occasionally in utility pole, from five to sixty feet up; hole round, 1½ inches across; interior cavity from eight to twenty-four inches deep.

Comment
This unique woodpecker works cooperatively in family groups to defend a territory, excavate nest holes, and brood and feed young. Juveniles of previous

clutches may stay home as helpers for several seasons until the chance to establish their own territory presents itself.

The focus of these family cooperatives is the main granary tree. In readiness for winter, birds diligently collect acorns and store them singly in holes drilled in soft bark of Douglas firs, in dead oaks, or in utility poles. Holes and nuts are selected for a tight fit, the acorn flush with the surface or slightly counter-sunk, making it awkward for rodents and other birds to pillage. Families use the same tree(s) generation after generation, drilling thousands of holes an inch or so apart. Trees with 20,000 holes are on record, and one super-granary had some 50,000. It is crucial that granary trees, described by Washington biologist Ken Bevis as "heritage sites to these woodpecker tribes," be left undisturbed for these unique birds.

REF: A(W)—623; GO—198; NG—266; P(W)—222

Northern Flicker

Colaptes auratus

Until recently also "Common Flicker"; previously "Yellow-shafted" (*C. auratus*), "Red-shafted" (*C. cafer*), or "Gilded" (*C. chrysoides*); folk names have included "high-hole," "clape," "pigeon woodpecker," "yellow-hammer," "yarrup," "hairy wicket," "wake-up," "yawker bird," "walk-up," "ant-bird," among many others; "Flicker" from Anglo-Saxon *flicerian*, "fluttering of birds," although word is also highly echoic of bird's call; *Colaptes* from Greek *kolapto*, "to peck with the bill, chisel"; *auratus* from Latin "golden," referring to undersides of wings and tail.

Description

Larger than robin; short-legged, solid; in flight shows bright salmon-red underwings, boldly speckled undersides, and bright white rump; bold black bib across top of breast; long, strong, slightly down-curved bill; in western red-shafted phase, neither sex has a horizontal red dash on back of head; crown and neck brownish gray; throat and sides of head gray; back and wings light brown with black barring; male only has red "mustache" from corner of mouth extending back under eye.

Behavior

Strong, markedly undulating flight with several rapid beats on up-swoop, wings folded for down-swoop; unlike other woodpeckers, spends much time on open, grassy ground, hopping awkwardly about searching for ants; drums during mating season, sometimes on buildings; courting couples go through elaborate "dance" duet on tree limbs, flaring wings and tails, bobbing and moving heads in circles; noisy, calls a staccato, strident "*yuk-yuk-yuk-yuk*," a more deliberate "*wicker, wicker, wicker*," or a single, loud "*kleee-yer.*"

Range

Migratory; breeds right across the continent from tree line to subtropics; habitat is open woodland, parkland, pastures, suburban yards, and parks; borderline between western "Red-shafted" and eastern "Yellow-shafted" is in Dakotas and eastern Montana; breeds and winters throughout Pacific Northwest.

Food

Ants, mostly from ground; insects; in-season fruit, nuts, seeds; suet, peanut butter, and, perhaps, sunflower seeds at feeders.

Nest

Prefers to excavate hole in tree or snag with punky heartwood; also uses utility poles, fenceposts, buildings, natural tree cavities, or nest boxes; known to use holes in banks and cliffs; excavated hole is two inches in diameter, from twenty inches to sixty-five feet up; old flicker holes are important to other birds and small mammals; starlings frequently evict flickers.

Comment

Writers of this and previous generations have made special note that the flicker is "a bit of an oddball" or "a rebel in the family ranks" among woodpeckers. Worldwide it is one of only three that are true migrators, the others being the Yellow-bellied Sapsucker and the Wryneck of Eurasia, the least woodpecker-like member of the clan.

The flickers until recently were listed as three species, but these have been "lumped" into one, renamed the Northern Flicker. What are now designated as three races have, except for the underwing colors that gave them their names, very similar plumage patterns. Both sexes of the "Yellow-shafted" have a crescent of bright red encircling the back of the head; the "Red-shafted" and "Gilded" don't.

The really important plumage difference is sex-related; all males, otherwise identical to the females, have a colored "mustache." The Yellow-shafted's is black, the others', red. In the name of science a deceptive "mustache" was painted on a mated female flicker. Her erstwhile lifelong mate promptly attacked her and drove her away. Reconciliation followed removal of the misleading insignia. Interestingly, where the races meet and interbreed, the essential mustache may come out red on one side, black on the other. Except to sometimes befuddled birdwatchers, it doesn't seem to matter.

-PSAWATZKY-
1992 ©

Perhaps because of their migratory ways, and occasional intermarriages, atypical flickers frequently show up where they "don't belong." In the winter of 1991–92, a male Red-shafted showed up at my yard in central Vancouver Island wearing all the proper insignia of his race, but sporting a red blaze on the back of his head, the clear mark of a Yellow-shafted ancestor. Ken Bevis of Ellensburg, Washington, had a yellow-shafted, black-mustached bird spend the winter of 1992–93 in his neighborhood, far east of where the field guides say it should have been.

REF: A(W)—642; GO—194; NG—264; P(W)—226

Pileated Woodpecker

Dryocopus pileatus

"Pileated" from specific name, which is from Latin *pileum*, "a cap," which refers to bird's prominent crest; formerly "cock-of-the-woods" or "logcock," red crest resembling rooster's comb; *Dryocopus* compounded from Greek *drys*, "a tree," and *kopis*, "a dagger."

Description

Crow-sized; with wings folded, is predominantly black except for white stripe on each side of the long neck and side of face; white chin, narrow white eyebrow stripe; both sexes have conspicuous red crest, male's being larger, and he has red "mustache"; in flight, white lining on underside of wings flashes prominently.

Behavior

First clue to presence may be deep, vertically oblong holes freshly chipped out of trunks of trees and snags, often close to ground; litter of chips especially obvious in snow; very wary except where it has had a chance to become habituated to people in protected areas such as national or large urban parks; on quiet days in mature woodland the loud, irregular whacking noise of this bird at work is usually the first active sign of its presence; call a loud, strident succession of "*kyak-kyak-kyak-kyak*"s often increasing in volume, very similar to flicker with the volume turned up.

Range

Nonmigratory; considered obligates to mature forest, hence limited to regions where tracts of mature deciduous and mixed forest occur, including parks; may frequent agricultural areas and urban areas adjacent to mature woodlands; favors habitat near water; widely scattered throughout Pacific Northwest, where mature forest exists, including extreme northern and western Washington, northwestern Oregon, and southward anywhere west of the Cascade–Sierra

P. SAWATZKY ©
1990

summit; depending on supply of mature trees, home territory may be up to 5,000 acres, with feeding sites widely scattered through it.

Food

Insects, especially carpenter ants, which it regurgitates to feed its nestlings; occasionally visits feeders for suet; said also to take nuts, meat scraps, hamburger; observed eating elderberries.

Nest

Hole usually thirty to fifty feet up; in Pacific Northwest it appears that a snag or punky-cored trunk at least twenty inches in diameter is essential; en-

141

trance 3 to 3½ inches wide, somewhat longer; typically wider across the bottom than across the top.

Comment

Pileateds have a professional's keen eye for signs of carpenter ants and can detect their presence in trees that seem perfectly sound to lesser sleuths. Indeed, the first outward sign that a big, apparently sound tree is harboring ants is often a pileated's fresh, gaping hole near the base of it.

In response to early settlement, shooting, and logging, populations plummeted, to the point where the species was thought to be threatened. But their numbers, particularly in the eastern parts of their continental range, are increasing. This may be due to the birds' latent ability to adapt to cutover or fragmented forest habitat, combined with the gradual recovery of tracts of woodland to the point where sufficient mature trees have reappeared. Growing public intolerance of indiscriminate shooting may also have helped these beautiful birds reestablish themselves.

REF: A(W)—703; GO—194; NG—274; P(W)—222

Crow Family

Family Corvidae

The corvids—crows and their allies—are an avian success story. Able to survive in virtually every terrestrial habitat on earth, they are a testament to the benefits of being masterful generalists. In other words, they are adaptable.

By hedging on their options they have missed the benefits, and avoided the risks, of specialization. They are predators, but lack the power and weaponry of hawks and owls. They feed on dead animals, but cannot soar effortlessly aloft all day, surveying a huge circle of earth like that master scavenger, the vulture. But, unlike these two, which will starve when there is no meat to be found, crows simply look for something else—seeds, green shoots, insects, garbage, shellfish, et cetera, et cetera, et cetera.

Essentially they are just oversized songbirds. Even the bulky raven faces his harsh world in the highest Arctic on dickybird feet innocent of destructive capacity. Its bill is large and businesslike, but more a handyman's tool than a specialized instrument.

Brains Over Brawn

If there is one thing they can claim as special, it is their intelligence. There is no absolute way of measuring this attribute in humans, and not even a reliable approximation of any scale to rate one species of animal against another. But in comparison to other birds reacting to similar situations, the crow and its kin do seem to be "smarter." They learn quickly, and have long memories. Convincingly, they possess the highest brain-to-body weight ratio of any bird.

The popular literature repeats a seaside anecdote on how Herring Gulls and crows both attempt to feed on mussels. Neither is strong enough to smash the shells, nor pry them open with its beak. Both have learned to fly aloft with a mussel and crack it by dropping it. With the gulls, it is a hit-and-miss operation, because often as not they bomb them fruitlessly onto soft mud. But the crows have learned to drop them onto the rocks.

Corvid intelligence isn't the lovable smarts of, for example, the porpoise. It is a defiant craftiness with a bent for larceny that humans find irritating, even threatening. Nest-building ravens have been seen pulling wool from the rumps of resting sheep, more to the disgruntlement of the shepherd than the sheep. Branded as pests of agriculture and of game birds, they have been persecuted relentlessly. They simply respond to the plots against them by becoming more skillfully evasive. Crows are noted for their uncanny ability to sense the presence of a concealed gun, and to spot the difference between a shotgun and a similarly shaped cane.

The crow family tends to be rather long-lived. A raven in captivity lasted for twenty-nine years, and wild Blue Jays have survived to fifteen. This of itself does not suggest a high IQ, but it is an advantage permitting both the time, in youth, to learn, and an extended adulthood in which to apply the accumulated experience.

Finally, for what it's worth as a measure of their braininess, this family boasts the only native North American birds that can be taught to imitate human speech. Starlings share this talent, but they aren't native birds.

Country Bird Moves Uptown

Throughout their range in North America, several species of corvids, initially swept aside by the impact of settlement, have learned to capitalize on the changes humans have wrought. In any frontier mining, fishing, or logging town, crows and ravens are as bold as street pigeons, often hanging about the downtown business sections in such numbers as to be nuisances. Squadrons of them ensure that the contents of any garbage cans left open will soon be strewn about. Auto insurance claims are occasionally paid to repair dents caused by ravens' dropping bones or frozen globs of refuse onto cars from on high.

In some major western cities, magpies have gone urban, thanks in part to a change in human behavior. At one time it was quite acceptable for a townsman, particularly a retired farmer or rancher, to blast away at any "varmint." Nowadays, however, civic authority takes a dim view of gunplay within city limits. So the cheeky bird, finding abundant food, protection from the wrath of human enemies, and sanctuary from most of its natural predators, has moved in to stay.

Grown abundant, it has become the focus of controversy, condemned by some for its noisiness, its destructiveness, its domination of feeders, its habit of strewing refuse about, and its reputation for raiding small birds' nests.

"Good" and "Bad"

In nature there is an endless interplay of actions that can be misinterpreted according to human values as either "good" or "bad," even for activities that don't relate to human interests. These biases obscure the real roles of the species they affect and, in the case of the "bad" animals, make them targets of unwarranted persecution.

Unhappily, crows, magpies, ravens, and, to a lesser degree, the jays are branded as "bad." All corvids will congregate around dead animals, to feed on the rotting flesh, a habit finicky humans find ghoulish. Other emotions intervene; all corvids are nest predators, feeding on the eggs and nestlings of other birds. On a purely emotional level, this is abhorrent; bird lovers feel pity for the bereaved parents, hunters fume over the loss of "their" game birds.

The answer for genuinely interested nature watchers is to learn more about the survival imperatives of the animals around them, to let real knowledge supplant prejudice and emotion. The important thing to keep in mind is that in nature there is no altruism and no vindictiveness, only the unbreakable rules of survival and reproduction.

Predators as Prey

It may help in overcoming our judgmental prejudices to realize that the scoundrel crow family is as much accountable to the laws of survival as any wild thing. Corvids, especially the young, provide food for larger predators. I have found the headless carcasses of young ravens lying near the nest tree, victims of Great Horned Owls. At our rural cottage I occasionally find scatterings of blue feathers on the snow, and the signs that a jay had been ambushed by a cruising goshawk.

Along with some species of gulls, the crow family has the most varied diet of any birds. They eat grain, green shoots from gardens, berries, dried fruit, carrion, eggs and nestlings, small terrestrial animals, insects, fish, and all manner of human refuse, and will hoard surplus food. Interestingly, "*pica*," the Latin word for "magpie," is also a medical term describing an unusual craving for unnatural things, such as a child who eats dirt or paint.

Hoarding, and migrating, are responses to life in environments where food resources are unreliable or vanish altogether, as in our mid-continental winters. Of this family represented here, only the crow is a true migrant; the rest have adapted well enough to tough it out with occasional foraging migrations when conditions in their home territories are unusually stressful.

Gray Jay

Perisoreus canadensis

Lackluster "Gray" replaces "Canada" of former name; "whiskey-jack" is the woodsy English version of Algonquian/Cree *wiskatjan*; European writers syllabize call of Siberian Jay as "*whisk-ee*"; *Perisoreus* is Greek for "to heap up," i.e., to store up, hoard; *canadensis* is Latinized "of Canada."

Description

Slightly larger than robin; off-white face and forehead, shading softly into smoky gray, accentuates the overall soft, puffy look; back of head, neck, and indistinct stripe encircling eye gray to gray-brown; no crest; back, wings, and tail soft gray, underside lighter gray; bill of modest proportions; tail long.

Behavior

Actions deliberate, unhurried; flight often a smooth, floating glide; accomplished mooch, training picnickers to share food by approaching them with an air of poised expectancy, not above helping itself with well-timed grab if passive appeal doesn't work, hence the alternate bush name "camp robber"; compulsive

food hoarder; call a clear, descending "*quee-oo*" whistle; other sounds include typical jay repertoire of squawks, chortles, and imitations.

Range

Optionally migratory, in some areas readily moving from high-altitude summer range to lower levels in winter; parts of some populations also migrate north–south; subject to occasional irruptive appearances out of normal haunts; in Coast and Cascade Mountains of western Washington and Oregon, extreme northeastern Washington, and adjacent northern Idaho; isolated population in Klamath Mountains of California.

Food

Omnivorous; fruit, seeds, meat, insects, carrion; in north, quick to scavenge at wolf kills; at feeder, takes suet, larger seeds, table scraps.

Nest

Large, thick-walled; well lined with fine grasses, bark shreds, feathers, hair, fur, spider and insect cocoon webbing; usually three to ten feet from snow surface, but occasionally much higher; usually close to trunk of small to midsize conifer in open woods, almost always on sunlit side; eggs very pale greenish splattered with olive and paler gray, especially at large end.

Comment

Gray Jays have elaborated on food-caching to a degree that not only allows them to survive the harshest of high-alpine winters, but to begin nesting well before they end. Compulsive hoarding of food during mild seasons is the means to this end. Their habit of storing food where subsequent snow won't bury it, aided by a prodigious memory, sees them and their brood through the shank end of winter. See Midwinter Nesting in Chapter 6, Those Fascinating Birds, for a fuller account of Gray Jay nesting behavior.

REF: A(W)—727; GO—224; NG—302; P(W)—256

Steller's Jay

Cyanocitta stelleri

Named after Georg Steller, German physician and biologist with Bering's 1740 expedition to Alaska; *Cyanocitta* from Greek *cyanos*, "blue," and *kitta*, "a jay."

Description

Large, tall-crested, dark bird; sooty head, throat, and neck blend into dark blue of body; darker flecks on wings and tail; long, fan-shaped tail.

Behavior

In family groups for awhile after young fledged; a confident, unafraid regular in yards, gardens, and orchards, but wary and evasive in its preferred upland habitat; voice a tuneless, raspy "*yaaak-yaaak-yaaak*," but imitates musical calls of other birds.

Range

Coastal populations nonmigratory, but interior populations partially migratory; in various types of coniferous and mixed-wood forest; retreats from upper altitudes in winter when it becomes more evident in valleys and coastal lowlands; absent from southwestern Oregon and southern Idaho, otherwise a common bird throughout the Pacific Northwest.

Food

Omnivorous; insects, small vertebrates, seeds in summer, switching to acorns, pine seeds in winter; at feeder, fond of peanuts, sunflower seeds, suet, baked goods, table scraps.

Nest

Well-made, bulky base of twigs, dead leaves; cup of mud and grasses, lined with fine grass, root fibers, hair, pine needles; in bush or tree, usually conifer,

eight to sixteen feet up, but can vary greatly, including being located in cavity in tree or even in building.

Comment

These largest of North American jays are accomplished mimics, frequently leading birders on wild goose (or eagle, or owl) chases. They have even been heard to give a perfect imitation of a Common Loon.

REF: A(W)—735; GO—222; NG—302; P(W)—254

Scrub Jay

Aphelocoma coerulescens

Previously also "California Jay"; "Scrub" from affinity to low thickets; *Aphelocoma* from Greek *aphelos*, "smooth," and *koms*, "hair," because this is a crestless jay; *coerulescens* from Latin *coruleus*, "dark blue."

Description

Robin-sized, but bill heavier and fan-shaped tail longer; head, wings, and tail dark blue, especially obvious during gliding flight; back dull brown; white throat outlined by incomplete blue necklace; flanks pale rust; belly soft gray.

Behavior

Social; territorial, pairs defending home turf year-round; scatter-hoards acorns, burying them by tapping them into ground with bill; short, undulating flights on shallow wingbeats, ending in glide; harsh voice a rasping "*skreek?*" or a harsh "*chek-chek-chek-chek.*"

Range

Nonmigratory, but may be seasonally nomadic; favors drier uplands of oak–pinyon, chaparral, juniper cover; at home in suburbs, parks; from extreme southeastern Washington through foothills of Cascades in Oregon through coastal pine–oak woodlands of northern California; center of abundance the Sacramento Valley; in recent years extending range northward, increasingly frequent in Puget Sound area.

Food

Insects, seeds, fruit, eggs, nestlings; in winter switches to acorns, pinyon seeds; at feeder, sunflower seeds, suet, corn, scraps.

Nest

Thick cup of twigs mixed with moss, grasses, weed stems, lined with finer plant fibers; usually in low shrub three to ten feet high.

-P. SAWATZKY-
-94 ©

Comment

Christmas Bird Counts over the past few years have turned up Scrub Jays where they have no business being, such as Astoria, Oregon, and around Puget Sound.

Jays being jays, theft provides an important source of food—acorns pilfered from the "granaries" of Acorn Woodpeckers. Looking on the bright side, the jays bury some of their loot up-slope from the granary pole and, in some cases no doubt, up-slope from the parent tree. This "uphill planting" performs a service for the oaks whose shed seed, on its own, could at best stay in place under the tree, or bounce and roll downhill.

REF: A(W)—630; GO—222; NG—300; P(W)—254

Clark's Nutcracker

Nucifraga columbiana

"Clark," of Lewis and Clark expedition of 1803 to Pacific Northwest; "Nutcracker" from bird's method of feeding; *Nucifraga* from Latin "nut" and *frango*, "break"; *columbiana*, after river near which Clark collected type specimens.

Description

Built like half-sized crow; canvas-gray body; wing dark with white patch prominent in flight; central feathers of tail dark, outer ones white; curved dagger bill much longer than that of similar Gray Jay.

Behavior

Slow, crowlike wingbeats; around mountain resorts a bold, persistent beggar of handouts; industrious hoarder of seeds, which it buries in ground; voice a flat, grating *"caaa"* or *"craaa."*

Range

Nonmigratory, but may range to lower elevations in times of food shortage; in Pacific Northwest most common in pine and Douglas fir forest above 5,000 feet, but occurs down to 2,000-foot level; found in north-central and northeastern Washington, central and western Oregon, through Idaho except extreme south, not in northern California.

Food

Omnivorous, but dependent mainly on Douglas fir seeds, and on pine seeds, which it buries in great numbers prior to winter; at feeders, takes peanuts, sunflower seeds, suet, table scraps.

Nest

Large bowl-shaped base of twigs, sticks, and bark, built up with inner cup of bark and grass filled in with punky wood powder; inner cup lined with grass, bark, and other plant fibers; sometimes a plaster layer (mud, duff, soil) between base and inner cup; in dense conifer, often toward end of a branch.

Comment

Like the crossbills, with which it shares a conifer-dependent life-style, the nutcracker must periodically abandon its preferred habitat when the seed crop fails. Judged by major irruptions of these birds out of their mountains, pine seed production collapses every ten to fifteen years. Unlike crossbills, but very much like jays, the nutcracker hedges against famine by storing from 20,000 to 30,000 pine seeds in caches on exposed south-facing slopes where mountain winds scour off the snow, and the sun keeps the earth from freezing solid. It is aided in its hoarding by a throat pouch with a capacity of ninety or more pine seeds, plus whatever it can load into its bill. It also has a mental map grid capable of accurately relocating seed caches by orienting to nearby marks such as stones. Experimenters have moved the marks and found the bird's recovery probes changed location by the same amount. It has been seen to dig down through a foot of snow with great accuracy to recover buried seeds.

The life-giving pine crop permitting, it shares with the crossbill the ability to nest very early in the season, brooding its young in heavy, well-insulated nests and feeding them on regurgitated seeds.

REF: A(W)—726; GO—224; NG—302; P(W)—256

-P. SAWATZKY -
1992 ©

Black-billed Magpie

Pica pica

"Black-billed" as distinct from "Yellow-billed" of California; sometimes "American" Magpie; "Magpie" has two roots, "mag" from diminutive for "Margaret" (although connection is a mystery), "pie" possibly from same root as "piebald," an animal with a patchwork of contrasting colors, or from Middle English *pie*, "magpie"; Latin *Pica*, "a magpie."

Description

Pigeon-sized, slim; very long-tailed, strikingly beautiful; head, neck, upper breast, and back iridescent black; tail and wings dark iridescent blue-green; belly white; in flight, outer wing primaries flash white, and horseshoe-shaped white mark on back very evident.

Behavior

All movements graceful, flowing, particularly when springing about among branches; level flight on measured wingbeats, almost languid, wings stroking the air; travels in small, loose groups; congregates around garbage dumps, road kills; call a strident, rasping "*yek-yek-yek*," repeated rapidly or in a single, drawn-out, ascending "*yaaag?*"; usually very wary and alert.

Range

Regionally and optionally migratory, depending on severity of winter in breeding range; circumpolar, in North America a western native, from Alaska south to New Mexico; not a bird of wet, dense coastal forests, stopping on the dry side of the Coast Range; otherwise found throughout entire Pacific Northwest, preferring open land with scattered groves, brushy gullies, wooded valleys.

Food

Omnivorous scavenger/predator; at feeders, hauls suet away in bulk chunks until it is all gone, a good reason for dispensing it in sturdy wire screen holders with ½ inch or smaller mesh.

Nest

Unmistakable; huge, loosely interlaced structure of twigs, often thorns, up to three feet in height woven around a cupped nest of mud and fibers, completely enclosed except for one or more side entrances; in small tree or large bush, from six to sixteen feet up; takes forty to fifty days to build.

Comment

This is the same bird notorious in European folklore as a noisy scold and thief. On this continent it is a western bird, possibly once closely associated with the Great Plains bison. With the loss of the great wild herds, and subsequent settlement, it suffered a setback. But it has reclaimed its former domain, and expanded.

Its legendary wariness is a response to persecution for its purported depredations on game-bird eggs and for pecking at wounds and warble fly sores on the backs of cattle, a food source it evolved to exploit on bison. Sometimes it deepens these wounds enough to injure or kill the animals, which unaccountably seem not to be troubled by the probing bills deep in their flesh. In its turn, the magpie is prey to the wintering goshawk and Great Horned Owl, at a time when other game is scarce.

REF: A(W)—564; GO—224; NG—304; P(W)—256

American Crow

Corvus brachyrhynchos

In older references, "Common" Crow; Anglo-Saxon *crawe,* "crow" imitative of call; *Corvus* Latin for "a crow"; Greek *brachys* is "short" and *rhynchos,* "beak," because beak is shorter than a raven's; this and the Northwestern Crow, *C. duratus,* are held by some to be the same species.

P. SAWATZKY
1991 ©

Description

Glossy black; told from raven by considerably smaller size, relatively smaller bill, lack of hackle feathers at throat, and square tail (raven's is fan-shaped); best diagnosis is voice, the raven's a variety of croaks, the crow's a basic "*caw.*"

Behavior

Social; out of breeding season may rove and roost in very large flocks; wary, alert, and sharp-eyed; flight on steady wingbeats with little gliding unless circling or coming in for a landing; forages on ground in cultivated fields, roadsides, garbage dumps; scavenges dead animals; voice a loud, harsh "*caw,*" may be very noisy especially around nest when young are begging from old birds, and when a group is "mobbing" an owl or hawk.

Range

Migratory in regions of severe winter weather, nonmigratory in benign conditions; winters along entire coast west of the Cascades, but stays away from dry rain shadow of the Coast Range; very large numbers winter along the Snake River valley; in the Puget Sound area interbreeds with Northwestern Crow.

Food

Totally omnivorous, taking seeds, fruit, insects, carrion, buds and shoots, eggs, nestlings; at feeder, suet, seeds, corn, grain.

Nest

Large bundle of coarse twigs, usually well up in major crotch on trunk or branch, obvious from a distance when tree is leafless; bowl made of shredded bark, grasses, vine stems, lined with moss, grass, fur, feathers; most frequent used-nest-of-choice by Great Horned Owls and some hawks, which don't make their own.

Comment

If the average person were asked to name four birds, one of them would almost certainly be the crow. Very likely that person could also do a fair impression of a crow.

Although that hoarse "*caw*" is the only call we associate with this plentiful bird, it is nevertheless employed with great eloquence. To a listening human its inflection, duration, frequency, pitch, volume, and tone can clearly communicate fear, alarm, suspicion, curiosity, anger, hunger, and "come hither." As to its clever adaptability, clergyman and lecturer Henry Ward Beecher summed up the crow in a trenchant comparison: "If men wore feathers and wings, very few of them would be clever enough to be crows."

REF: A(W)—685; GO—226; NG—306; P(W)—252

Northwestern Crow

Corvus caurinus

Sometimes the "San Juan chicken" in those islands; in Old English the *crawe* was said to *crawan*, in Middle English becoming *crowe* and *crowen*, out of which evolved "to crow," which only roosters do in modern English; *Corvus* is Latin for "a crow"; *caurinus* Latin for "Northwestern"; increasingly considered to be the same species as the American Crow, *C. brachyrhynchos.*

Description

To all appearances a slightly smaller, more lightly built version of the American Crow; best differentiating feature their differing voices.

Behavior

Very social; a beachcomber, pulling apart high-tide windrows of seaweed, winging a few feet into the air to drop small shellfish onto the rocks; hangs about in towns looking for scraps; equivalent of American Crow's "*caw*" is a reedy, untuned "*caaa*"; also dry, clicking rattle more mechanical than vocal.

Range

Nonmigratory; coastal strip, and adjacent mountain slopes from extreme northwestern Oregon all the way to southwestern Alaska coast; range demarcation with American Crow obscured around Puget Sound and midway up Olympic Peninsula.

Food

Omnivorous, habitat providing shellfish, crabs, marine carrion; garbage; grain, especially corn; fruit.

Nest

A bulky mass of twigs under large cup of grass, mud; inner lining of fine grass, bark fibers, hair; in tree or shrub at varying heights, on rocky ledge, occasionally on ground under boulder or stump; often nests in loose associations.

Comment

Crows quickly become rooftop hang-abouts if garbage cans are left unlidded. Another attraction is pet food. Many well-meaning householders fill their pet's back-step food bowl before leaving for work in the morning. The overfed dog or cat, once it has nibbled a bit on the oversupply of food, is indifferent when the crows swoop in to clear out the dish in minutes. Thinking that Spot or Fluffy has wiped the platter clean in their absence, their owners recharge the dish to the brim.

So much rich food artificially supports a huge overpopulation of crows. In nesting season this mob is very nearly as efficient at cleaning out songbirds' nests as it is food bowls.

In natural habitat, nest predation by crows is a manageable impact for small

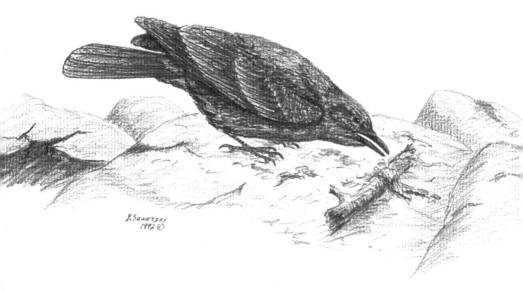

P. SAWATZKY
1992 ©

birds. The crows themselves are widely distributed in their own nesting territories; there are few surplus nonbreeders. Small birds have plenty of cover to conceal nests in. But in suburbia, nesting cover is fragmented into narrow lines and isolated clumps, ideal for surveillance by nest predators. When those predators patrol in large flocks, songbird nesting success can be cut to zero.

For many species of songbirds, suburbs are breeding "black holes" where territory-seeking adults go, but from which no young ever emerge. It would help if we all kept the lid on, and put Fido and Fluffy on a diet.

REF: A(W)—754; GO—226; NG—306; P(W)—252

Common Raven

Corvus corax

Sometimes "Northern" Raven; "Raven" from Anglo-Saxon *hraefn*, "raven"; *Corvus* is Latin for "crow"; *corax* Greek for "a raven," akin to *krazo*, "croak."

Description

Big, black; distinguished from crow by larger size, relatively more massive bill, shaggy throat feathers, wedged tail (crow's is squared off), and voice; equivalent of crow "*caw*" is a grating, guttural, resonant croak.

Behavior

Usually seen in pairs or small family groups, except at food sources such as garbage dumps, where it may congregate by the dozens; more inclined than crow to circle aloft and soar, and frequently indulges in rolling, tumbling, diving aerial games, especially at onset of breeding season in late winter; voice a highly variable repertoire of throaty honks, squawks, and an unexpectedly musical, bell-like "*tok*"; fur traders called it "barking crow"; vulturelike in ability to detect carrion, kills.

Range

Nonmigratory, but may be seasonally nomadic; worldwide in northern hemisphere, from high Arctic to subtropics; absent to unusual in northwestern and north-central Washington, otherwise widely distributed throughout Pacific Northwest, favoring mountains, less-populated hill and desert terrain, forested coasts.

Food

Everything; "kills rabbits and birds" says a British field guide; where wolves occur, forms close relationship in winter, following packs to feed on kills and wolf droppings; feeds at road kills.

Nest

A large mass of sticks, twigs on cliff ledges, in trees (usually large conifers); may build new nest on top of last year's.

Comment

On a number of occasions I have noted that a solitary raven approaching a scrap of food on the ground for the first time goes through an elaborate routine. Surveillance comes first, from varying angles and elevations. The ground approach proceeds by hesitant stages and nervous retreats, ever nearer until the bird is close enough to stretch forward, stab and recoil, and pause. Slightly reassured it repeatedly jabs, bounds back, springs up on flapping wings until the prize is finally snatched and yanked back or flipped overhead.

Students of bird behavior say it is a test that evolved to make sure potential carrion is really dead. Possibly so, but I call it the "trap dance," learned from generations of ancestors that learned to rob the still-ubiquitous, baited leghold trap without falling into the hidden, snapping jaws.

REF: A(W)—685; GO—226; NG—306; P(W)—252

P. SAWATZKY
1991

Titmice

Family Paridae

The short form for "titmouse" causes North Americans to flinch. But "tit" in this case is from the Norse *tittre*, a general term for anything small or little. Perhaps via the Vikings and their well-known practice of dropping in to stay, the word became Middle English *tit*, meaning "small." "Mouse" is a case of linguistic mistaken identity, for it has nothing to do with mice, arising instead from the Anglo-Saxon *mase* or *mose*, a term for small birds. It would be a quibble rendered hopeless by time and long custom to suggest that the plural should really be "titmouses."

Titmice are a widespread family of forty-six species, ten of them in North America, inhabiting a wide variety of habitats from subarctic to tropical. They missed only Australia, New Zealand, and South America.

Although in some cases separated by great chunks of geography, the family resemblance between our chickadees and several species of Eurasian tits is obvious; the Marsh, Sombre, and Willow Tits could pass at first glance as Black-capped Chickadees, the Siberian as a Boreal. The latter in fact shares the Boreal Chickadee's territory in central Alaska and in neighboring Yukon and the Territory of MacKenzie. Their dissimilar voices would likely be the first give-away, although the Marsh Tit's call is described as including a *"chikkadee dee dee"* along with a sneezelike *"pitchoo"* and a nasal *"chay."*

In suburbs, towns, farms, and adjoining parklands and forests, the versatile chickadees often forage in the company of nuthatches, woodpeckers, bushtits, and kinglets. These loose aggregations trickle through the treetops, filling the air with chirps and tweets that sound for all the world like amiable chit-chat. Such mixed "guilds" no doubt confer an advantage for someone; perhaps the food search of one species uncovers sources for another, perhaps with more eyes on the alert, there is better security against predators. Given the chickadees' opportunistic ways, one wouldn't be surprised if they turned out to be the ones that profited most from these integrated outings.

Snake-in-the-Hole

There is an interesting relationship between snakes and Tufted Titmice. Where they can get them, the birds habitually weave discarded snakeskins into their nests. This is a habit shared by the Great Crested Flycatcher, another cavity nester. The Flycatcher occasionally even allows part of the skin to dangle outside the nest entrance.

There is a further link between snakes and the titmouse family. Most titmice, including all chickadees, are cavity nesters. There are certain obvious advantages to a snug hole, safe and sheltered behind sturdy wooden walls. But, as pointed out in the section on woodpeckers, it can turn into a trap when a squirrel or weasel is filling the entrance hole and there's no fire exit. Brooding females, when so threatened, will open their mouths, hiss loudly, and move their heads back and forth in a manner clearly imitative of a snake's threat gestures. If this bluff doesn't scare off the predator, it might at least make it hesitate just long enough for the bird to escape.

High Ingenuity Quotient

All members of the titmouse family share the trusting nature and the bold, inquisitive behavior that make our chickadees such favorites at feeders. No doubt the urge to examine anything new that comes to their attention is an adaptation to a harsh environment where opportunism in the search for food can mean the difference between life and starvation.

Inquisitiveness and ingenuity go hand-in-hand. An experimenter in Britain discovered that tits learned to retrieve a bit of food on the end of a long string tied to a perch. The birds would haul in with their beaks, clamp the loose loop under one foot, and haul in again until the food was reeled in. They could handle up to two feet of line.

In his book *A Complete Guide to Bird Feeding,* John V. Dennis recounts this experiment but notes that in his own efforts to duplicate it, his Carolina Chickadees and Tufted Titmice simply fluttered directly to the food, grabbed the string and hung there with both feet while they scooped the prize.

One wonders if Mr. Dennis made things too easy for his subjects by providing string thick enough to cling to. Perhaps the use of monofilament fish line or thread would foil that overly ingenious business of going directly to the end of the string. It would be a more searching test of our North American titmice, and most heart-warming to their fans if they passed it.

Black-capped Chickadee

Parus atricapillus

"Chickadee" imitates call, although "Chickadee-dee-dee" would be more accurate; *Parus* Latin for "titmouse"; *ater* for "black," *capillus* Latin for "hair of the head."

Description

Very small, active; tiny bill; body plumage soft, fluffy; crown, back of neck, throat, and bib black; cheeks, sides of neck white; back gray-beige; wings, tail

P. SAWHTZKY ©
1990

slate gray with edges of feathers lightly frosted; flanks tinged with buff, belly off-white; sexes identical.

Behavior

Acrobatic, hyperactive, excitable, vocal; undeterred by cold weather; usually first "customers" at new feeder; feed by fluttering hurriedly to feeder, selecting seed, flying off; crack sunflower seeds by clutching them tightly against perch with one foot, hammering them open with beak; in winter travel in family groups; famous "*chicka-dee-dee*" call augmented in late winter with clear, slow "*seeeee-feé-bee*" whistle; also soft twitter.

Range

Nonmigratory, but some may irrupt out of range or to lower altitudes in severe winters; common coast-to-coast, from tree line south; found in woodlands of all kinds, especially those near water; treed homesteads, parks, suburban yardscapes; found in varying levels of abundance throughout Pacific Northwest.

Food

Insectivorous by preference, gleaning winter twigs, bark for eggs, pupae, dormant adult insects, but supplementing this with weed seeds, fruit; in the wild picks scraps from remains of predator kills; at feeder keen on sunflower seeds, nuts, peanut butter, suet, much of which it stashes away.

Nest

Nests and shelters in winter, in tree holes it cleans out of punky knotholes; in winter adults huddle together; can sometimes be tricked into using nest box if it is first filled with wood shavings.

Comment

These beady-eyed charmers have done more than any other bird to convert indifferent householders into dedicated feeders. Their unquenchable, bubbly good nature is often the only evidence of life on bitterly cold winter days. The light tap-tapping from the edge of the shelf is familiar to those with windowsill feeders, indicating that a chickadee is hammering open a sunflower seed. Clean around feeders, they don't congregate on platforms in a squabbling, defecating bunch as House Sparrows and finches do. Compulsively inquisitive and trusting, they are the easiest of birds to tame, learning quickly to take seeds out of hand, then to search clothing, lips, and ears for hidden tidbits.

REF: A(W)—663; GO—228; NG—310; P(W)—258

Mountain Chickadee

Parus gambeli

Parus Latin for "titmouse"; *gambeli* from William Gambel, first ornithologist to spend several years, in the 1840s, in California.

Description

Only chickadee with striped face, dark line through eye, white stripe over it; slightly larger than very similar Black-capped.

Behavior

In all respects a chickadee; tends to move and forage in tree crowns rather than in lower vegetation; voice huskier than Black-capped's, similar in tone to Chestnut-backed's, a slightly hoarse "*tzik-a-zee-zee.*"

Range

Nonmigratory but can be seasonally nomadic; resident in the mountains of western North America from Mexican border to Alaska; absent as a resident from wet coastal forests; mainly a highland breeder, favoring conifer forest up

- P. Sawatzky -
- 94

to tree line; in winter may descend to lowland woods, orchards, and residential areas; there is a dense winter population center in the Cascades near Upper Klamath Lake in west-central Oregon.

Food

Insects, seeds; at feeders, seeds, suet.

Nest

In a cavity; digs its own, but more ready than other chickadees to nest in boxes and vacated woodpecker holes; nest a thick pile of moss, grass, plant fibers, fur.

Comment

Like other chickadees, this one readily joins other species in winter to forage in loose flocks through the woods; at this time it may be found in the company of whatever other species of chickadees may be resident in the area.

Nest holes are essential to the breeding success of species that use them, especially if they cannot dig their own. A vivid illustration of this is recounted in the *Book of North American Birds,* a Reader's Digest publication. Arizona observers recorded an attempt by a pair of Violet-green Swallows to usurp a Mountain Chickadee hole while the owners were out. The pitched battle that broke out upon the chickadees' return lasted for more than an hour. The birds fought in the air, grappled on the ground, pecking and buffeting. Several times a swallow grabbed a chickadee by a wing or foot and yanked it out of the hole. The chickadees eventually won. The defeated swallows could have lost their lifetime chance to raise a brood.

REF: A(W)—733; GO—228; NG—310; P(W)—258

Boreal Chickadee

Parus hudsonicus

"Boreal" means "of the north," "Chickadee" imitates its call; *Parus* is Latin for "titmouse"; *hudsonicus* means "of Hudson Bay."

Description

Similar in size, plumage pattern to Black-capped; coloration resembles the Chestnut-backed, but back is less ruddy and cap is dark brown; chin and throat black; flanks a ruddy brown wash; overall color tends to beige rather than gray.

Behavior

Shares acrobatic, fluttery energy of all chickadees, but less trusting, more subdued; often forages with other chickadees, nuthatches, kinglets, and smaller

-P.SAWATZKI-
-94 ©

woodpeckers; call definitely a chickadee's but thinner, wheezy "*sik-a-day-day*," drawled out, like slow Black-capped with laryngitis.

Range

Nonmigratory, but occasional winter nomad south of usual range through boreal forest and southern tundra; more adapted to coniferous (spruce–balsam) forest than other chickadees; present in northeastern Washington, northernmost Idaho.

Food

Omnivorous; winter gleaner of small branches, twigs, conifer needles for dormant insects, larvae, eggs, and scraps from predator kills; comes less readily to feeders than Black-capped or Chestnut-backed; once there, shares its cousins' delight with sunflower seeds, suet, peanut butter.

Nest

Hole cleared out in decayed stub of conifer or birch, often quite low, almost never higher than ten feet; prefers swampier, more enclosed habitat than Black-capped.

Comment

Of the two species of chickadees whose range straddles the top of the continent, the Boreal ranges farthest north. Where it occurs south of its major range, in disjunct pockets of woodland, the woodlands invariably turn out to be boreal relicts.

Some guides suggest the Boreal is less visible than the other chickadees due to its preference for foraging in the interiors of dense conifers, coming less readily to the tips of branches. This habit, and its more remote range, make the Boreal seem scarcer than it really is.

REF: A(W)—744; GO—228; NG—312; P(W)—258

Chestnut-backed Chickadee

Parus rufescens

Parus Latin for "titmouse"; *rufescens* Latin for "reddish."

Description

Smaller than other chickadees; distinguished from them by rich chestnut sides and back; black on crown rather faded out, brownish, otherwise the head and throat same as Black-capped.

Behavior

Typical chickadee; in natural surroundings tends to forage higher in trees than Black-capped; least musical of chickadees; voice hoarse, shrill; "*tzeek-a-zee-zee*" call delivered with agitated rapidity; most frequent utterance a nervous "*tzee-deee.*"

Range

In a strip along the west coast of the Pacific Northwest west of the Cascade–Sierra Mountain divide, and in Douglas fir forests east of the Cascades crest; in areas where its range overlaps with that of the Mountain Chickadee, it occupies the lower elevations.

Food

Insects, seeds, occasional fruit; at feeders, sunflower seeds, suet.

Nest

In stub or dead tree, usually low, rarely more than ten feet high; nest a cup of plant fibers, hair, fur, feathers on a thick base of moss.

-P. SAWATZKY -
1992 ©

Comment

   In certain favored areas of northern Washington, it is possible to have four species of chickadees at the same feeder.

REF: A(W)—744; GO—228; NG—312; P(W)—258

Plain Titmouse

Parus inornatus

"Titmouse" from Norse *tittre*, "small," and Anglo-Saxon *mose*, "small bird"; *Parus* is Latin for "a titmouse"; *inornatus* is Latin for "unadorned" or "plain."

Description

Chickadee-sized; except for pert crest, virtually fieldmark-free; upper body and wings uniform brownish gray, underparts dingy white; bill noticeably larger than in chickadee.

Behavior

Not social, feeding singly or in mated pairs; acrobatic, lively; voice a raspy, agitated "*sika-dee-dee-dee*" similar to chickadee song, and a repeated "*weety weety weety*"; other calls syllabized as "*seedly-dee,*" "*tee-wit tee-wit,*" et cetera.

Range

Nonmigratory; in western and southwestern United States; favors drier, open woodland, particularly where oaks grow; extreme southern Idaho and Oregon represent northernmost boundary of range; the Sacramento Valley is the center of abundance.

Food

Acorns, seeds, insects, spiders, fruit; comes readily to feeders for suet and sunflower seeds.

Nest

In cavities; may partially excavate own tree hole in punky wood; may use birdhouses; nest a cup of moss, grass, weed stems, lined with fine fibers, fur, feathers.

Comment

The titmouse and chickadee are relatives; a family resemblance is obvious to anyone who has fed both. The two divide their territories partly on winter food choice. In summer both feed on a varied fare of insects, spiders, and other invertebrate prey. In winter the chickadees keep to their insect diet as much as possible, scouring twigs and bark for eggs, pupae, and dormants. They also add weed seeds to their menu.

But the titmouse turns to tree mast, principally acorns, in winter. These are shed by the tree each autumn, which means that in areas of significant snowfall they'd be buried out of reach of the titmouse. Nut trees can also be capricious producers, in some years failing completely to bear a crop. Animals dependent on them, as the titmouse is, would be severely stressed during such years. But the chickadee's insect and seed diet is a hedge against such privation. Some species of insects might languish in some years, some weed seeds fail. But, as any gardener can swear to, there has never been a total "crop failure" of either weeds or insects.

REF: A(W)—627; GO—230; NG—308; P(W)—260

Bushtits

Family Aegithalidae

The Aegithalidae are not a plenteous family; in the two genera found worldwide—the Long-tailed Tits and Bushtits—there are only seven species. Just one of these occurs in the Western Hemisphere, undoubtedly explaining why the first part of its former name, "common," was recently acknowledged to be redundant in North America, and dropped. You'll find "Common Bushtit" in all but the more recent guides. These may also list the Bushtit as a member of the Paridae family, the one that includes the chickadees and the verdin. There is still debate over where it truly belongs.

In the meantime, we can be happy that the Pacific Northwest is a place where this lone New World Bushtit can be found, in some locales in good numbers. Like a lot of birds, possibly in response to man-altered habitat, it is pushing its population boundaries northward and eastward.

Bushtits are almost as tiny as kinglets. Their voices, in keeping with their size, are thin, wispy, and so high as to strain the upper limits of (in my case) the middle-aged ear. Falling ventriloquistically from trees high above, the soft peeps deny you a sonic fix however much you might crane upward and swivel and tilt your head. When you mingle this bit of a bird with kinglets or chickadees, the challenge to the middle-aged ear and eye, to say nothing of the middle-aged neck, is considerable. The field guides try to help by pointing out that while kinglets have minimal fieldmarks, Bushtits have none at all worthy of the designation. The exception is a southwest race, the "Black-eared Bushtit," that sports dark smudges of eye shadow. If you find yourself looking at a tiny bird that appears to be fieldmark-free and has no crest, it's a Bushtit.

In areas where Bushtits are relative newcomers, museums and nature columnists report that one of their most frequent queries in winter is about "a small, plain bird with a long tail eating suet at my feeder."

As if to compensate for being a diminutive gray-brown puff of anonymous feathers, the Bushtit constructs one of the most impressive nests you are likely to encounter. It is a well-woven pouch of fine materials hung from a thin branch. It may take the pair from two weeks to more than a month and a half to build. Although there is no serious effort to conceal the nest, if it is disturbed at any time during construction, egg-laying, or incubation, the pair will desert, break up, and try again with new mates. After the young have fledged and left the nest, the old pair may still use it as a winter roost.

Nest-building skill runs in the family. The nest of the Cape Penduline Tit of Africa has a dummy entrance in the side that leads to a dummy nest chamber.

The real entrance is a woven tube above the decoy hole that the bird closes in its passage to and from the real nest chamber below the false floor of the fake chamber. Some African tribespeople collect Penduline nests and use them for purses and carrying pouches.

Bushtit

Psaltriparus minimus

Formerly "common bushtit"; *Psaltriparus* from Greek *psaltria*, "a harpist," and Latin *parus*, "a titmouse"; *minimus* is Latin for "least."

Description

Small; tiny bill, long tail; gray-brown overall, with no obvious field marks; adult female has straw-colored iris, male's is dark.

P. SAWATZKY
1992 ©

Behavior

Ceaselessly acrobatic, flitting, hanging, pecking on twigs, branches, and leaves from low shrubs on up to tall trees; except during breeding season travels in busy, dispersed groups, constantly calling; frequent members of mixed foraging "guilds" with chickadees, kinglets; voice a thin, high "*tseep*" or lisping, nervous twitter.

Range

The mountainous West and Southwest of North America, down into Central America; favors open woodland, especially oak and pinyon–juniper habitat; in varying densities through most of the Pacific Northwest, especially in the Sacramento Valley and the Chehalis River valley in Washington; is trending northward into Canada.

Food

Insect eggs, larvae, pupae, and adults; spiders; some fruit; found to be keen on suet, peanut butter, or mixtures of two at feeders.

Nest

Woven pouch hung from small twigs; seven to ten inches deep, three to four inches wide at bottom; entrance through side at top; fine fibers, plant down, algae, cocoon silk, felted and bonded with spider webbing; thickly lined with small feathers; wall as much as ½ inch thick at bottom.

Comment

Vancouver Island naturalist Bill Merilees in his book *Attracting Backyard Wildlife* relates his observation of Bushtits flying repeatedly through the spray from a lawn mister until their feathers got so soaked they had to dry off before they could fly again.

Bushtits were until recently not regarded as likely feeder birds, but have now established themselves in some areas as regular visitants. Some bird feeders report special success with a blend of dripping fat, peanut butter, and rolled oats pushed into holes drilled in a small tree trunk.

REF: A(W)—662; GO—232; NG—312; P(W)—260

Nuthatches

Family Sittidae

In one of the many introductions to birding books that he has written over the years, Roger Tory Peterson attributed the base level of interest in birds to " ... the White-breasted Nuthatch type of birdwatcher who feeds birds on the shelf outside the kitchen window and goes no further afield."

I took this as a tribute to the bird, and to the fact that it is one of the most consistent of visitors to winter feeding stations, often the first one to acknowledge a newly placed offering. For many of us, the faithful nuthatch is second in our affections only to the irrepressibly cheerful chickadee.

Nuthatch "faithfulness" in mated pairs extends through their mutually held territory to each other, and is a year-round bond. The sentiments of their human hosts notwithstanding, this is simply a matter of their behaving in their own reproductive interests. Constancy may be a response to their need for ready-made tree holes to nest in.

Safe, secure holes in trees, particularly if you are in the second-hand market, are a scarce item. The absence of a suitable hole means that they cannot breed. It is therefore crucial for those who already have a territory, nest site included, to hang onto it. And they can maintain better security if they stay on their turf and have a mate to help run off claim jumpers.

"No Trespassing"

Nuthatches are not noticeably quarrelsome at feeders. But confronting an aroused one is something one does not do lightly, particularly in the "no trespassing" zone around their nests. The body language is eloquent. Wings and tail are raised and flared, exposing otherwise concealed patterns of white that are a warning flash that cannot escape notice. The stiletto bill and the beady eyes are directed at the enemy with no-nonsense intensity. The tensed body is cocked toward the adversary and rotated jerkily back and forth, like a mechanical toy. The threat is unmistakable.

I once watched two embattled birds confront both Gray and Red Squirrels over possession of an old flicker hole in a poplar in my yard. It was the doughty birds that raised their brood that year, in that tree.

The European version of the Red-breasted Nuthatch enhances the defenses of its nest hole by plastering the entrance with mud until it is barely able to squeeze in. This serves to keep out larger preemptors, especially starlings. Our Red-breasted smears spruce, pine, or fir gum around the entrance hole. This may well be a behavioral relict from a Eurasian ancestor, its original purpose diffused because our species has continued to evolve since arriving here in the absence of starlings, an omission latterly restored, unfortunately. The pungent, sticky gum might obscure the scent of the nest, its gooeyness repel trespassers. One reference noted that a nuthatch itself was found dead in the entrance to its nest, stuck in the resin.

A further variant on this behavior is to be found in the White-breasted, which has been seen rubbing the bark near its nest hole with blister beetles or ants which secrete irritant chemicals when so abused. It is a commonly enough observed behaviorial peculiarity to have been named "bill sweeping." The strong-smelling and/or repellent vapors thus deposited could be a way of deterring nest-robbers like squirrels, or of masquerading telltale scent.

In common with many overwintering birds, all three of our nuthatch species store surplus food. A feeder with a generous supply of sunflower seeds can trigger a marathon of activity, as happened with a solitary male Red-breasted that arrived at my city windowsill early one October. He made a collecting flight from the shelf to nearby oaks once every forty-five seconds on average for extended periods. Before vanishing abruptly, he had hundreds and hundreds of seeds poked into the rough bark of the oaks. Whether his disappearance was a decision to resume his journey south, or the intervention of a neighbor's cat, one can only guess.

There are twenty-one species of nuthatches throughout the world. They are unique in their ability to climb down trees (or rocks or walls) headfirst as easily as they can climb up. Scanning surfaces for food from the top down rather than from the bottom up must have been an adaptive breakthrough in its time. It gave some innovative proto-nuthatch a slight edge over its more conventional relatives. Descendants fortunate enough to inherit the knack prospered by it and eventually evolved into a group of separate species.

Refinements

Nuthatches share with a lot of other scanners and probers a white chin and/or breast. Reflections off this bright surface into shadowy cracks, holes, and undersides would throw useful light onto food items concealed in them.

If you look closely at a nuthatch fixed in place you will see that it has one leg out behind, on the "up" side, with the oversized hind claw firmly hooked onto the surface. The other foot is placed well forward, i.e., down, for steadying support.

There are other refinements that the nuthatch brings to its trade. One of them has to be a highly developed skill at selecting cracks and notches that will hold a nut or seed in place solidly enough for the dextrous bill to hack apart. The Brown-headed Nuthatch of the southeast even uses bits of wood as tools to pry up loose bark in its search for hidden insects. If it is available, nuthatches will also attempt to cover hidden seeds with bits of bark or shreds of lichen.

Red-breasted Nuthatch
Sitta canadensis

"Nuthatch" from "nuthack," original name brought to Americas by English colonists; *Sitta* from Greek *sitte*, "nut-hatch"; *canadensis*, Latinized "of Canada," reflecting major range of bird.

Description

Shares slate-blue back, wings, tail of larger White-breasted; distinguished from it by smaller size, narrow black line through the eye, and white line above eye, and also by rust to brick-red breast, belly, flanks, thighs, and tail coverts; color of ruddy underparts varies with individuals; sexes similar, but female crown dark gray, ruddy parts less pronounced.

Behavior

Very similar to White-breasted, foraging head-down on tree bark; family groups forage together in late summer and fall, otherwise solitary; a busy, businesslike but dithery feeder bird; diligent hoarder of larger seeds and suet; voice similar to White-breasted but weaker, higher-pitched, a thin, nasal "*yank-yank*"; also makes a clear, soft note, "*hit*," very high, repeated several times.

Range

Conditionally migratory; breeds across continent in boreal forest right to tree line; much more a denizen of coniferous forests than White-breasted; in Pacific Northwest nests in montane coniferous forests, occurring in higher abundance in mature forests with closed canopies and lots of snags; very high population center in northeastern Washington in Spokane area, a lesser center in Cascades southeast of Eugene; in "invasion" years may appear anywhere in the region, including atypical marshlands and desert lowlands.

Food

In summer, insects, spiders; in winter, insect dormants, eggs, seeds of conifers; tends to search branches, cones, and twigs rather than trunks as White-breasted does; may forage with other species; in the wild, picks tidbits from predator kills; at feeder, a lover of sunflower seeds and suet.

Nest

Either ready-made cavity in tree or one excavated in punky wood, hence height highly variable; occasionally uses nest boxes; entrance smeared with spruce or balsam fir gum; female reported to fly directly into hole, presumably to avoid contacting resin.

Comment

The little Red-breasted closely resembles the European Nuthatch, *Sitta europaea*, with which it shares the habit of plastering the rim of its nest hole. Observers note that by the end of the nesting season, parent Red-breasteds acquire a very tatty appearance from the resin stuck on their feathers.

REF: A(W)—707; GO—234; NG—314; P(W)—262

White-breasted Nuthatch

Sitta carolinensis

Seventeenth-century British colonists brought "nuthack" with them, descriptive of familiar European bird's habit of wedging nuts into cracks, hacking husks off with bill; with dialectic drift it became "nuthatch"; vernacularly "ass-

P. SAWATZKY ©
1990

up"; *Sitta* from Greek *sitte*, "nuthatch"; *carolinensis*, "of Carolina," where first described.

Description

Sparrow-sized; large head and short neck, tail, and legs impart compact, torpedo shape; back slate-blue; crown, back of neck black; wings mainly slate-blue with indistinct lines and flecks of black and white; stubby tail slate, outer margins pattern of black, white especially prominent when tail flared; sides of face to above eye, neck, breast off-white; thighs and under-tail brick-red; prominent dark eye set in white; bill slender, sharp, slightly upturned; sexes similar, except female's head gray.

Behavior

Perches, feeds, and forages head-down on vertical surfaces; stance squat; scans world with neck craned back; cracks nuts, large seeds by wedging them into crevices, whacking at them to chip off husks; winter call a flat, nasal note repeated urgently several times, best imitated by a falsetto "*yaank*" whilst holding nose.

Range

Migratory from northern parts of range; nests continentwide in mature deciduous and mixed woodlands, as far north, but not into, boreal forest; in Pacific Northwest also found in purely coniferous woodlands; drawn to cities, towns, parks, and homesteads with enough big trees to qualify as "woodlands."

Food

Searches tree trunks for insects, spiders, in all stages; nuts, some berries, larger seeds; not picky at feeders, taking seeds, especially sunflowers, suet, peanuts, baked goods, some kinds of table scraps; diligent hoarder, jamming seeds into cracks in bark; readily tries anything, often preceding even chickadees to new feeders.

Nest

In tree cavities, usually those ready-made by decay or woodpeckers, but may excavate its own shallow cavity in well-rotted wood; occasionally accepts nest boxes or uses crannies in buildings; may line entire cavity thickly with coarse grass, twigs, leaves, chips.

Comment

Nuthatches' ability to work head-down is unique; even the tree-adapted woodpeckers hitch awkwardly backward when descending. Their trim shape, air of urgent busyness around feeders, bold plumage pattern, and upside-down orientation make them unmistakable. Confusion is only likely between it and the smaller Red-breasted, where they co-exist.

REF: A(W)—708; GO—234; NG—314; P(W)—262

Pygmy Nuthatch

Sitta pygmaea

Sitta from Greek "nuthatch"; *pygmaea* from Latin *pygmaeus*, "a pygmy," this being the smallest North American nuthatch.

Description

Squat, compact, very short-tailed; head and hindneck gray-brown, including area around eye; back and tail slate-blue, wings slate with frosting of light blue-gray; sides of face and throat white, underparts cream-buff; whitish mark as if brushed lightly on back of neck.

Behavior

Social outside of breeding season, sometimes in large groups; perches and forages head-down on tree trunks; busy, energetic, vocal, often chattering continuously; unlike other nuthatches, voice is not nasal; call a rapid, piping "*pit-pit-pit*" and a high, extended "*te-dee te-dee*" resembling, as noted by Howard Ennor in *Birds of the Tri-Cities*, some notes of the American Goldfinch.

Range

Nonmigratory, but occasionally moves into lowlands adjacent to mountain habitat; scattered through pine forest areas of western and southwestern United States and central Mexico; very closely associated in Pacific Northwest with Ponderosa Pine, Douglas fir, and Lodgepole Pine biome; high concentration in northeastern Washington centered on the foothills around Spokane.

- P. SAWATZKY -
1992 ©

Food

Insects at all stages, occasionally hawking them like a flycatcher; seeds, mainly of pine; at feeder, takes seeds, suet.

Nest

In cavity, usually self-made, generally twenty feet or more up a tree, snag, or post; willing to use second-hand hole, including nest boxes; interior well padded with bark shreds, plant fibers, moss, hair, wool, leaves, and feathers.

Comment

This busy little stub-tail has the peculiar habit of cramming any cracks or holes around its nest with hair or fur, finding a ready source of these in owl castings.

Where the pines are—Ponderosa, Jeffrey—is where this bird is. *Birds of the Okanagan Valley*, Cannings et al, notes that winter suet feeders set up near stands of Ponderosa Pine often have Pygmy Nuthatches "crawling over them like hungry mice."

REF: A(W)—709; GO—234; NG—314; P(W)—262

Creepers

Family Certhiidae

Until the 1970s our Brown Creeper was *Certhia familiaris*, considered to be a member of the same circumpolar species the English call the Treecreeper. *C. familiaris* still denotes the Eurasian bird, and older American field guides still give this name. However, ours has been accorded full species status and is now *Certhia americana*.

Bark Specialist

Many birds, especially winterers such as nuthatches and woodpeckers, are foragers in and under bark, but the Brown Creeper is the most bark-dependent specialist. It not only searches on it for food, but utilizes it for winter roosting and for nesting. Other cavity nesters may build under a buckled slab of bark if nothing else is available, but the creeper will rarely use anything else.

Some writers note that if you nail a slab of bark to a tree by the ends, being careful to hump it outward in the middle to leave a decent space of several inches between it and the trunk, the Brown Creeper might use the contrived cranny as a winter roost, or even a nest. I wonder if a strip of carpet, or some other suitable discard, would be an acceptable substitute for the bark, providing it blended in fairly unobtrusively with the surface of the "host" tree.

As befits a bird that spends its working day hitching itself ever upward, the creeper's feet are long-clawed and strong. It also shares with woodpeckers a tail equipped with stiff, pointed hackles that serve as a brace while the feet are clamped into the bark. They very likely also snaggle into the surface, preventing backslide when the bird hitches upward, which it does by moving both feet simultaneously in a quick hop. Woodpeckers and nuthatches, in contrast, move their feet in sequence, in a very quick motion that seems like a hop, but is in fact a very quick step.

Closet Machismo

Surprising for one so timid and retiring, the male turns into an exhibitionist like the rest of us during courting time. He woos his prospective mate with a burst of song, described in Noble Proctor's *Song Birds* as "a wonderful, descending musical jumble of notes," a generous review of a talent most other music critics classify as meager. Then this drab little elf turns athletic with a fast, spiral flight upward around the tree trunk he has selected for his display. The female may join in this flight, allowing herself to be pursued in the same dizzy spiral.

If, ultimately, she is sufficiently impressed, the two of them go to work building a nest behind his pre-selected slab of loose bark. He helps fetch the raw materials, she does the weaving; the project can take as little as six days, or as long as a month. Nests are situated between five to fifteen feet up. Observers report that the nest tending is done with typical creeper reserve. Adults approach it the same way they do their foraging, landing below it, spiraling upward in those rapid, jerky little hitches until, with one quick hop, they just vanish behind their shield of bark.

Brown Creeper

Certhia americana

"Creeper" from way it moves close against the bark of trees as it forages; *Certhia* from Latin *certhius*, "a creeper"; *americana*, latinized "of America"; in older guides species name is *familiaris*, Latin for "homelike," hence friendly.

Description

Slim, very small, with slender, down-curved bill; longish tail with stiff, pointed feathers flared slightly against the bark; upper plumage a camouflage pattern of buff spots, streaks and lines on brown base; belly, breast, and chin white.

P.Sawatzky ©
1990

Behavior

Shy and retiring; quietly searches bark of larger trees by starting near the base, hitching upward in short, quick jumps in a spiral around trunk until it is well up, then flying quickly down to base of another tree; favors mature trees, especially along woodland edges; call a very high, faint "*tsee*"; song described in the Peterson Guide as a thin, sibilant "*see-ti-wee-tu-wee*" or, if you like, "*trees, trees, trees, see the trees.*"

Range

Nonmigratory in mild coastal woodland, partially to fully migratory inland, depending on severity of winter; bird of mature river valley, coastal and lakeside woodlands, both deciduous and coniferous, and montane dry-belt pine forests; at home in well-treed urban parks, golf courses; nowhere abundant, it is widely distributed in winter throughout the Pacific Northwest.

Food

Scans rough-barked trees for spiders, insect eggs, pupae, adults, using its sharp, decurved bill as a fine probe; rare visitor to feeders, where it takes suet; may be coaxed to specific trees if bark is smeared lightly with suet or suet/ peanut butter mix.

Nest

Almost invariably—and unique in—nesting behind or under loosened slabs of bark on recently dead trees; nest may be compressed into shape of a sharply upturned crescent by confines of space; base of twigs, grass stems, bark shreds often arranged to block off most access to the space beneath the bark, lining of fine bark threads, grass, root fibers, spider silk, mosses, occasional feathers.

Comment

This little bird is professionally inconspicuous, preferring the other sides of big trees when you are trying to get a look at it. The thin, ventriloquistic call, when it chooses to give it, doesn't help much. No surprise, therefore, that it is often listed as "rare" or "infrequent," a status conferred by people who possibly just didn't look long and hard enough.

Some bird feeders have noticed that creepers seem to pay more attention to trees in the vicinity of feeders. The reason could be that they are gleaning fragments of seeds and fat left on the bark where other birds wiped their bills after feeding.

REF: A(W)—709; GO—234; NG—314; P(W)—262

Kinglets

Family Muscicapidae, Subfamily Sylviinae

The name of this family comes from Latin *musca*, meaning "a fly," and *capere*, "to take," hence "flycatcher." The subfamily name is from Latin *silva*, for "a woods," hence *sylviinae*, "of the woods."

It would take approximately 100 Ruby-crowned Kinglets to make a pound. I have never had the unhappy task of weighing a dead one, but several references assure me that they run from just under 4 to 4.5 grams, the greater figure just equaling 0.16 ounce. The Golden-crowned is even tinier, the smallest songbird in North America. The smallest-size leg band will stay on a Ruby-crowned, but is too big for the Golden-crowned. At an average length of 3½ inches (nine centimeters), the Golden-crowned is slightly smaller than the Anna's Hummingbird.

For most Northwesterners, even those who live in coniferous woodland habitat, kinglets are not very obvious birds. In summer they favor a heavy cover of evergreens, often back among the muskeg and mosquitoes where wayfaring humans don't occur. And even when the two do meet, the birds are so small, so busy and unobtrusive, and often so well up in mature spruce that they aren't noticed. Experienced birders say that the nests are so small and so well camouflaged up near the roof of the evergreen canopy that they defy detection.

As befits a relative of the thrush family, the Ruby-crowned is noted for its clear, vibrant song, astonishing hearers that so small a creature can belt out so much volume. But the Golden-crowned, unlike its virtuoso cousin, has a weak, small voice that is easily lost to human ears in its dense evergreen habitat.

Gathered in larger flocks, and with fewer of the bigger, noisier, and more colorful birds around to distract the eye, they are more noticeable in winter. Of the two, the Golden-crowned is more plentifully represented in the Pacific Northwest in winter.

In winter, kinglets of both species can be seen foraging in mixed "guilds" of bark gleaners: chickadees, titmice, creepers, and nuthatches. John Dennis, in his *A Complete Guide to Bird Feeding*, says they may occasionally follow these other birds to feeders, but that they rarely become regulars. When a kinglet does show up, he notes, it outperforms even the chickadee in its acrobatic ability to poke into awkward places. It is at a feeder that one can best appreciate the miniature proportions of this animated bird. Seen next to a kinglet, a chickadee looks positively hulking.

Although both species of kinglets winter in the Pacific Northwest, the Golden-crowned is the more plentiful. Neither of these very similar birds is noted for its affinity for feeders. Therefore, a species account of the Golden-crowned suffices.

Golden-crowned Kinglet

Regulus satrapa

Old World warbler, gnatcatcher, and kinglet subfamily; in larger family that also includes thrushes; "Golden-crowned" from small dash of yellow on crown, "Kinglet" meaning "little king"; *Regulus* Latin for "little king"; Greek *satrapa* meaning "a ruler," i.e., one who wears a golden crown, an example of taxonomists' picking a solitary physical mark for double emphasis.

Description

Tiny, round-bodied; olive-green, grayish; short-tailed; delicate, fine-pointed bill; crown stripe, bright orange in center bordered by yellow edged in black, visible only at close range or when raised in display; dusky line through eye, off-white line over eye; legs proportionately thinner than any other small wintering bird; sexes differ only in that female has no orange in a yellow crown.

Behavior

Restlessly flits about, usually near tips of branches, often well up in conifers; so active, field marks other than diminutive size are difficult to see; constantly flicks wings; often forages by hovering near twig tips; gleaner of smallest twigs and conifer needles; may forage in mixed parties of titmice, creepers, chickadees, nuthatches; call a hurried, thin, high-pitched "*tsee-tsee-tsee*"; song a very high, weak, rapid trill, preceded by an almost inaudible, ascending series of about four "*tsee*" notes.

Range

Migratory; breeds in boreal and montane forests, hence resident in much of Pacific Northwest; winters irregularly everywhere throughout region where suitable tree cover occurs.

Food

Insects, eggs, larvae, pupae gleaned from twigs, needles; sap from sapsucker tap-holes; infrequent feeder visitor, then taking only suet and perhaps peanut butter.

Nest

A neat little suspended pouch cunningly hidden beneath foliage at tip of evergreen bough, often very high; well camouflaged with moss, lichen; lined with feathers set so tips will fold down over eggs when parent is away.

Comment

On the occasions when people can observe wintering kinglets, they cannot help but be amazed that such small creatures can generate and hold enough warmth to survive. No doubt the physics of size and wind chill *do* foredoom many of these undersize bundles of energy to a quick, shivering end. But heavy losses are soon replaced; each female that survives to mate and nest can brood up to ten eggs the following summer, so many that they crowd two-deep in her tiny nest.

REF: A(W)—735; GO—252; NG—322; P(W)—268

Thrushes

Family Muscicapidae, Subfamily Turdinae

The Muscicapidae family includes Old World warblers, kinglets, gnatcatchers, Old World flycatchers, and the thrushes and their allies. As well as the thrushes proper, the subfamily Turdinae includes bluebirds, solitaires, and the familiar robin. In the genus *Turdus,* the true thrushes, there are more than sixty species and they are found on every continent except Australia. No other single genus of songbird is so widespread. Wherever they occur, there is at least one species that is a common yard and garden bird.

The niceties of bird nomenclature were not uppermost in the minds of English immigrants piling off the boats to tame seventeenth-century America. Thus, any bird with a reddish breast, or even a suggestion of ruddiness about it, was dubbed a "robin" after the familiar red-breasted bird of British fields and gardens. At one time the Eastern Bluebird was a "robin," the towhee was a "ground robin," the oriole was a "golden robin," and the Cedar Waxwing a "Canadian robin."

The American Robin vies with the Red-winged Blackbird as the most common bird in North America, and with the House Sparrow as the most familiar. Unlike the sparrow, it is not a human-dependent street bird. It is just as much at home in the rain forests of the Pacific Northwest coast or the upper reaches of the boreal-tundra transition zone as it is dodging lawn sprinklers in suburbia. But people so associate it with the latter scene that their first reaction on encountering it in the wilderness is a surprised: "What is our robin doing away out here?"

"Cheer-up!"

The thrushes are noted for their great voices, and although the American Robin is not rated as the greatest songster of them all, its dawn carol is one of the best-known and loved of nature's sounds. It is not a continuous cascade of warbling, like that of the finches, but a series of clear, whistled phrases, separated by the briefest pauses. To some the clipped phrases sound like football signals and they have nicknamed the robin the "quarterback bird."

The main recital is the one that heralds the dawn, often well before the sun has even tinted the horizon. At the height of the concert season, in late March or early April when the males are consolidating territories in anticipation of the females' return, the singing can go on for most of the day. But when the intensity diminishes, dawn and dusk are the principal singing periods.

Ernest Thompson Seton published his observations on a variation in birdsong that can be readily observed in robins because their singing is so loud, and they sing from regular vantage points. At times a bird will abruptly begin singing in a muted, distant-sounding voice. Seton noted that a singing male, if made uneasy but not frightened off by something close at hand, would keep on singing, but with his bill shut. He said he had noted this habit in several other species.

Sex and Violence

Lust and fence-line disputes have been sources of bloodshed and legal fees among humans for as long as our history can recall. Put them together, and you have the potential for rivalry of awesome, or farcical, proportions.

Male robins compete with such frenzy in the territorial/mating game that at times they behave as if completely addled. In addition to wild low-level pursuits on the wing, accompanied by rapid "*git! git! git!*" shrieked at trespassers, male robins have worked themselves into frazzles attacking their own images in windows, windshields, hubcaps, and rear-view mirrors. The cue to aggression being the ruddy breast of a male rival, they have tackled similar-colored socks, handkerchiefs, and other items on clotheslines, and ornaments and discarded toys on the lawn.

Domesticity

Although the female robin selects the site, builds the nest, and does all the brooding, the male nevertheless proves to be a dutiful helpmate, feeding the nestlings and assuming full babysitting chores when his mate builds a new nest and starts brooding a second clutch. The harassed male can then be seen scouring lawns for food with his brood dogging his heels and begging loudly when he pulls up an earthworm. These fledglings reveal their species' thrush ancestry; their breasts are dappled with brown spots on a washed-out background.

At this time there are a couple of things that can be done to give robins a hand. Keeping the family cat shut in while the baby robins get over the "stupid" stage of life may help at least one or two make it to early adolescence. It may also be a real help to nest-building, if the weather is dry, to leave a pie plate of good stiff mud on or near the birdbath, or to turn on the lawn sprinkler where it will create a muddy puddle.

Foraging robin pairs recently demonstrated that new knowledge about animal behavior doesn't have to come from costly expeditions to remote sites. By watching four pairs of robins working the lawns of a Kansas college campus, an observer discovered that they subdivided their territories roughly in half along an east–west axis when searching for food. The female always searched one half, the male the other. Such an arrangement enhances the pair's foraging efficiency by minimizing competition between them and avoiding overlapping searches.

In common with other thrushes, robins are omnivorous to a certain degree in that they freely switch from preying on invertebrates, principally earthworms, to gathering fruit and berries. They do not seem to be very interested in seeds. Their liking for fruit has frequently brought them to grief with farmers and orchardists trying to grow soft fruits and berries.

The Varied Thrush, a cousin of the robin, normally confines itself to the western rim of the continent. But every now and then flocks of them rove eastward in the fall. They end up, to the delight of birders, in the Midwest, the Atlantic States, and rarely even on Sable Island a couple of hundred miles out in the Atlantic off the southern coast of Nova Scotia.

American Robin

Turdus migratorius

"Robin" diminutive of "Robert" and of French origin; in England "redbreast" was original name, then "robin redbreast," then "redbreast" was dropped; *Turdus* is Latin for "a thrush"; *migrator* is Latin for "wanderer."

Description

Rather leggy, long-tailed bird; dark gray tail, back, wings, darker head; brickred breast and belly; chin light with dark, vertical streaks; broken white eyering; lower belly and undertail coverts white; beak yellow; female same as male but paler.

P. SAWATZKY
1991 ©

Behavior

Most commonly seen hunting worms on lawns, alternately tipping forward to scan the grass intently or standing erect when alert for danger; runs and hops; most wintering robins form large flocks and take to heavy bush, where they seem to be much more elusive than their summer equivalents; song famous as harbinger of spring, a loud, clear, distinctly separated series of "*cheery, cheery, cheer up, cheerily*" phrases; call of alarm a sudden "*cheep!*" or rapidly repeated "*git-git-git!*".

Range

Partially migratory in Pacific Northwest; breeds continentwide, and north to beyond the tree line; winters throughout the Pacific Northwest.

Food

Mixture of insects, earthworms, fruit; may be encouraged to feeders with raisins, berries, fresh or dried fruit, shredded coconut; early spring migrants may be driven to feeders if late snowstorm blankets natural food sources.

Nest

Substantial base of twigs, straws, stems mortared from inside with heavy layer of mud formed into deep, round cup; inner lining of fine grasses; in fork of tree or solid branch, in tangle of vines, on ledge or beam about buildings; from six to thirty-plus feet above ground.

Comment

I read that in times of drought if nest-building female robins can't find a source of mud, they will pick up beakfuls of dirt and take them to water to mix their own. Failing even this, some will build entirely without benefit of mud.

Basically a bird of open forests and edges, it very likely benefitted when logging and settlement changed forested areas to fields, pastures, and orchards, and when agriculture and settlement brought trees to the open plains. Whatever its historic niche, today's robin seems to have a foot firmly in two worlds, the backyard and the backwoods. In different habitats, the same bird acts like two different species.

REF: A(W)—587; GO—244; NG—330; P(W)—274

Varied Thrush

Ixoreus naevius

Also sometimes "winter robin," "Oregon robin"; "Varied" suggests more multicolored or patterned plumage than that of most thrushes; *Ixoreus* from

Greek *ixos*, "mistletoe," and *oreos*, "mountain," from a European mountain thrush associated with mistletoe berries; *naevius* is Latin for "spotted" or "varied."

Description

Shape and size very close to robin; male upper parts slate-blue, underparts orange with black band across breast; wings gray-blue with two orange bars, orange frosting on edge of primaries; wide black patch on side of face, orange eyebrow strip; female duller-colored, with khaki brown in place of male's blue.

Behavior

Social outside breeding season and in migration; sometimes forages on lawns, hopping like a robin, otherwise feeds on ground, scratching energetically among

-P. SAWATZKY -
1992 ©

shrubs and trees; shy, secretive, hiding quietly in upper branches when flushed from ground; song a sustained, high, buzzing note, swelling in volume, then fading into a silent pause, then repeated on a different pitch; call a low "*took*" or soft buzz.

Range

Migratory in north and in interior, nonmigratory along coast and in milder zones; breeds from Alaska to extreme northwestern California; favors shady, dense, coniferous forest from seaside to upper mountainside; winters along coast west of Cascades and the Sierra.

Food

Snails, worms, insects, berries in summer; dried or frozen berries and fruit, and acorns in winter; attracted to yards and orchards in winter by berry bushes, orchard fruit left on trees; may visit feeders for sunflower seeds, raisins, apples, suet.

Nest

From six to twenty feet up, usually in conifer, concealed next to trunk; bulky base of twigs, weed and grass stems, dead leaves, bark shreds; cup of mud, grasses, moss, and dead leaves collected wet, which dry into papier-mâché consistency; lined with fine, dry grasses.

Comment

It is interesting to note the varying attempts by authors to describe the song of this bird of the deep woods: "Unmusical," "eerie," "remarkable," "bell-like," "buzzing," "matchless truth and purity of tone," et cetera. I manage a passable imitation with a high-pitched plastic whistle, humming softly as I blow.

The berries of Mountain Ash are a strong attractant for this bird, especially those that have fallen to the ground. It follows that pulling the berries off the tree and scattering them generously on the ground beneath it will enhance your chances of attracting Varied Thrushes.

REF: A(W)—720; GO—246; NG—328; P(W)—274

Waxwings

Family Bombycillidae

There are only three species of true waxwings in the world. Two, the Cedar and Bohemian, occur in the Pacific Northwest. Their closest relatives in North America are the Silky Flycatchers, a connection acknowledged in the waxwing family name: Bombycillidae is a compound of Greek and pseudo-Latin meaning "silk tail."

If you see one of these elegant birds in summer, it is almost certainly a Cedar Waxwing. It will likely be perched on a prominent lookout from which it will launch aerial pursuits of flying insects. This easygoing fruit eater turns out to be a very adept flycatcher, agile enough to capture even swift and maneuverable dragonflies.

The flycatching is a response to the needs of its new hatchlings. They require a starter diet high in protein, a demand fruit cannot fill. After a few days on the booster menu, fruit gradually replaces insects, and then in generous quantities. A parent waxwing transports berries in its crop; one was seen to disgorge thirty chokecherries at the nest, popping them one after another into the waiting gapes of its young.

While its first cousin the Cedar is hawking after insects over a pasture or pond, the Bohemian Waxwing is doing the same thing farther north, probably from the edge of a boreal bog.

In the fall, both migrate, the Cedar south to more benign winter holdings, the Bohemian south and east into the summer range of the Cedar. A winter waxwing in the Pacific Northwest could be either one, the Bohemian more likely to be found in the northern, forested areas, the Cedar to the south. But numbers vary greatly from season to season and in accordance with the availability of dried and/or frozen tree fruit.

Both birds travel widely; banding shows that Bohemian waxwings banded in Saskatoon, Saskatchewan, came from breeding areas west of the Rockies. A Cedar Waxwing juvenile banded near Kingston, Ontario, on the north shore of Lake Ontario in August 1980 was shot February 13, 1981, in Morelia, Mexico, 2,140 miles distant.

Avian Dandy

The waxwing's elegant figure, slightly more rotund in the Bohemian, is impeccable in sleek plumage that always looks as if the wearer is freshly groomed for a formal night out. The colors are tastefully subtle, shades of rich gray-brown melting into fawns with a suggestion of saffron. The few highlights—most noticeably the jaunty crest, complemented by a velvet-black line through the eye, a natty bar of deep yellow at the end of the tail, a tiny daub of red on the wing—accentuate the overall statement of restrained elegance.

About thirty years ago, birders started noticing the occasional Cedar Waxwing with orange instead of yellow at the end of the tail. In the intervening years, the incidence of orange-tipped waxwings has markedly increased. The most plausible explanation is that the color comes from the berries of ornamental yew, which has come into fashionable use as a landscape plant over the last thirty years, and which is a favorite winter food of waxwings.

For all its nattiness, the waxwing personality is that of a gentle, easygoing wayfarer, fond of dining well in good company, as polite as it is handsome. In *Wings of the North*, Candace Savage notes that the beguiling trustfulness of the bird is shown in accounts of their taking string from outstretched hands, and of trying to pull hair from a person's head, all in the interests of collecting nesting materials.

The "Plume Trade"

Incredible though it is to us now, at one time millions of songbirds, and others, were shot every year to supply feathers for women's hats. The brutality and waste of the "plume trade" outraged many, but the influence and money of the fashion industry frustrated all efforts to put a stop to it.

Then Frank Chapman, ornithologist for the American Museum of Natural History, staged an inspired protest that helped change the course of nature preservation in North America. He went "birding" on the streets of Manhattan, recording the feathers in women's hats. Prominent among the forty species he listed were Northern Flicker, Snow Bunting, Northern Bobwhite, and Common Tern. But the most frequent species identified was Cedar Waxwing, a bizarre tribute to their lustrous beauty. The sharp-eyed Chapman noted only one Bohemian plume in his fashion-parade inventory. There would undoubtedly have been more except that their remote breeding range kept them safe from the feather hunters' birdshot.

Nature-lovers of the day, spurred by Chapman's imaginative protest, launched an impassioned campaign appealing to the conscience of the fashionable to stop wearing feathers of wild birds. The plume and millinery industry retaliated, claiming that 83,000 American workers would be plunged into unemployment if the plume hunt were stopped. In a barrage of counter-publicity they dismissed the charges of cruelty and scoffed at the threatened extinction of certain species. The dismissive rhetoric and dubious assurances ring familiar to those of us in touch with today's heated debate over fur trapping.

The bird preservationists eventually won out. Fashions changed, and the thousands of "threatened" workers simply switched to turning out featherless headgear. Birds such as Snowy Egrets slowly recovered from the brink of extinction.

Feathered Gourmands

Birds that feed on fruit trade quality for quantity. Fruit is less nutritious than insects and most seeds, but is often available in great abundance. Waxwings feeding on cotoneaster berries consume three times their weight of them every day. To process such bulk, they have a short gut designed for fast throughput; passage from beak to the top of your car can take as little as sixteen minutes. This need to eat hugely has gained waxwings an undeserved reputation for gluttony. They are often seen gorging on fruit and then lolling about like overstuffed Christmas dinner guests.

Now and then this feeding pattern brings them to embarrassment when they load up on fermented fruit. Householders then report in some alarm that their ornamental crab is full of birds fluttering and falling about for all the world as if they were drunk, which indeed they are.

The "wax" that gives the birds their name is exuded from the tips of the feather shafts of the secondaries on the wings of both sexes. Its presence varies considerably, being nonexistent to sparse in young birds, most pronounced in breeding adults. I have read the opinion that these protect the feather tips from fraying as the birds flutter about in branches gathering fruit. Most writers, however, take this uncertain and obscure field mark to be a visible badge of fitness and maturity among the birds themselves.

Bohemian Waxwing
Bombycilla garrulus

Common name likely arising from vagabond "Bohemian" winter wanderings, rather than with any link to western Slovakia where they are only occasional visitors; "Waxwing" from waxy substance on tips of secondary wing feathers; formerly called "silk-tail"; Greek *Bombyx*, "silk," *cilla* is invention from Latin mistakenly coined to mean "tail"; *garrulus*, from Latin *garrula*, "chattering", waxwing's crest making it resemble European jay, *Garrulus glandarius*.

Description
Robin-sized; elegant; smooth plumage is subtle blends of soft grays, rich ochers; trim, sharp-tipped crest, narrow black mask through eyes, black chin; bill small, black; cluster of waxy tips on wing secondaries difficult to spot; best told from smaller, more slender Cedar Waxwing by cinnamon undertail coverts, white bar and flecking on dark wings, and broader yellow band at end of tail.

Behavior
Always in busy flocks, especially in winter around fruit-bearing trees like Mountain Ash, firethorn, ornamental crab, Russian Olive; calls constantly while feeding or in flight; tame; shares habit with Cedars of sitting in a close row on a branch, passing a berry or bright object back and forth; call a weak, trilling, slightly buzzy "*tzeee.*"

Range
Erratically migratory; circumpolar; breeds in boreal forest of western Canada, and in western mountains down to extreme northern Washington; wanders widely in winter, especially frequent and abundant visitor to northwestern Washington.

Food

Fruit eater, optionally insectivorous, particularly when feeding nestlings; might visit feeding stations to try frozen fruit, berries, or raisins, prunes, dates; best attractants are berry or fruit-bearing trees that hold fruit over winter.

Nest

Usually in conifer on forest edge near clearing, lake, marsh; five to twenty feet up; cup of conifer twigs, lichens, and grass, lined with hair, down.

Comment

The North American range maps for the Bohemian suggest that it could be a recent immigrant from Siberia, spreading south and east from a toehold in Alaska. If true, this might account for its not breeding in the boreal forests east of Hudson Bay or in Newfoundland, at least not yet. Cedar Waxwings, in contrast, breed in a broad band right across the continent. Could they be much earlier arrivals from the same forebears of the Bohemian, evolved into a separate species?

Should a flock appear to feed on the frozen fruit of a nearby tree, get out

P. Sawatzky ©
1991

the binoculars promptly and give their beauty and charming sociability a long look. They travel far and wide in search of food and, once they have plucked every berry, will not be back again.

REF: A(W)—747; GO—258; NG—344; P(W)—282

Cedar Waxwing
Bombycilla cedrorum

Has been called "cedar bird" from association with this tree, and "cherry bird" for its diet of fruit; like Bohemian, secondary wing feathers bear red tips resembling the wax once used to seal envelopes; Greek *Bombyx* means "silk" in reference to family link to silk-tails, *cilla* is Latin non-word in error thought to mean "tail"; Latin *cedrorum* means "of the cedars."

Description

Smaller than robin, slimmer than Bohemian; plumage silky, smooth; obvious crest sharp-pointed, backswept; color predominantly a blending of soft browns melting to fawns, beiges, khaki; narrow satin-black face mask elegantly lined in off-white, chin dark; belly and flanks pale yellow; undertail coverts white and unusually long, extending well toward end of tail; rump and base of tail gray; squared-off tail has wide, dark subterminal band; end band is bright yellow or saffron; unlike Bohemian, darkish wings have no bars or yellow checkmarks; voice a high, thin, metallic trill.

Behavior

Sweeps about in fast-flying flocks, constantly calling; settles into fruit trees or berry bushes, feeding busily in an amiable, well-mannered scramble; may grab berries on the wing by hovering at bunches; may eat plucked berry by tossing it into the air and catching it; quite tame, especially when preoccupied with eating.

Range

Migratory; a North American species, breeding in a wide band across continent from coast to coast; nests throughout most of Pacific Northwest wherever woodland habitat offers a combination of insect life and fruit-bearing shrubs and trees; frequent, often abundant winter visitor to suburban yards and parks where it seeks fruit and berries of ornamentals.

Food

Fruit, petals, buds most of year; during nesting reverts to flycatcher ancestry to feed insects to young for a few days before gradually switching to fruit; may come to feeders for raisins, frozen berries, dried fruit.

Nest

    In open woods, hedges, orchards, shelter belts; on horizontal limb well away from trunk, six to twenty feet up; a bulky, loose base of twigs, weed stems, grass; cup of grass, plant fibers lined with rootlets, fine grasses, plant down; might appear at first glance to be a clump of debris caught by chance in a cleft in a branch; occasionally nests sociably, close together in same or nearby trees.

Comment

Both our waxwings have inspired lyrical prose in generations of writers, not only about their dapper beauty, but about their charming manners. Together in an ornamental crabapple in winter or a birdbath in summer, they are gracious about sharing space and waiting turns. Courting couples sit close together, passing a petal or berry back and forth, doing a sedate little side-step dance. Their devotion doesn't end with ritual; if one of a couple is killed, the survivor may call disconsolately for a couple of days.

Among birds that households have rescued and adopted, a disproportionate number of successes seem to be waxwings. Their dietary needs of fruit are easily met and their placid nature allows them to accept their human benefactors without too much stress.

REF: A(W)—748; GO—258; NG—344; P(W)—282

Shrikes

Family Laniidae

Popular nature lore accounts for the fact that while most people have never seen a shrike, some know of the "butcher bird" and its ghoulish habit of impaling the bodies of its victims on thorns and barbed wire. The mythology further explains that without doing so the shrike would be unable to tear prey apart, lacking the powerful feet and sharp talons of full-scale raptors.

A secure meat hook might make it easier to pull larger prey apart, but is it crucial? Crows and magpies, likewise handicapped with dicky-bird feet, nevertheless use them very effectively to hold down large food items while they tug at them. The shrike's feet are at least as heavy, proportionately, as a crow's.

The idea that shrikes are compensating for weak feet, and that hawthorn shrubs festooned with little carcasses represent a food cache or larder, has been convincingly challenged by researchers in Israel. Reuven Yosef and Berry Pinshow, then of the Ben-Gurion University of the Negev, observed that if the collection of prey is a larder, it is a very poor one because it is obvious to every passing scavenger and pilferer. And while shrikes do employ thorns and barbs as meat hooks to dismember large prey, this may be more an incidental convenience than a necessity, because they also impale small, fragile items like crickets, and even inedible things such as snail shells.

Working with resident Great Grey Shrikes, the same *Lanius excubitor* we call the Northern, the two men demonstrated convincingly that the impaling habit could have arisen from a courting behavior display. It is demonstrated only by males, and the more conspicuous and well stocked his display is, the better able a male is to attract a female. For a year Yosef and Pinshow manipulated the displays of males in a cluster of territories, consistently depleting some, augmenting others, leaving a control group untouched.

When returning migrant females sized up the prospective mates, the ones with the boosted caches were chosen first, pairing an average of a month earlier than males in the control group. Subsequent nesting success was also markedly improved. The unfortunates whose caches were cleaned out every week all failed to mate and abandoned their territories.

These observations led to the conclusion that a good cache advertises to cruising females that the displaying male is more able to obtain food, whether by better hunting skill, his ability to recognize and defend a superior territory, or both. Either way, he will not only be a better provider for his offspring, but will pass to them genes reinforcing these traits.

One-on-One

The Northern Shrike is one of the relatively few predators that kills prey, one-on-one, that is close to its own size, and whose weapons are not so obviously superior to those of its prey. They have better success with smaller birds, but will attack and kill larger species. They have been seen pursuing robins, and there are accounts of their killing Evening Grosbeaks. Whether they have the skill of predators such as wolves in singling out individuals that are more vulnerable than their flock-mates is not known.

Northern Shrikes visiting my yard seem to be much more interested in the voles than the birds. I once watched one searching intently but calmly around a scrap lumber pile near my feeder. During its half-hour hunt it did everything except actually squeeze in among the boards to flush out the prey it knew was concealed among them.

In its pursuit of birds it is postulated that the shrike relies in part on what would be the ultimate disguise, its resemblance to an unthreatening songbird. Thus masked it gets close enough to an unsuspecting victim to pounce or launch pursuit before it bolts. Certainly this innocuous cover, if it is one, doesn't fool all birds. On the infrequent times when a shrike has appeared at my feeder, the reaction of the regulars has been one of alarm and/or panic. Some observers, however, report that victims will sometimes remain as if mesmerized as a shrike makes its fatal approach.

Failing a quick grab, pursuit on the wing can be a protracted chase in which, often as not, the intended meal outmaneuvers the hunter. If the victim is overtaken, it is buffeted to the ground and the shrike tries to dislocate the neck or pierce the skull with a well-placed bite. If the victim is struggling too vigorously for this, it will try to subdue it by hammering it about the head with its heavy bill, employing an unusually strong set of neck muscles. It may then hang up the body, a skill that begins as an instinctive reaction. In Robert Burton's

Bird Behavior, it is reported that young Loggerheads at twenty-two days of age start to hold food in their bills and to draw it along a perch in random fashion. If the food happens to catch on a twig or crotch, the bird immediately concentrates on dragging it repeatedly over the obstacle. In this way it very quickly learns to perfect the technique.

Northern Shrike

Lanius excubitor

"Northern," as distinct from the Loggerhead, a more southerly occurring relative; "Shrike" from Anglo-Saxon *scric,* "a shrieker"; also "butcher bird" from habit of impaling or hanging prey on thorns, barbed wire; *Lanius* from Latin for "a butcher"; *excubitor,* "a sentinel."

Description

Robin-sized; black-masked, boldly patterned in off-white, gray-black; belly, rump, undertail coverts white; wings black with white patch and frosting at ends of longest flight feathers; fan-shaped tail black with white edges; crown, nape, back smoke-gray; large head, heavy, straight, dark bill with sharp, pronounced hook; breast of juvenile with light lines, faint or absent in adult; sexes identical.

Behavior

Perches quietly on utility wires, dead branches, fence posts, alert for prey beneath; pumps tail upward; undulating flight on rapidly beating wings often low, ending in sharp swoop up to perch; may hover, kestrel-style, when hunting over grassy cover; chases small birds in pell-mell pursuit, occasionally around feeding stations; favorite hunting grounds on plains a dry slough with circle of willow; call a harsh "*shek*" or "*shak,*" song an extended medley of warbles, whistles, phrases from other birds' songs mixed with discordant notes.

Range

Erratically migratory; circumpolar; breeds throughout Alaska and in high taiga and tundra of Northwest Territories; in Pacific Northwest a shrike in summer has to be a Loggerhead, in winter very probably a Northern; erratic and uncommon winterer through region east of the Cascades, particularly in central and eastern Oregon; rare west of Cascades.

Food

Predatory on small birds, mice; may pursue insects either on ground or in the air; may take suet at feeding stations, but its primary interest there is other birds, mice, et cetera.

P. SHWATZKY ©
1990

Nest

Bulky, on foundation of twigs, cup lined with roots, hair, feathers; prefers dense conifers, height dependent on size of available trees; favors proximity of thorn-bearing shrubs.

Comment

Shrikes rarely visit feeding stations for the usual purpose; rather, they are attracted by the concentration of other birds and the presence of mice.

When one does call, it is an event fraught with potential for life-and-death drama at close quarters. Lacking an overwhelming size advantage and the powerful clutching, piercing talons that are hawks' and owls' primary killing tools, the shrike kills in an often protracted struggle in which the prey is buffeted to the ground and bludgeoned on the head with the heavy bill. Once subdued it gets the coup de grace from a bite through the neck or back of the skull.

A detached view of predator–prey relationships is hard to sustain when one sees beloved birds assaulted so brutally. But the shrike, and its prey, are following the dictates of behavior millions of years in the evolving. And it is the shrike that, over the past decades, has suffered an alarming decrease in its range and numbers. Viewing it at work, firsthand, should be regarded as a rare look into life's reality, definitely *not* an emergency to be interrupted.

REF: A(W)—728; GO—260; NG—334; P(W)—280

Starlings

Family Sturnidae

The scene is a wharfside market in Seattle on a warm June afternoon. A couple of musicians have pulled in a crowd, the inevitable guitar cases open in supplication on the tiles in front of them.

But they do not have the scene to themselves. A starling, recognizing prime turf when he sees it, is working their crowd. Not for this pro the passive, guitar-case–style appeal, nor the undignified scrambles the silly pigeons flap into over every tossed scrap. This guy is organized. He starts at one end of the front row of spectators, strutting briskly along, moving in close, pausing briefly but deliberately to fix each person with a beady eye. He is less like a panhandler than an usher taking up collection in church. Most of the crowd has munchies, and the bird does well—I throw him a chunk of my tempura.

I am at best a grudging admirer of starlings. But even well-entrenched prejudice cannot blind me to the beauty of this clever, businesslike bird. In the lowering afternoon sun the iridescence of his head and neck feathers shimmers. The bright yellow bill and the copper-pink feet and legs show up strikingly against the dark, mud-colored slate. The immaculate, satin-black body plumage radiates fitness and physiological prosperity.

The European or Common Starling is a scion of an Old World family tree of 103, 106, 111, or 130 species, depending on which authority you read. There are 3 in North America, all of them imports. Near Homestead, Florida, is a tiny enclave of Hill Mynas, descendants of escaped cage birds. The Crested Myna was introduced in Vancouver, British Columbia, in 1895. It spread only to nearby portions of Vancouver Island, where it hung on for many years, but has not been seen there recently. Apparently its tropical habit of not incubating its eggs for extended periods during midday has inhibited its reproductive success.

No such laxity inhibits the Common Starling; it is a determined, opportunistic breeder. With little hesitation it will attack birds as large as flickers and evict them from their nest holes. Observers have noticed that the starlings appear to wait patiently until the flickers have completed the excavation before making their move.

In combat with other species the starling uses a hold perfected for battle with its own kind. If one of a battling pair can get onto the other's back, it locks its feet into its opponent's feathers, grabs it by the back of the neck with its beak, and hangs on for dear life, sometimes as long as a half hour. This trick, combined with the fact that starlings work well as a tag team to gang up on opponents, enables them to vanquish bigger birds like flickers. The little starlings the pair then raises in the usurped premises are—wouldn't you know it—noted in their turn for being unusually hardy.

Blame the Bard

Shakespeare was inadvertently responsible for adding this ubiquitous nuisance to North America, although direct blame rests with a group called the American Acclimatization Society. Its self-appointed aim was to introduce to America every bird mentioned in Shakespeare's works. Regrettably, in *Henry IV,* Hotspur proclaimed, "Nay, I'll have a starling shall be taught to speak nothing but 'Mortimer'...." Accordingly, the Society ordered up a few cagefuls and turned them loose in Central Park, New York, on March 6, 1890. The initial eighty releasees were joined in April 1891 by twenty pairs of reinforcements.

Surprisingly, previous attempts to start the scourge had failed. However earnestly we might now wish it, do-gooders of the time did not recognize the initial failures as the disguised blessings they were. As early as 1872 there was a release in Ohio, and others preceded the infamous 6th of March in Central Park.

Whirlwind Takeover

The plague incubated in New York for six years before breaking out. It first swept the southern expanses of the continent, taking only a little more time to invade the environmentally harsher north. It is now listed as rare to casual in southern coastal and central Alaska.

Like House Sparrows, starlings are largely dependent on humans for their well-being and do not nest much beyond the confines of towns and farmyards. In breeding atlas maps that indicate the density of individual species, the dots for the starling may literally blacken settled areas. In places, however, there will be conspicuous holes of non-occurrence that turn out to be large parks where backcountry has been preserved from development.

Although common to abundant as winter stay-overs in the Pacific Northwest, many still migrate, joining with grackles and blackbirds to forage in the marshes, shorelines, and agricultural lands of the southern United States. The size of some of these integrated flocks is mind-boggling, by credible estimate the largest numbering 70 million. At roosts, branches break under the weight of the clamorous horde, and the accumulation of droppings beneath the trees sterilizes the soil.

The starling musters the standard adaptive repertoire that helps successful invasive species thrive—hardiness, assertive opportunism, a high birth rate, absence of homeland pathogens, and adaptability. Except for the reprieve from pathogens, these are attributes possessed by native birds the starling has displaced. What, then, confers its competitive edge?

First, it arrived preconditioned to life with humankind, an adaptive move that similar native birds like grackles are only now beginning to make. The second reason could be its unusual jaw musculature. Logically, most creatures that grip or chew with their mouths have powerful biting muscles; those required to open the jaws are relatively weak. But the starling jaw has two-way power. Pushed into your lawn, the bill can be forced open. Simultaneously the eyes are rotated forward to provide binocular vision down the hole. This "gaping" enables the bird to detect immobile as well as active prey.

Only a few members of the starling family possess this capability, and among the very few other songbirds that have it are the starling's wintering companions, grackles and blackbirds. Most soil-dwelling invertebrates are dormant and inactive in winter, a food source starlings are better-equipped to exploit than other birds, and at a critical time of year.

There is a further, gender-based refinement to the starling's winter feeding pattern. Males will flock to garbage dumps and feedlots where grain and other high-carbohydrate food is the most likely fare. But the females go their separate way to seek out invertebrates, rich in protein that is stored in the pectoral muscles in reserve for the demands of egg laying later on.

Booby-trapped Nests

Species of birds that breed in used cavities and old nests, either their own or others', save labor and time, and reduce the uncertainties of relocating. But their offspring run the risk of inheriting the swarm of lice, mites, and bacteria that multiplied during the tenure of the previous clutch. Some birds habitually add fresh sprigs of greenery to the nest during incubation and prefledging. It turns out that the plants selected for this, such as yarrow, agrimony, and cedar, have fumigant properties that inhibit bacterial and parasitic growth. How do the birds know which plants to select?

Two Pennsylvania researchers—L. Clark and C. A. Smeraski—discovered that during the nesting season, starlings develop a sense of smell comparable to that of a rat or a rabbit. They use this to sniff out aromatic green plants that have fumigant effects when brought into the nest cavity. After the nesting season, their olfactory powers diminish to the very low level they share with most other birds.

Starlings would not be starlings if they simply dealt with the pathogens in the usual way and then left the nest; they use the pathogens to sabotage potential competitors. Like most birds, they keep the nest clean of droppings up to the time the young begin to feather. At that point they stop both housecleaning and adding fumigant greenery. Thereafter, to quote *The Birder's Handbook,* the nest hole becomes heavily fouled and resembles "a pest-ridden compost," crawling with lice and thousands of mites. The older starling fledglings are hardy enough to tolerate such infestations. But what they leave behind is a biological "booby trap" fatal to the more fragile newly hatched young of any competing species that might reuse the nest.

Like the crow family, starlings have a reputation for "smarts." As cage birds they can be taught, as Hotspur proclaimed to our regret, to imitate human speech. In traps that securely confine other birds, starlings have been observed to take as little as two minutes to get out by lifting drop-doors or pulling hinged ones inward.

On a positive note, starlings probe out and eat the larvae and pupae of the Gypsy Moth and Japanese Beetle, introduced pests on which most other birds do not prey. It is also suggested that their probing bills spread the spores of insect diseases.

A final note on starling ingenuity: On a winter visit to Toronto in 1992, I bought a small bag of bird seed at the corner shop and set up a feeder for my hosts. The bag dribbled seeds on the kitchen floor, however, and when I looked more closely I found that one side was punched with little holes in the clear plastic. Later, on a stroll past the same shop, I noticed a starling on the sidewalk near the pile of seed bags, and stopped to watch. When not dodging the dogs and the passing feet, it hopped among the bags, punched its dagger of a bill through the plastic, gaped it open and dipped up millet with its tongue.

European Starling

Sturnus vulgaris

"Starling" from Anglo-Saxon *staer,* "star," plus diminutive "ling," possibly from fanciful likening of delta-winged flight silhouette to stars; *Sturnus* is Latin for "a starling"; *vulgaris* is Latin for "common."

Description

Robin-sized; chunky, short-tailed, dark; large head and long, straight, pointed bill; bill yellow from midwinter to early summer, otherwise brown; adult sexes identical except female eye has yellowish edge around iris; after late summer moult, body feathers are light-tipped, giving a heavily speckled appearance that diminishes by spring as tips wear off leaving the dark, iridescent, glossy summer plumage.

Behavior

Social; outside of breeding season gathers in large flocks, especially in migration and wintering; struts about probing ditches, pastures, lawns; aggressive at feeders among themselves and against other species; noisy; voice a series of whistles, squeaks, gurgles, chirps, and clicks in which it might imitate other birds.

Range

Partially migratory; found continentwide, even in the Arctic around human settlements; in areas and elevations of severe winter, almost all migrate; as you move from north to south, and from inland to coast, winter populations increase; irrigated farmland is prime wintering ground; banding has indicated that some birds from northern Washington and adjacent British Columbia migrate to California, where they winter with resident starlings.

Food

Omnivorous; "gapes" in soft soil and litter for insects and grubs; winter flocks congregate in garbage dumps, feedlots, irrigated land; at feeders, takes most seeds, sunflowers last; likes table scraps and suet.

Nest

Cavity nester, including holes in buildings, signs, and light poles; preempts Purple Martin and bluebird houses, if permitted; aggressively evicts flickers and

woodpeckers from tree holes; nest a collection of straw, weed stems, and trash with cup of fine plant fibers, feathers.

Comment

This abundant pest vies with the co-immigrant House Sparrow for the title of bird we most love to hate. Pushy and preemptive at feeders, it is particularly hostile to woodpeckers, which it seems consistently able to mob and vanquish.

You can make it awkward for them, and still provide for native species at your feeders, by not scattering feed on the ground, by dispensing seeds in hanging feeders, and by offering suet in containers accessible only through the bottom.

The starling's imitative repertoire extends to mechanical noises and mammals. Kris Fulsaas of Seattle, Washington reports that starlings near her yard "meow" in so catlike a manner that she often looks around the yard for a cat, only to realize that the noise is coming from a bird ten feet up on a wire.

REF: A(W)—590; GO—260; NG—346; P(W)—280

Sparrows

Family Emberizinae

This group includes the Old World buntings and their New World kin, our "sparrows." Our "sparrows" are not really the same as the Old World birds they were (mistakenly of course!) named after. Those of us who are slightly adrift about the kinships in this large group of songbirds are in good company; sparrows and "sparrows" have been, and remain, a source of contention among taxonomists.

To add to the confusion, our best-known "sparrow," the House Sparrow, is held by some (including Peterson in his most recent guides) to be no sparrow at all, but an Old World weaver finch. However, the American Ornithologists' Union's 1983 checklist places the House Sparrow in the Old World sparrow family.

Compared to the sociable finches, our sparrows are not enthusiastic feeder seekers, nor do they rove about in flocks. The exception to both these characteristics is the dapper junco. The even more elegant Rufous-sided Towhee readily comes to feeders, but like the other sparrows comes to feeders almost as an afterthought when it is already settled in the neighborhood for the duration.

Depending on where you hang up your feeders in the Pacific Northwest, you can expect anything from none at all to a half dozen or more sparrows. Which half dozen? As one scans the Christmas Bird Count summaries for the region, the cut-off point between the species we have a fair chance of seeing at our feeders, and the ones the average bird feeder will rarely, if ever, see, gets hazy. The ones selected here are the American Tree, Song, Fox, White-crowned, and Golden-crowned Sparrows, and the Dark-eyed Junco. Better luck next time to the Lincoln's, Savannah, White-throated, and other sparrows that did not make the cut. Nothing personal.

All in the Family

As anyone knows who has an older field guide to compare with recent editions, both the common and scientific names of birds are constantly being changed. These decisions are the result of deliberations by the American Ornithologists' Union which, among other revisions recently made, has changed the Canada Jay to the Gray Jay, the Baltimore Oriole to the Northern Oriole, the Sparrow Hawk to the American Kestrel. Such changes reflect an ongoing debate between "lumpers" and "splitters."

At one time the impetus amongst scientists was with the splitters, those who see in minor differences in physical form a reason to declare their possessors a separate species, or at least a subspecies. Conversely, the lumpers hold that many differences claimed by the splitters are superficial and do not justify setting up a separate species or subspecies.

Juncos, for example, were until recently regarded as four regional species, five counting the Yellow-eyed of Mexico. The regional species have recently been reassessed and found wanting sufficient differences to merit full species status. The differences between them, the lumpers assure us, are entirely sartorial and do not at all prevent juncos of the various forms from interbreeding wherever their ranges overlap.

Rufous-sided Towhee

Pipilo erythrophthalmus

Sparrow family. "Rufous-sided" because of the brick-red sides, "Towhee" imitative of the eastern form's call; other names are "chewink," "swamp robin," "ground robin," "jo-ree"; on west coast locally and formerly "spotted towhee" or "Oregon towhee"; Pipilo coined from Latin pipo, "to chirp"; erythrophthalmus from Greek words erythros, "red," and ophthalmos, "eye," hence "red-eye."

Description

A large, long-tailed sparrow dressed in bright contrasts; male head, bib, back, wings, and tail coal-black; white flashes on outer corners of fan-shaped tail, and white check-marks on back and wings; sides robin-red, belly white; eye a piercing red; female similar but much subdued, the black of the male replaced by sooty brown; some coastal forms very dark over all.

P.SAWATZKY
1992 ©

Behavior

Fitfully restless; stands and perches in tilted-forward posture, tail cocked up; generally busy near or on dense shrubbery, drops quickly into it at slightest disturbance; scratches busily about in leaf litter with quick forward hop and backward flick with both feet; song a "*chip-eeeeeeee*," the second note a metallic, one-note trill; call a harsh jaylike "*meeewwwww*."

Range

Migratory from north and interior of region, nonmigratory along the coast; breeds through most of United States and temperate parts of southern Canada; favors shrubby tangles around edges of clearings, along fences, thickets around yards and parks; in Pacific Northwest winters in western halves of Washington and Oregon, in southern Idaho, and throughout California.

Food

Insects, weed seeds, occasional fruit, berries; relies heavily on acorns where they are available; at feeders, takes sunflower seeds as first choice, millet as second; will go to high feeders placed amongst branches, but prefers ground feeding.

Nest

Usually a cup in the ground, rim level with surface, in thick shrubs, often sheltered by plant tuft; rarely above ground in brush tangle, or dense bush or vine; thick cup of grasses, bark shreds, rootlets, conifer needles, lined with finer grasses, occasionally hair; frequent cowbird "host."

Comment

There are four species of the genus *Pipilo* in North America, all of them westerners except for the Rufous-sided, which occurs right across the continent. Anyone familiar with the "*drink-your-teeeee*" call of the eastern Rufous-sided will not at first recognize the less-musical "*chweeeeeee*" of the western race. The two eastern syllables start disappearing in a distinct transition zone beginning in central Montana.

Efforts to imitate, or "syllabize," the calls and songs of birds have resulted in some heroic phonetics. "*Chick-a-dee-dee*" and "*caw*" are self-evident. And pub-crawlers immediately recognized a fellow tippler in the Olive-sided Flycatcher with his "*quick-three-beers.*" But more complicated vocalizations were not so easy. Ernest Thompson Seton had a go at the eastern Rufous-sided Towhee with "*chuck-burr-pill-a-will-a-will-a.*" Canadian ornithologist P. A. Taverner thought it sounded like "*dick-yoo, chiddle-chiddle-chiddle.*" The differences could be accounted for by the "ear-of-the-hearer" phenomenon, or to the fact that many species of birds have distinct regional dialects. My own interpretation of the towhees on my turf in Manitoba, where they are neighbors to coyotes, is "*keep-yeer-fleeeeeees.*"

REF: A(W)—598; GO—324; NG—386; P(W)—330

Fox Sparrow

Passerella iliaca

"Fox" because the eastern type species, and most races east of the Rockies, are a bright foxy brown. Choate in *American Bird Names* (p.143) explains the scientific name thusly: "L. (Latin) *Passer*, 'sparrow'; L. *-ella*, 'little'; hence 'little sparrow' for the genus which has one of our largest sparrows. *P. iliaca* … ; L. *iliacus*, 'relating to colic,' from L. *ilia*, 'the groin' or 'lower intestine,' the anatomical seat of the Roman bellyache. It is remotely possible that the taxonomist who named the bird had in mind 'flanks,' as this portion of the bird's anatomy is conspicuously streaked."

Description

Larger than House Sparrow; in the Pacific Northwest basically a large, dark brown sparrow with long, slightly notched tail; lighter underside has rows of heavy spots like upside-down *Vs*, clumping together in a ragged spot in the center of the breast; most likely to be confused with Song Sparrow.

Behavior

Scratches noisily on the ground, usually among trees or under bushes, flipping up leaves and debris behind it; this reflex is so strongly connected to feeding that the bird does it on feeder tables, sending seeds flying; voice strong and clear, song one or more slurred whistles followed by several short, musical "*churrrrrrs.*"

Range

Migratory; breeds in its various forms across the north of the continent, including most of Alaska, down the Rocky, Cascade, and Sierra Nevada mountains, and the Blue Mountains; familiar winterer in most of the region except southeastern Oregon and southern Idaho; most plentiful along coastal coniferous belt.

Food

Insects, worms, seeds scratched from beneath woodland ground litter; may occasionally also search through windrows of marine vegetation along beaches; at feeder, most seeds.

·P. SAWATZKY·
1992 ©

Nest

On ground; occasionally in thicket or low conifer branch above ground; a thick, deep cup of twigs, bark shreds, grass and weed stems, moss, lined with fine rootlets, hair, feathers.

Comment

The plumage coloration in this bird is quite variable in the Pacific Northwest. None of our indigenous races really have the bright, ruddy brown plumage that gave the eastern bird its name. The darkest form is the sooty brown race from the Northwest. A more reddish bird breeds in northeastern Washington, and a form with gray back and head breeds in northern Idaho and in migration shows up in eastern Washington and Oregon.

REF: A(W)—680; GO—342; NG—406; P(W)—324

Song Sparrow
Melospiza melodia

"Song" from bird's obvious talent; *Melospiza* from Greek *melos*, "song," and *spiza*, "a finch"; *melodia* from Greek/Latin, "a pleasant song."

Description

Same size as House Sparrow; inconspicuously plumaged; relatively long tail rounded at end; rows of heavy brown dashes on white breast and sides come together to form dark, ragged spot on upper breast; top of head brown, with narrow black streaks and broad midstripe of gray; the rest is a blend of browns, rusts, and tans; various West Coast races darker, larger than eastern type form; everywhere its song is the best "field mark."

Behavior

Not sociable; highly territorial in breeding season; ground feeder; pumps long tail during characteristically short flights; begins singing very early in season, often well before snow is gone where it winters over; sings from elevated perch in "chest-out" posture, feathers puffed out, head thrown back; song starts with three or four clear notes, then a rolling series of sweet warblings ending in a buzzy trill; no other sparrow sings so well; call note a distinctive "*chimp*"; easily attracted by a squeaking or "*pishing*" noise.

Range

Migratory; common to abundant over northern three-quarters of continent, excepting high Arctic tundra; found in open bushland, woodland and waterside edges, marshes, and in hedges, gardens, and parks in suburbia; winters almost everywhere through Pacific Northwest, except for the Salmon River region

of Idaho; is a year-round resident along the coast, along inland river valleys and other regions with a mild, moist climate.

Food

Mainly a ground feeder; weed seeds, insects added during nestling-feeding season; feeder choice is most small seeds, especially thistle and canary, plus sunflower; prefers low table or ground, but will follow other birds to higher feeders.

Nest

Often builds two or more per season, first one on ground, before leaves are out, second in low bush or tree; ground nest well concealed under tuft, shrub, or fallen branches, with base of grass, weed stems, leaves, bark fibers, cup lined with fine grasses, rootlets, hair; tree nest similar, in bush or small tree eighteen inches to three feet up, sometimes up to thirteen feet; high rate of cowbird parasitism.

Comment

This drab little virtuoso is born with its song in its head, and will tenaciously sing the basic Song Sparrow melody even if it is raised experimentally with domestic canaries. But it develops best when it absorbs its father's song along with its daily fare of insects and regurgitated seeds. Having done this, it then proceeds in early maturity to invent its own unique song, using variations on many basic themes. The average male has eight to ten separate, extended recitals, but some prodigies have as many as twenty. Thoreau syllabized this bird's basic pattern as: "*Maids, maids, maids … hang on your tea kettle-ettle-ettle-ettle.*" Latter-day imitators suggest "*sweet*" in place of "*maids*."

In *Birds of Nova Scotia*, Tufts, always interesting, recounts a story of a farmer whose cat, in the summer of 1952, brought in a male Song Sparrow. A check revealed no apparent injury to the bird, so the farmer released it, expecting that it would flee out of sight in haste. Instead, it flew to a nearby branch, shook itself vigorously, and burst into song. A message in there, perhaps?

REF: A(W)—681; GO—342; NG—392; P(W)—324

American Tree Sparrow

Spizella arborea

Name bestowed by early English settlers who mistook it for similar, unrelated, red-capped European Tree Sparrow; has been called "Arctic chipper" and "Canada sparrow"; "Sparrow" from Anglo-Saxon *spearwa*, "sparrow"; *Spizella* from Latin *spiza*, "a finch"; *arborea* from Latin for "a tree."

P. SAWATZKY
1991 ©

Description

Slightly larger than chickadee; fox-red crown, small chestnut patch on sides of breast at shoulder; only sparrow with a dark "stickpin" spot on plain, smoky-white breast; sides of head, neck, and breast light gray; brown wings have two irregular white bars; tail plain dusky with outer feathers edged in white; back heavily streaked with black, buff, and brown.

Behavior

Travels in loose flocks in winter; busy ground feeder; constantly flashes light edges of outer tail feathers; feeding call an icy, tinkling "*tseewit,*" call note a silvery, high "*tseet*"; often sings in winter, "*sweet sweet sweet,*" followed by a series of fast warbled notes, last phrase dropped in pitch.

Range

Migratory; tundra breeder, from northern edge of boreal forest to Arctic coast, through most of Alaska east to Labrador; strictly a winter bird of the Northwest region; frequents weedy fields, marshes, roadsides, and forest edges in upland and drier areas of region, avoiding wet forest of the coastal belt; nowhere plentiful here.

Food

Weed and grass seeds; readily comes to feeders for sunflower, millet, and other seeds.

Nest

On ground, against moss hummock or under woody shrub; rarely, in low shrub; base of twigs, weed stems, rootlets, shreds of moss and lichen, fully lined with feathers, hair.

Comment

The "winter chippy" is the sparrow most commonly seen and heard throughout its huge wintering range in the United States. Its presence, and the fragile notes of its song, are a sure sign of winter. Its centers of greatest abundance are in the corn belt of the Midwest. There it is one of the most frequent feeder visitors, preferring the ground but moving readily to tables and shelves.

REF: A(W)—581; GO—338; NG—398; P(W)—280

Golden-crowned Sparrow

Zonotrichia atricapilla

"Golden-crowned" from the sulphur-yellow stripe on the top of the head; *Zonotrichia* from Greek *zone*, "a band," and *trichias*, "a thrush"; *atricapilla* from Latin *atrus*, "black," and *capilla*, "hair"; we thus have the common name describing one part of the bird's head and the scientific name another, since the gold band is bordered by black stripes.

Description

House Sparrow-sized; crown of head black with broad, yellow stripe down the middle that changes sharply to gray at back of head; viewed from side, head may appear black; sides of face and throat gray; sexes identical; in winter, head markings are dull, obscure; upper body a pattern of browns, beige; breast and belly uniform light tan-gray.

Behavior

Moderately social; shows site attachment in winter, either singly or in small flocks; ground feeder, preferring to be in or near dense, broken cover; skims the ground in flight from one patch of shelter to the next; voice a clear, flutelike whistle; cadence of song suggests tune of "Three Blind Mice," often syllabized as "*oh, dear mee.*"

Food

In winter, seeds, buds, fresh leaves, and shoots; at feeder, small seeds, grain, chick scratch on ground.

—P. SAWATZKY —
1992 ©

Range

Migratory; nests in subalpine timberline on southwestern and western coasts of Alaska, throughout montane British Columbia except in the extreme southeast, into northern Washington; common wintering bird from British Columbia border south, west of the Cascades and the Sierra; rare to uncommon east of the Cascade–Sierra highlands.

Nest

On the ground at base of low shrub or tussock, or under overhanging plants; thick cup of small twigs, bits of bark, fern leaves, grass stems, dead leaves; lined with fine grasses, hair, feathers.

Comment

Other sparrows might puzzle the neophyte birder, but there is no doubt about the elegant Golden-crowned. Perhaps because of its relatively limited range, it presents itself in a dependably consistent form, not one of the dozen or so "morphs" that Song and Fox Sparrows come in. Its uniformity may also be sustained in part by its migration pattern. According to Munro and Cowan, and Jewett, referred to in *Birds of the Okanogan Valley*, these birds go south in the fall through the high country of the Coast Ranges and the Cascades, but come back north in spring up the coastal lowlands.

REF: A(W)—750; GO—340; NG—404; P(W)—316

White-crowned Sparrow

Zonotrichia leucophrys

Formerly "Puget Sound" sparrow in that locality; *Zonotrichia* from Greek *zone*, "a band," and *trichias*, "a thrush"; *leucophrys* from Greek "white" and *ophrys*, "eyebrow," for the white line over the eye.

Description

"Stripe-crowned" would be more descriptive, since the outstanding field mark of the adult bird is its puffy, black-and-white striped head; a regional coastal race has somewhat dingy white stripes; chin whitish, underparts plain gray; back and wings brown, bill flesh-colored; crown distinctly dome-shaped compared to that of most sparrows.

Behavior

Erect posture constitutes a field mark; runs rapidly about on the ground, usually perches no higher than eye level; puffs up crown when agitated; many regional dialects to its short song, but basic form is one or more deliberate, plaintive whistles followed by several short trills ending in two or three quick descending notes; call a metallic "*chink.*"

Range

Migratory and residential; nests right across subarctic and arctic Canada, south in high alpine habitat through Rockies and Pacific Northwest; a resident population breeds on coastal belt from Canadian border to southern California; migrants of the Arctic-nesting Gambel's race are commonest winterers east of the Cascades and can be very abundant during fall and spring migrations.

Food

Weed seeds gleaned from the ground; buds, berries; at feeder will take sunflower seeds, millet, chicken scratch, other small seed; prefers ground, but will soon learn to use higher feeders.

-P. SAWATZKY-
1992 ©

Nest

Cup of grass stems, dead leaves, conifer needles, bark shreds, moss, lined with root fibers, hair, feathers; under grass tuft, fern, or at base of stunted shrub; rarely in a bush or low tree branch off the ground.

Comment

Migration is gender-linked, the females of any given population tending to migrate farther south than the males.

The Birder's Handbook refers to a study done by Gary Fugle at the University of California, which demonstrated that brightness of the crown pattern is the key status signal. Adult males with bright stripes are at the top of the heap, with juvenile females, which have the dullest striping, at the bottom. By brightening up the headdress of subordinate individuals with a painted stripe job, Fugle found that they immediately rose a notch or two in sparrow hierarchy.

White-crowneds are one of many ground-nesting species in which the females, disturbed at the nest, will scurry away on the ground in a hunched, head-down "mouse run," some giving a distinct mouselike squeak. If the trick works, would-be egg predators are decoyed away from the nest and end up with nothing but a brisk turn of exercise when the scurrying "mouse" flies off.

REF: A(W)—682; GO—340; NG—404; P(W)—316

Dark-eyed Junco

Junco hyemalis

Frequently called "snowbird"; "Dark-eyed" as distinct from the Yellow-eyed or "Mexican" junco; all but most recent field guides specify "Slate-colored Junco," "White-winged Junco," "Oregon Junco," "Gray-headed Junco"; newest guides list these as races of *hyemalis,* former species name for Slate-colored; *Junco* from Latin *juncus,* "a rush," which has no traceable link to juncos; but Latin *hyemalis,* "winter," clearly refers to their appearing only in winter in south-temperate regions.

Description

Rotund, dark, sparrow-sized; stubby, flesh-tinted bill shows up brightly against charcoal face and throat; longish tail black, white edges of outer feathers usually concealed; "Oregon" male head and cape jet black, sharply demarcated from reddish brown back, ruddy flanks, and white belly; Slate-colored is slate-gray on entire upper body; females are subdued counterparts of males.

Behavior

Strongly social ground-forager; readily joins other birds to table, shelf, or even hanging feeders; may scuff down through light snow cover to reach bare ground; flicks white outer tail feathers from under centrals, especially just before takeoff, flashing them conspicuously in flight; call a rapid, plaintive burst of "*deets*"; soft twittering in flight; song a largely one-pitch trill, like Chipping Sparrow with more tuneful pipes.

Range

Migratory, flying only far enough south, or to lower altitudes, to reach adequate forage; breeds throughout boreal, montane, and adjoining mixed-wood forests from coast to coast; "Oregon" is the most common year-round junco in the Pacific Northwest, joined in most winters by the Slate-colored over most of the region.

-P.SAWATZKY-
·1994- ©

Food

Insects during breeding season, seeds in winter; at feeding stations will readily take to sunflower seeds, all small seeds, crumbs, occasionally suet and peanut butter.

Nest

On ground, in open woodland, forest edge; concealed in tree roots, under debris, rock, tussock, occasionally in ferns, on rubbly slope; rarely, in low shrub or conifer; small cup of bark shreds, stems, light twigs, lined with fine grasses, rootlets, hair; prefledged nestlings precociously active afoot, able to scramble away from nest and hide if danger threatens.

Comment

The juncos that recently lost their species accreditation were lumped together because their differences, the lumpers assure us, are largely sartorial, and they freely interbreed where their nesting ranges overlap.

Junco migration is divided along age and gender lines. Females when they migrate travel farther south than males, but juveniles of both sexes remain farther north than adults. A pattern noted by bird feeders north of the juncos' wintering range is that they show up in spring, usually before the snow has gone. They stick around for several weeks, vanish for a week or so, then seem to reappear for awhile. What actually happens is migration in two pulses, the males in the vanguard, followed in due course by the females.

REF: A(W)—731; GO—334; NG—402; P(W)—332

Cowbirds and Other Blackbirds

Family Icteridae

This family is exclusive to the Western Hemisphere and includes the bobolink, orioles, meadowlarks, blackbirds, and cowbirds. Icteridae is from Greek *ikteros*, "jaundice." This ailment, named for the yellowing of the skin it causes, was supposed by the ancients to be alleviated if the sufferer were lucky enough to see an oriole, many species of which are also yellow. The Old World orioles belong to the Oriolidae, a family not related to our orioles.

The ninety-odd species of our blackbird family are a notably diverse lot, not only in their appearance but in their behavior. Among its number in the Pacific Northwest is the brightly plumaged Northern (formerly "Baltimore") Oriole, a noteworthy singer that weaves a delicate hanging pouch nest. Then there is the somber Brown-headed Cowbird, which "sings" in a strangled squeak, and as far as can be determined retains no vestige of an instinct for building a nest of any kind.

Numbers are the "bottom line" indicator of any species' success, although they are certainly no guarantee of survival, as demonstrated by the lamented Passenger Pigeon. Its population at the time Europeans began their assault on the Americas has been credibly estimated at 3 billion. It could, in such awesome abundance, have been the world's most plentiful land bird, a place now probably occupied by starlings or House Sparrows.

In North America, our "top bird" could now be the Red-winged Blackbird, an avian success story in its ability to cope with habitat alterations inflicted by modern humans. If you lump it in with other blackbirds, as well as grackles and cowbirds, which band together in their wintering grounds to form massive flocks, there is no doubt about which family is the one of greatest apparent abundance.

Many blackbirds share with starlings the ability to forage by "gaping." They force the bill into rotting wood, clumps of vegetation, flowers, curled leaves, packed ground litter, and moist sod, and then bring into play a special set of strong jaw muscles enabling them to force the bill open. This makes available to them sources of food such as buried insects, slugs, and worms to which surface-foraging birds do not have ready access. See the write-up on Starlings, family Sturnidae, for more on "gaping."

Adaptability, and the attendant opportunism, have been the ticket to success for species that have become plentiful as an offshoot of human impact. In the early days of bird feeding, blackbirds of any kind were rare visitants; the appearance of a Red-winged Blackbird at a northern Michigan feeder in 1921 was an occasion for publication. Now, often to the dismay of bird feeders in the blackbirds' wintering territory, they are all too ready to come to the banquet board.

Blackbirds are similarly abundant winterers in the coastal and more southerly reaches of the Pacific Northwest. Here we have two family members unique to the coast, the Bicolored, a race of the Red-winged, and the Tricolored, a separate species but in many ways very similar to the Red-winged. Since all three join the huge foraging flocks that range winter fields and marshes, the Tricolored is included in the species account of the Red-winged.

Our "Friend"

The versatility of the blackbird family is amply demonstrated by the Brown-headed Cowbird. This unassuming bird has evolved to occupy the niche of the nest parasite amongst our American songbirds. It prospers along with the works of agricultural and urban humankind. Where it winters, it benefits from our feeders.

To what degree does our inadvertent benevolence sabotage the well-being of other birds, including our favorites at the feeder? While the cowbird is not a winter feeder bird in most of the Pacific Northwest, it is expanding both its breeding and wintering range. During the summer of 1993, I had a dozen of them at my feeder. Here, far, far from cattle country, they are at home and flourishing, bold witnesses to an astonishing population explosion and a remarkable range extension.

Given the direct impact it has on our songbirds, plus the evidence of its expanding its winter presence here as it has elsewhere, a general discussion of nest parasitism and of the cowbird's natural history is relevant in any book on Pacific Northwest birds.

Members of widely varying families of birds have independently evolved into nest parasites. The best known of those is the cuckoo of Europe, *Cuculus canorus*. Our North American cuckoos build their own, not surprisingly rather half-hearted affairs. Some honeyguides of Africa are parasitic and, of the cowbirds of the Western Hemisphere, some are parasitic, some are not. There is even a parasitic duck.

Needless to say, with the variety of species that have taken to parasitism, both their strategies and the effect upon their hosts vary greatly. One of the easiest parasites to foster is the young of the aforementioned duck, the Black-headed of South America. Uninhibited by favoritism, the female dumps her eggs into the nests of any other duck species, as well as those of coots, ibises, spoonbills, herons, storks, and gulls, all of which accept the extra egg. When the duckling hatches, all it needs is two days' brooding, then it swims off alone and commences to feed itself.

A changeling of entirely opposite behavior is inflicted on hosts by two species of African honeyguide. Like its newly hatched nestmates, the honeyguide chick is naked and blind, but unlike them has a powerful hooked beak with needle-sharp tips that cross at the ends. It repeatedly bites the host's chicks until they die of multiple lacerations and punctures. Alone, it incessantly imitates the food-begging cries of not one, but two of the hosts' chicks. Halfway through the six-week nestling period, the deadly hooked ends of the beak become blunted. By the time it is ready to leave the nest, it weighs twice as much as each of its foster parents.

A New Relationship

The Brown-headed Cowbird is known to have laid in the nests of more than 200 species. Some—like waterfowl, killdeer, hawks, and even humming-birds—are manifestly unsuitable foster parents. And its hosts are similarly naive; many of them uncritically accept a cowbird egg even though, from its size and pattern, it is obviously a plant.

One supposes, therefore, that this is a relatively new relationship; neither party has had the time to evolve sophisticated responses to the other's tactics. The cowbird's egg is usually larger than those of the host, which gives the chick a size advantage. It also has an incubation period of eleven to twelve days, which may give the cowbird nestling a short but critical head start in the nests of some hosts.

Once hatched, the cowbird has its own suite of options to play. Programmed to wriggle under anything it touches in the nest, and to maneuver it to the rim and over, it gets rid of eggs and fellow nestlings. Or, blessed with a loud voice, a huge mouth, and ravenous appetite, it may simply hog all the food and starve its foster siblings to death right in the nest. In some circumstances, however, it may have to share; there are plenty of examples of its coexisting with apparently healthy nestmates.

One puzzle worth pondering is how young cowbirds avoid what should be a severe identity crisis. Every cowbird you will ever see has to have been raised by other birds, but it will not have imprinted on them. Once fledged, it joins its own kind.

Pre-dawn Infiltration

Identity problems or not, come the nesting season a young female cowbird knows exactly what to do. She stakes out a piece of good nesting habitat, but apparently does not drive other female cowbirds away from it; they seem able to sort out their spacing without territorial aggression. Males court her, and she mates with one or more of them. Patroling her territory, she cues onto potential hosts by their nest-building activities and keeps them under close surveillance.

Her own egg-laying is apparently triggered by the presence of one or more of the hosts' eggs in their nest. If she laid an egg in an empty nest, the foster parents would likely desert or eject the egg. Most songbirds, by the way, lay an egg a day, early in the morning, then stay away from the nest until they have a full clutch. The cowbird usually removes one of the host's eggs and eats it, sometimes the day before laying her own egg, sometimes the day after. She makes her calls in early dawn, before the owner lays her own daily egg. On the critical day of egg-laying the cowbird works quickly, taking no more than two minutes to do the job. Sometimes her sit-and-run hit takes no more than five seconds. Then she's gone, forever.

The literature cites cases of two or more cowbird eggs or nestlings in one nest. The usual explanation is that more than one cowbird has parasitized it.

A cowbird's first round of egg-laying (one hesitates to call it a "clutch"), in which she usually lays six eggs, all of them in different nests, may be followed by one or two more rounds, depending on the availability of host nests. During a good season she could lay twenty or more; some authors claim forty.

The question then is, why aren't there more cowbirds than there are? Almost certainly there are more cowbirds than there *were*, particularly compared to the period after the demise of the bison and before its replacement by the domestic cow.

There are, for the cowbirds, problems in dealing with birds that have had time to evolve countermeasures. Some birds, such as robins, catbirds, Blue Jays, Eastern Kingbirds, Cedar Waxwings, and Brown Thrashers, either puncture or eject cowbird eggs. This rejection is an odd-egg-out reflex; if given several cowbird eggs and one of their own, they eject their own! Some warblers tend to nest in loose association with Red-winged Blackbirds and sustain a lower incidence of parasitism because the aggressive blackbirds drive off trespassing cowbirds. Cowbird chicks in American Goldfinch nests frequently die of malnutrition on the straight diet of seeds the goldfinch nestlings thrive on.

What with normal predation added to the evasive tactics of their hosts, cowbirds have to lay large numbers of eggs to sustain their numbers. According to *The Birder's Handbook*, a recent study shows that only 3 percent of cowbird eggs result in adults. The handbook doesn't specify whether this study was done in populations of birds that have evolved adaptive countermeasures. If so, the survival data for cowbirds operating amidst populations of naive birds could be much higher.

Red-winged and Tricolored Blackbirds

Agelaius phoeniceus and *A. tricolor*

Formerly, and regionally, "swamp blackbird," "red-winged starling," "marsh blackbird," "redwing," "soldier blackbird," and (best description of all) "red-shouldered blackbird"; "Tricolored" (and *tricolor*) from red and white of epaulette, and black of body; *Agelaius* from Greek *agelaios*, "flocking"; *phoeniceus* is Latin for "red," from crimson or purple dye made in Tyre from shellfish and traded by the Phoenicians.

Description

Slimmer than robin; adult male glossy black with bright red shoulder patch partially edged in yellow, white in the case of the Tricolored; adult female sparrow-patterned, dusky-flecked brown above, pale undersides boldly streaked in dark brown; first-year male a strong pattern of dull black and rusty brown, shoulder patch dull, flecked with brown.

Behavior

Very social; Red-wingeds nest in a community of territories, Tricoloreds nest in dense colonies; in autumn both forage in flocks large enough to be major pests in grain crops; flocks visit feeders, eat hurriedly, then depart; Red-winged males show stronger tendency than females to form one-gender groups; both very agile, quick to adapt to hanging feeders; Red-winged song a very distinctive, musical "*onk-la-reeeee*," with extended emphasis on the final trill; Tricolored song a more nasal version, "*on-kee-kaaaa*"; Red-winged call an emphatic "*chack*"; alarm note a down-slurred "*tee-err*"; Tricolored call a nasal "*chemp*"; flocks in winter to feedlots, golf courses, orchards, and farmyards.

Range

Northerly populations of the Red-winged are migratory, progressively less the farther south you go; breeds throughout the continent from northern margin of boreal forest south to Central America; breeds throughout Pacific Northwest wherever wetlands, low meadows, or irrigated land are found; common winterer/year-round resident wherever coastal marshes, river valleys, and reservoirs provide generally ice-free conditions. The Tricoloreds' winter center of abundance is southwestern Oregon and adjacent northwestern California.

Food

Omnivorous; feed on the ground and at the seed heads of field crops, including small grains, corn, and sunflowers; weed seeds, grubs, and insects; at the feeder, cracked grain, sunflower seeds.

Nest

Red-wingeds nest in cattails, sedges, rushes, near or over shallow water; in willows, weed clumps, grass tussocks in dry areas; base of sedge stems, grass, rootlets bound to surrounding stems with strips of plant fiber (milkweed where available); cup lined with fine grasses; from three inches to fourteen feet off the ground. Tricoloreds' habits similar, except that nests are very close together, sometimes in immense colonies that extend from marshland into neighboring shrubbery and trees.

Comment

The distinctive voice of the Red-winged male is as much a field mark as his sleek, black coat and shoulder flashes. So is his defense behavior. When a visitor

P. SAWATZKI
1991 ©

nears a nesting group, the males announce themselves by fluttering aloft in a peculiar, awkward-looking display flight calculated to show off the bright red "epaulettes" to best effect. If the interloper doesn't get the message, the riled-up males will swoop, delivering smart buffets to the head the closer the prowler gets to the nest. If blackbirds choose a garden hedge to nest in, their aggressiveness can be a considerable nuisance.

There is a color phase of the Red-winged, the Bicolor of central California, that has a red epaulette without the yellow border.

REF: Red-winged: A(W)—456; GO—298; NG—420; P(W)—308

Tricolored: A(W)—457; GO—298; NG—420; P(W)—308

Brewer's Blackbird

Euphagus cyanocephalus

"Brewer's" after American physician/ornithologist Thomas M. Brewer (1814–1880); *Euphagus* from Greek *eu*, "good," and *phago*, "to eat," unclear whether reference is to the edibility of the bird, or to its own appetite; *cyanocephalus* from Greek *kyanos*, "blue," and *kephale*, "head."

Description
Slightly smaller than robin; male all-black with yellow eye; iridescent, the head purple, the body greenish, brightest in late winter and spring; female brownish gray with no streaking as in female Red-winged.

Behavior
Strongly social; in winter joins foraging flocks of Red-wingeds and grackles; feeds on ground by "gaping," a habit it may use even among loose seeds on a feeder shelf; call a harsh "*chack*," song a wheezing creak, "*tuk-tuk-ksheee.*"

Range
Migratory, but more likely to stay the winter the closer to the coast one gets and the farther south; originally a western bird, now breeding east of Great Lakes; favors open, brushy habitat on field edges, ditches, streams.

Food
Insects, spiders, weed seeds, grain; may occasionally wade and dabble in shallow water; at feeder, chicken scratch, sunflower seeds.

Nest
From low shrubs to trees as high as 150 feet up, often conifers; in tall sedges, or on hummocks of vegetation growing in water; even occasionally in tree cavity or on broken snag; sturdy base of fine twigs and grasses, cup of grasses, pine

-P. SAWATZKY-
1992 ©

needles, plant fibers often mortared with mud or cow manure; lining of fine rootlets, hair.

Comment

Elsewhere on the continent blackbirds have demonstrated their versatility by becoming regular, and in many cases all too plentiful, feeder birds. In John Dennis's *A Complete Guide to Bird Feeding,* they are dealt with in a chapter titled "Things That Go Wrong" under a subhead "Unruly Guests." Depending on where you feed birds in the Pacific Northwest, both the Red-winged and the Brewer's Blackbird can be rated anywhere from unusual to overabundant. The Christmas Bird Count results show an abundance center in central to northern California.

REF: A(W)—551; GO—298; NG—422; P(W)—306

Brown-headed Cowbird

Molothrus ater

Also and/or formerly "buffalo bird," "cow blackbird," "cow bunting," "lazy bird," "cuckold,"and "eastern," "Nevada," or "common" cowbird; "Cowbird" from habitual association with grazing cattle; Greek *Molothrus* applied in confusion instead of *molobrus*, "a parasite, greedy person"; *ater* Latin for "black."

Description

Smaller than robin; stubby, sparrowlike bill; male appears black at a distance, but close up, dusky brown head and neck are visible; body iridescent black; female dull gray-brown, very faintly streaked underparts.

Behavior

Seasonally social, in summer solitary or in loose pairing groups, in winter may join other blackbirds and starlings in large foraging/roosting flocks; visits feeders singly or in small groups; forages on ground, walks about with tail tilted

P. SAWATZKY

up; in warm seasons hangs around cattle, perched on their backs, pursuing insects underfoot; during breeding season males maintain vigil from a tall tree-top, calling periodically; courting song of male a low gurgle with squeaky "*glug-glug-ge-leek*"; call a high-pitched, sibilant whistle followed by two lower notes, syllabized as "*wheeeee-tse-tse*"; alarm note an abrupt "*chuck.*"

Range

Migratory; throughout continent in open woodland and agricultural lands, and in suburban yards and parks; plentiful in summer throughout Pacific Northwest; winters almost exclusively along coastal lowlands from Canadian border to Baja California.

Food

Insects, especially grasshoppers; cutworms; weed seeds and grain; at feeders, most seeds, small grains, cracked corn.

Nest

None; brood parasite in other birds' nests; Yellow Warbler may react to cowbird egg by rebuilding on top of it, sometimes creating a stacked nest three or more layers deep.

Comment

The cowbird is North America's answer to the cuckoo of Eurasia, famous for laying its eggs in other birds' nests and leaving all the work of brooding and feeding to the deceived foster parents. Rather drab, a somewhat retiring, even polite, feeder guest, it has been the subject of much study because its reproductive strategy is anything but unassuming. Once a bird apparently linked to the Great Plains and its herds of bison, it has spread, with industrialized humans and their bulldozers, crops, and cattle, far beyond where it, and the buffalo, once roamed.

REF: A(W)—679; GO—300; NG—422; P(W)—310

Finch family

Family Fringillidae, Subfamily Carduelinae

Depending upon which reference one consults, and its date, the family Fringillidae totals more than 500 species, the largest in the bird world. Within this group are some 125 species (again writers differ) comprising the subfamily Carduelinae, 9 of these being the Pacific Northwest's familiar native finches. The contradictions arise because bird classification is a constantly evolving process that renders old references ever more obsolete. It generates debate and jobs within the ornithological establishment, and it is good for the field guide business. But unless you are very sensitive to the scorn you might suffer by appearing afield with a guide that is two or three names out of date, don't rush off to the bookstore.

Finches are regarded, along with the corvids (jays and crows) as the most recently evolved birds; some species show high levels of specialization, others, great adaptability. Whatever the route to survival, finches have been very successful at colonizing new territories and exploiting new niches. It was the finches of the Galapagos Islands that helped Charles Darwin formulate his monumental theory of evolution. From a single species that somehow reached these remote islands evolved a variety of new species to fill the available niches.

One of the most famous of these is the Woodpecker Finch. Lacking the natural equipment to probe into holes for wood-boring grubs, this bird uses a twig or thorn held in its bill. It not only selects suitable probes, but trims and clips them, thus demonstrating both ingenuity of a high order and sophisticated tool use.

Finches are predominantly seed eaters, with stout bills, heavy skulls, and strong jaw muscles for cracking tough husks and crushing hard seeds. The Eurasian Hawfinch, with a bill even larger than that of our Evening Grosbeak, can exert a force of more than ninety pounds, sufficient to crack olive pits.

Most finches have a crop for storing food and a powerful gizzard for grinding it up. Some feed their young exclusively on a milky porridge of regurgitated seeds, others may provide a mix of seeds and insects as a starter formula, switching exclusively to seeds as the nestlings develop.

Compulsive Songsters

A feature common to the carduelines is their singing ability. While most birds sing only in their nesting territories in the breeding season, carduelines sing wherever they happen to be, and at any time of year.

The familiar canary, bred from the wild Serin of the Canary Islands, *Serinus canaria*, has been a domesticated cage pet from at least as early as the time of the ancient Greeks. The variety that has brightened generations of homes from its wire cage was imported into Italy from the Canary Islands in the sixteenth century. Easy to keep on a simple diet of seeds, it is now bred in an astonishing variety of plumage colors and patterns.

Its singing ability is legendary. In the early years of this century, British fanciers taught a bullfinch to whistle "God Save the King." The bird invariably hesitated at the end of the third line, and if he paused a bit too long, a canary in the next room, which had picked up the melody on its own, would chime in and finish it for him.

The finches of our northern winters are famous throughout the continent (and the hemisphere, for the five that are circumpolar) for their erratic, usually massive winter migrations, or "irruptions." The degree of irruptive behavior of these northern finches depends on the diet of each species. The American Goldfinch, the least "northern" of the lot, is also the most consistently migratory. It feeds primarily on the seeds of low-growing weeds, particularly dandelions and thistles. These either scatter upon ripening or are covered by snow in winter. Thus, with their northern food supply very likely to be buried, goldfinches fly far enough south to avoid the problem, in all winters staying over, in greater or lesser numbers, in the milder regions of the Pacific Northwest.

In contrast, other wintering finches such as crossbills find their natural food higher up in spruce and pine trees well above the snow, which may be one reason they do not follow a set migratory pattern.

Feeding above the snow level is no guarantee of stability, however. Crossbills are the most irruptive northern finches. Years of superabundant spruce cone crops alternate with years of sparse production over vast expanses of boreal forest. Crossbills have therefore evolved into foraging nomads, migrating west–east as well as south in search of productive tracts of evergreens. Finding them, they not only settle in to feed, but may commence nesting. They are on record as raising broods every month of the year throughout the Northern Hemisphere where conifer forests happen to have produced abundantly for that particular season.

Pink Finches

The males of four species that can occur in the Pacific Northwest are pink or reddish to varying degrees: the Purple, Rosy, House, and Cassin's Finches. Species accounts of the House and Purple, the two most likely to turn up at feeders here, are provided below. The Cassin's and the Rosy nest in isolated mountainous parts of the region, and rate as rare and irregular winter visitors at lower elevations. Interesting though they are in their own right, they are so unlikely to visit feeders anywhere in the region that they did not justify species accounts.

A Word About "Grosbeaks"

The name "grosbeak" has been applied as a handy descriptive name to several birds in different subfamilies, all of whom bear similarly heavy-duty bills. The result has been slightly confusing; Evening and Pine Grosbeaks aren't really grosbeaks, taxonomically, but are members of the Cardueline Finch subfamily. Cardinals, Rose-breasted and Black-headed Grosbeaks, and Lazuli Buntings are true grosbeaks, members of the Emberezidae family. This is why, in properly ordered reference books and field guides, Evening and Pine Grosbeaks are illustrated amongst the goldfinches and Purple Finches, not among the true grosbeaks.

Pine Grosbeak

Pinicola enucleator

Finch family. "Pine" from usual habitat; *Pinicola* from Latin "pine" and *colere*, "inhabit"; *enucleator* is Latin for "one who shells," descriptive of the birds' habit of husking spruce cones.

Description

Chunky, robin-sized; short, dark, strongly curved bill; adult male dusky-pink, sometimes with patches or flecks of gray; darkish line through eye; moderately long, dark, slightly forked tail; wings dark with two white bars; subadult male soft gray with crown and rump rusty rose; adult female gray with shading of olive to russet on crown and rump; larger than other pink finches (crossbills and Purple), with relatively longer tail and no bold striping like Purple.

P. SAWATZKY ©
1990

Behavior

Sociable; flocks often segregated by gender and age, females and immatures in separate groups from adult males; placid, sometimes very tame; call a gentle, high-pitched "*tew-tew-tew*"; song is a brief, pleasant, unenergetic warble.

Range

Nomadically migratory; northern boreal forest breeder, circumpolar in distribution; in Pacific Northwest, breeds in northern Cascades and northern Sierra Nevada; may appear in winter almost anywhere in Washington, western Oregon, and north-central Idaho.

Food

Particularly fond of ash tree seeds, and buds and catkins of poplars; mainstay is spruce seeds, periodic failures of this source accounting for their drift south in some winters; readily accepts sunflower seeds at feeders.

Nest

Loose, bulky platform of twigs, fibers, lichens; midheight in a conifer or birch, or low in juniper or underbrush.

Comment

"Ridiculously tame" is the phrase used for these easygoing birds in *The Birder's Handbook*. Tufts, in *Birds of Nova Scotia,* recalls days at the turn of the century when boys could hit them with snowballs and kill them with their slingshots. I have never encountered any so foolishly trusting, but around the feeder they are calm and gentle birds, exhibiting none of that otherwise typical hyper finch aggressiveness.

Occasional reference is made to their apparent evolution away from dependence on tree seeds to a diet of buds, fruits, and weed seeds, and that they are especially fond of crabapples. *Birds Around Us* says they relish cranberries, either canned or fresh. For several winters past I have therefore stored a bag of high-bush cranberries in the freezer where they await the opportunity to test the postulated change of tastes of these loveliest of winter birds.

REF: A(W)—725; GO—316; NG—436; P(W)—342

Purple Finch

Carpodacus purpureus

"Finch" is from Germanic *fink,* and Anglo-Saxon *finc,* but ultimate roots are possibly from Indo-European *pingo,* echoic of birds' calls; *Carpodacus* is from Greek *carpos* for "fruit" (i.e., seed) and *dacos* for "biting"; *purpureus* is

Latin for "crimson," more descriptive of bird's color than misleading English "purple."

Description

Roger Tory Peterson's "like a sparrow dipped in raspberry juice" is most apt description of male; color brightest on head, rump, lighter on throat, breast, flanks; dark ear patch on side of head, lighter eyebrow streak; dark brown wings checked and lined with subdued pattern, all with rose wash; tail dark, well notched; females, immatures heavily streaked on breast and back in browns, light beige; belly off-white; at first glance male could be mistaken for male Pine Grosbeak or crossbill, and its similarity to the Cassin's, Rosy, and House Finch males makes differentiation a challenge.

Behavior

Sociable; flocks may be divided by sex and age, all-male or all-female-and-immatures; aggressive behavior at feeders intensified by crowding; flight fights have been observed in which grappling pairs thrash straight up for many yards and fall back to ground, still struggling desperately; calls a musical "*churr-lee*" and sharp "*tink*" in flight; song a rapid, clearly enunciated, rich warble, ending with down-slurred "*too-eee*," delivered from treetops, occasionally also from flight with no loss of exuberant energy.

Range

Variably migratory; irruptive from breeding range in northern boreal forest and adjacent mixed woodlands of Canada; regular winterer along a band west of the Cascades through Pacific Northwest south through California.

Food

Primarily seeds; some tree buds and poplar catkins; insects and berries in summer; sunflower seeds are favorite feeder fare, but will eat other seeds and suet, if "flowers" run out; will use high shelves; agile enough to use hanging feeders.

Nest

Well up in tall conifer if available, otherwise at variable heights in deciduous trees or shrubs; well-hidden cup of fine twigs, grasses, and rootlets selected to blend into surroundings.

Comment

In his *Joy of Birding*, Chuck Bernstein notes that warblers do not really warble, that Purple Finches and goldfinches do. Among my warmest recollections of bird feeding at our cottage are bright late-winter days when the trees in the yard were thronging with these merry finches. About noon each day they would fill the sheltered valley with song.

Recalling these idyllic interludes brings to mind an incident related by Seton in *The Birds of Manitoba*. On May 14, 1884, he "collected" a male Purple Finch. Shooting birds was then the standard method of verifying sightings, but it seemed a trifle ghoulish of him to go on and note that he blew it away "in full song." We can be thankful that the ready-made technology of modern cameras, binoculars, and field guides has made bird "collecting" almost completely unnecessary.

REF: A(W)—723; GO—316; NG—440; P(W)—342

House Finch

Carpodacus mexicanus

"House" for association with dwellings; locally and formerly "California linnet"; *Carpodacus* from Greek *carpos* for "fruit," *dacos* for "biting," apt for bird that eats the "fruit" (seeds) of plants; *mexicanus* is Latinized "of Mexico" where type specimens were collected in 1776.

Description

Slimmer than slightly larger Purple Finch; male has brown cap; "headband" over eyes, and the throat, breast, and rump are orangey red, brighter and more clearly demarcated than in male Purple; wings and back brown-patterned without the raspberry wash of the Purple Finch; underbelly more streaked than in Purple; in some males, the colored areas, especially breast, are copper yellow; female brown-streaked overall, with facial pattern much less noticeable than in female Purple.

Behavior

Sociable; comes very readily to feeders, sometimes in noisy, take-charge bunch where it may displace House Sparrows; travels with siskins, Purple Finches; call notes shrill "*wheer*" or sharp "*pit*"; habits resemble those of House Sparrow, except that both sexes sing, a cascade of sweet notes and whistles mixed with slurred, harsh "*wheer*" notes in descending pitch.

Range

Largely nonmigratory; originally native to Southwest United States and Mexico; first recorded in western Oregon and Washington in the 1940s, and since has spread throughout the region; is especially at home in cities, suburbs, and farmsteads.

Food

Very much a seed eater, consuming very few insects; occasional fruit, berries, nuts, especially from ornamentals in urban areas; an orchard pest in California, where it strips trees of buds; at feeders, goes for most small seeds and sunflowers.

Nest

In either cavities or trees; cavities include buildings, birdhouses, tree holes, or old nests of Cliff Swallow, robin, oriole; tree nest an untidy collection of twigs, grasses, and debris, lined with same material; five feet or higher in dense foliage in vine, shrub, or tree.

Comment

This native finch is an ongoing sensation in the bird world by virtue of its becoming a successful "exotic" in its own country, and its explosive colonization of new range. The excitement began in 1941 when pet shops in Brooklyn, New York, were caught selling "Hollywood finches" shipped in from California. To avoid prosecution under the Migratory Bird Act, some dealers let their stock go. The "Hollywood finch" has now spread throughout most of the eastern United States and adjacent Canada, and is still expanding its range. According to Terry Root in *Atlas of Wintering North American Birds*, they use feeders so much that the shape of their bills has changed, allowing them to open sunflower seeds more efficiently than their western counterparts can. Fast-track adaptability!

Whilst all this energetic expansion was going on in the east, the Southwestern population was spreading east and northwest. It seems that this versatile bird has found a great ally in humans and is taking full advantage of the alliance in both its established and its introduced populations.

Their colonization pattern is interesting; the first pioneering birds are migratory, leaving their new territory in winter. But as subsequent generations acclimatize themselves they become sedentary, redirecting their traveling urge to scouting out, and settling, new frontiers.

Like many aggressive colonizing species, the House Finch has achieved superabundance in parts of its new territory. In California its taste for buds and blossoms of orchard trees has made it a major agricultural pest. And bird feeder catalogs now advertise "House Finch–proof" feeders.

Given the westerly push of the transplanted eastern population, and the eastward shift of the original western population, the two will soon reunite, if they haven't already met and melded somewhere in East Texas or Oklahoma.

REF: A(W)—588; GO—316; NG—440; P(W)—342

Evening Grosbeak
Coccothraustes vespertinus

Finch family. "Evening" assigned in 1823 by American ornithologist W. C. Cooper, who first recorded it one evening northwest of Lake Superior; "Grosbeak" from French *gros*, "large," and *bec*, "beak"; *Coccothraustes* from Greek *kokkos*, "kernel," and *thrauo*, "shatter," nicely describing feeding method; *vespertinus* Latin for "evening."

Description
Chunky, robin-sized with thick, heavy bill; males in bold pattern of black, white, yellow that can't be mistaken for any other winter bird; females shaded gray-buff on head (darkest), back, breast, belly, rump; wings and tail black with white marks; chalky white bill of both sexes peels in late winter to uncover light lime-green breeding color.

Behavior
Sociable, in noisy flocks of a half dozen, often many more; crowds onto feeders with considerable jostling and bickering; tame when habituated to presence of feeder attendant; undulating flight, accompanied by strong "*keer*" notes; call a clear, musical chirp; song a robust, rambly warble.

Range
Erratically and massively migratory; breeds southward from Canadian border through coniferous uplands of Rockies including northern and southwestern Idaho, northern and western Washington, the Cascades in Oregon, Klamath and Sierra Nevada of northern California; depending on coniferous cone crop may winter in breeding range, but can turn up virtually anywhere in Pacific Northwest in some winters.

Food
Conifer seeds, juniper berries, maple seeds; seeks out salt from treated roadways and livestock licks; huge appetite for sunflower seeds at feeders.

Nest

Shambly cup of twigs thinly interwoven with lichens and plant fibers; usually well up in tree, preferably conifer, close to trunk in crotch or well out on limb concealed in twigs.

Comment

It used to be called the Sociable Grosbeak; this or "wandering" or "western" would be more descriptive than the meaningless "Evening." The ornithologist (Cooper) who named it is the same fellow after whom the Cooper's Hawk is named.

It has been noted from the early 1800s as an irregular winter visitant throughout the East, sometimes appearing in great numbers in New England and down the East Coast. Once breeding strictly in the West, it has rapidly shifted eastward. Its expansion is attributed to a combination of agricultural settlement, the accompanying widespread planting of box elder with their abundant winterfast seeds, and winter bird feeding.

What seem to be irregular, aimless wanderings may in fact be a flexible itinerary of alternative paths that the birds follow in search of winter feed. Certainly they range far; birds banded at Seven Sisters in eastern Manitoba have been reported from Newport, Tennessee; Cedar Rapids, Iowa; Hale, Michigan; Owen, Wisconsin; Coulee City, Washington; and Bemidji, Minnesota. The fact that they have the longest wings in proportion to their size of any of the other North American finches suggests they evolved in response to the benefits, and demands, of long-distance flight.

REF: A(W)—717; GO—310; NG—442; P(W)—344

Crossbills

Family Fringillidae, Subfamily Carduelinae, Genus *Loxia*

Carduelinae is rooted in another Latin word, *carduus,* "thistle," and it means "goldfinch." The cheery "thistlebird" is thus the flag-bearing species for the branch of the finch family that includes so many of the familiar native seed eaters so welcome at winter feeding stations across the Pacific Northwest.

Worldwide there are only three species of crossbills; our Red and White-winged range throughout the Northern Hemisphere and are joined in Eurasia by the Parrot Crossbill, *Loxia pytyopsittacus.* All of them closely resemble each other, and all are specialized to harvest the seeds of cone-bearing evergreens. Such differences as there are arise from further specialization, according to which particular conifers a species is most closely associated with.

A Food Specialist

In spite of the obvious, vast abundance of cone-bearing trees in the subarc-tic reaches of the Northern Hemisphere, there are difficulties connected to a conifer-dependent existence. Conifers are unreliable sources of very small seeds, housing them under tough scales in cones that open when it is in the tree's interests to release seeds to the wind. Cracking ripe but unopened cones is hard work, demanding special tools and skills.

The twisted beak of the crossbill is such a tool. As a fledgling it has a normal bill. But at four weeks the ends of the bill begin to twist sideways, one to the right, the other to the left. Which does which is varied, some birds being left-crossed, some right. The jawbones themselves are straight; only the horny outer sheaths are crooked.

A Red Crossbill attacks a spruce cone by gripping it solidly with its powerful, oversized feet, perhaps first clipping the cone off for more convenient handling on the nearest steady perch. It inserts the tip of the upper mandible under a cone scale, bracing the lower mandible against the outside of the scale at the bottom. With special muscles it moves the jaws sideways in a lateral shearing action to pry the scale out, aiding this move with a twist of the head. This cracks the cone scale vertically. Holding it open, the bird inserts its large, muscular tongue equipped at the tip with a cartilaginous cutting edge and shears off the enclosed seed.

This shucking process is carried on with rapid, assembly-line efficiency. A flock of crossbills working through a grove of conifers creates a sound like falling rain, what with the noise of the snapping scales and the shower of debris hitting the ground. It should be pointed out that other species of birds—grosbeaks, siskins, and others—are also conifer-seed eaters, and shuck cones with their conventional beaks. In the fight for survival, however, extra efficiencies in the exploitation of a major food source can save crucial energy, confer that extra bit of nourishment, and otherwise spell the difference between life and death when margins are small.

Anyone who has tried to force apart the hard, thick scales of an unopened Lodgepole Pine cone discovers that it is built to stay resolutely clenched until time, or the heat of a forest fire, melts the cementing resin and it opens to release its imprisoned seeds. Spruce cones are large but the scales can be pried open, while the larch bears the smallest and least-armored cones.

The Parrot Crossbill of Eurasia is associated with pines and has the largest and heaviest bill, the larch-harvesting White-winged the lightest, and the Red, reflecting its affinity for spruce, in between.

Feast and Famine

Another problem for conifer-dependent seed eaters is the trees' irregular seed-bearing cycle. With no obvious, consistent connection to environmental causes, such as weather, they alternate a year of abundant cone production with several years of meager yield. The only consistencies seem to be that all the trees of a given species over great expanses of northland do it in rhythm.

Nut-bearing trees follow a similar regime. Even cultivated ones retain their own agenda, frustrating orchardists' best efforts to optimize growing conditions and otherwise to beguile them into "forgetting" their imprinted capriciousness.

It has been postulated, in a scenario that has its detractors, that the northern conifers use this mechanism to starve out the populations of animals that feed on their seeds. Unlike many plants, they do not have a system of traded benefits in which the plant provides food in exchange for pollination, seed dispersal, or some other inadvertent service. The cone-seed eaters are predators, the seeds, their prey.

Operating in a system of evolutionary one-upmanship, each side has developed its own strategies. The trees alternately swamp the predators with so many seeds they cannot possibly eat them all, and then cut production almost entirely to starve them out. Given the vast expanses over which this supposedly managed famine is wrought, it is for the numberless, unwitting seed eaters a calamity of awesome proportions and incalculable misery. Red Squirrels instinctively hedge against this feast-and-famine regime by storing, in feast years, two winters' worth of spruce cones, as many as 15,000.

Crossbills do not have this option. What they do have is the ability to nest whenever and wherever there is sufficient food. For, while conifers over great areas might synchronize their seeding schedule, it is not continentwide, nor is it coordinated among species. Thus, when the White Spruce of Alaska–Yukon abruptly fail, the regional Black Spruce or tamaracks might partially fill in. If they do not, perhaps the spruce of boreal Minnesota have produced a bumper crop.

This imposes a fly-or-die option in which the birds in huge numbers erupt from their breeding grounds in an urgent search for food. Whether salvation is a matter of luck or whether there are subtle clues that tell them where to look is not known. Whichever is the case, they sometimes show up in swarms, in places far removed from their normal haunts.

Cameron B. Kepler in *The Encyclopedia of Birds* reports that from a batch of migrant crossbills banded in Switzerland, some were recorded the following fall and winter in southwestern Europe, while others appeared in later years in northern Russia, 2,500 miles from the banding site. The suggestion is that, however widely crossbills rove, they retain fidelity to a home range and may return there if they survive long enough.

Historic Invasions

If they find a land of plenty where several conifer species are producing bountifully, with cones ripening in sequential seasons, the opportunistic birds will keep on nesting as long as the food holds out, irrespective of the weather. Their ability to raise young in the bitterest of conditions is discussed in Mid-winter Nesting in Chapter 6, Those Fascinating Birds.

Irruptions of crossbills have been so massive they have been written into history. In A.D. 1251 Matthew Paris wrote about the unusual birds that invaded England and devastated the apple crop. Chroniclers in Europe, Japan, and North America have noted the mysterious and sometimes destructive invasions of strange birds that abruptly appeared and then vanished, not to be seen again for generations.

When they show up at our feeders, they demonstrate that, while they are highly specialized foragers, they have not lost the adaptability that typifies the finch family. They can turn their bent bills to sunflower seeds, even suet. And in keeping with their exotic appearance, they often betray an exotic taste for highly unusual foods. Amused observers have watched them eating ashes, frozen dishwater, tea leaves, charcoal, bits of mortar, spots of frozen dog urine in the snow, and salt. They frequently suffer heavy mortality on highways when they go after road salt. Perhaps these unpalatable substances help to counteract the sticky resin that they constantly encounter in their normal feeding.

Red Crossbill

Loxia curvirostra

Finch family. "Crossbill" descriptive of the seemingly misshapen beak; *Loxia* from Greek *loxos*, "crooked"; *curvirostra* is Latin for "curved bill."

Description

House Sparrow-sized; ends of large bill crossed; tail short, notched; adult male dull red with sooty brown wings and tail; abdomen and undertail coverts

P. SAWNSSKI ©
1990

gray; female olive-buff on back and head with close pattern of brown check-marks; belly, undertail, and rump olive-yellow; wings and tail dark.

Behavior

Social, usually in flocks, chattering in flight; swarm through conifers like miniature parrots, climbing with bills and feet; grip cones with feet, expertly pry open the scales; at close quarters, as at a window feeder, further parrotlike behavior obvious in use of the large tongue to work kernels out of sunflower seeds; often very tame and easily approached; call a repeated sharp *"jit-jit-jit,"* song a melody of vigorous canarylike warbles punctuated with clear *"too-tee too-tee too-tee-tee"* whistles.

Range

Nonmigratory, but highly nomadic; core habitat is northern and mountain coniferous forests, but wanders erratically within this range and occasionally far out of it, winter or summer; sometime visitant in great numbers anywhere through Pacific Northwest where conifers are bearing seeds.

Food

Seeds of spruce, larch, fir, pine; may also use elm seeds, and in times of starvation will eat fruit, including orchard apples; nestlings fed a porridge of regurgitated seeds and fluid; at feeder, takes sunflowers, nutmeats, cracked cereal grains.

Nest

In conifer at edge of woodland; usually high up, well concealed among twigs at end of branch; bulky base of twigs, built up with grasses, lichen, bark shreds; lining of fine grass, hair, fur, feathers; punky wood worked in as filler in winter nests; eggs pale bluish white with purplish brown specks and scrawls near the large end; only female broods, fed by male.

Comment

One of the real delights of winter feeding is to have a flock of these unique northerners share space with you. If you happen to have a grove of conifers nearby, some of them might decide to settle in and raise a brood, as a pair did in the winter of 1987–88 at my feeding station in Winnipeg. From late January to early March, the male and female regularly fed at my office window tray, an arm's length from my word processor. Whether they succeeded in raising any young I do not know, for none came to the feeder. They shared the close-by spruce with Blue Jays, and the neighborhood was prowled by the inevitable skulk of cats. I also wondered if sunflowers were an adequate substitute for the nestlings' natural diet of conifer seeds.

REF: A(W)—721; GO—322; NG—436; P(W)—340

White-winged Crossbill

Loxia leucoptera

Finch family. Wings are actually black, with two white bars, making the common British name "Two-barred" more descriptive; *Loxia* from Greek *loxos* "crooked"; *leucoptera* from Greek *leucos*, "white," and *pteran*, "wing."

Description

House Sparrow-sized; ends of bill crossed; short tail notched; adult male dusky rose, eye darkly shadowed; wings black, with white tips on tertials and two bold white bars; female yellowish olive under lines of brown spots, with white bars on dark wings.

Behavior

Social, flocks chattering in flight; often very tame and trusting; parrotlike in climbing about conifer cones and twigs with bills and feet as they forage, and in use of large tongue to husk sunflower seeds at feeders; call a single, clear "*peet*" or a rapid, raspy "*jeet-jeet-jeet*" in flight; song a sustained series of canarylike warbles and trills punctuated by harsh rattles.

Range

Circumpolar; irruptively migratory from home range in boreal and mountain evergreen forests in Northern Hemisphere; somewhat more northerly in North American breeding range than Red Crossbill; erratic winter visits determined by presence of sufficient numbers of seed-bearing conifers.

Food

Seeds of conifers, especially larch; at feeder, takes sunflower seeds, peanuts, cracked grains, occasional suet.

Nest

Indistinguishable from that of Red Crossbill; bulky, base of twigs carrying cup of grasses, lichens, bark shreds, leaves, lining of rootlets, lichen, punky wood, hair, feathers; usually well up in conifer, on end of branch, well hidden; eggs pale bluish or greenish white spotted or splotched lightly with dark purple at large end; male feeds female during incubation and for first few days of brooding, his calling and hovering flight song a clue to nest location; like Red, nests at any time of year.

P. SAWATZKY
1991 ©

Comment

Both the Red and White-winged are noted as food specialists, their breeding governed by the abundance of conifer seeds, their irruptive migrations by scarcity of this wild crop. Observers note that the White-billed feeds on larch seeds, borne in a small cone of relatively flimsy construction compared to the much heavier spruce and pine cones favored by the Red. Tools matching task, the White-winged's bill is noticeably less rugged than the Red's.

REF: A(W)—722; GO—322; NG—436; P(W)—340

Redpolls

Family Fringillidae, Subfamily Carduelinae, Genus *Carduelis*

This genus includes goldfinches and siskins; *Carduelis* is Latin for "goldfinch."

Redpolls are circumpolar, and in both Eurasia and North America have the same scientific names. In English field guides our Common Redpoll is simply the Redpoll, and our Hoary is the Arctic. Whether they should continue to be two species is a question that birders and taxonomists on both sides of Bering Strait continue to debate. Peterson, in the most recent edition of his field guide to western birds, treats them as one species, stating that the Hoary is " ... now regarded as a northern population of the 'Common' Redpoll." The Audubon field guide to western birds, however, says that in areas where their ranges overlap, they do not interbreed, " ... although some experts consider them two forms of a single species."

The problem for birdwatchers and taxonomists is that between the extremes of the darkest Commons and the lightest Hoaries, the distinguishing field marks gradually blend from one to the other. In this continuum there is no point where everyone would agree that "up to here they are all Commons, beyond here, all Hoaries." This suggests that they do in fact interbreed, and that they will be reclassified as one species.

During migratory rambles, Hoaries mingle indiscriminately with Commons. Therefore, bird feeders will continue to squint through their binoculars and field guides, hanging on the pickets of indecision between a genuine Hoary and a pallid Common.

Like the other "northern" finches, redpolls are "all-or-nothing" erratic migrants, appearing in huge flocks one winter, totally absent for several seasons following. Several winters ago, a farmer near our cottage left part of a small field of sunflowers unharvested. By late winter redpolls swarmed like locusts over the ranks of frozen stalks. In the last two winters, however, we have been lucky to have one or two of these birds at our feeder all winter.

Whatever their winter abundance, they vanish in spring from all of the Pacific Northwest to return to their tundra homeland. As an adaptive adjustment to this harsh environment, redpolls are better able to withstand cold temperatures than any other songbird yet studied. Their short incubation period of ten days is a further survival advantage in the hurry-up summer of the high Arctic.

In common with many other northern birds, redpolls often show remarkable tameness. There is at least one record of a bird-bander able to just pick them off her window feeder, and there are many accounts of these bold little birds captivating people by alighting on their heads and shoulders as they reloaded their feeders. This tameness is often attributed to the birds' northern origins, where they have no contact with humans and have therefore not learned to fear them. Another theory is that they are conditioned by the uncertain productivity of their environment to suspend normal caution and go for food whenever the chance presents itself.

They are very fond of birch seeds, which they harvest in three stages. They first flutter and climb about in the trees, swallowing some seeds, but knocking most of them out of the tiny cones onto the snow below. They then pick the seeds off the snow, gulping them hurriedly and storing them in the diverticulum, a bilobed pouch similar to a chicken's crop, about halfway down the gullet. This done, they fly to a sheltered spot, or to their nighttime roost, where they can regurgitate the seeds at leisure, shell them out, and swallow them. This minimizes the time spent on food collecting, and consequent exposure to predators and harsh winds. It also gives the bird a bedtime store of food for snacking on during the long night.

Common and Hoary Redpolls

Carduelis flammea and *C. hornemanni*

Finch family. "Redpoll" from color of cap or "poll," from Middle English *pol(le)*, "top of the head"; "hoary" refers to frosty appearance of plumage; *Carduelis* is Latin for "goldfinch"; *flammea* is Latin for "flame-colored," from pink wash on some parts of male plumage; *hornemanni* after J. W. Hornemann, Danish scientist.

Description

Chickadee-sized; both sexes have satiny, dark red forehead patch, black chin; pale rump and flank lightly streaked with brown; back slightly darker, more heavily streaked; two pale bars on brown wing; stubby, sharp, conical bill; tail sharply forked; males have pink wash on breast, often on rump; Hoary is like

Common veiled in hoarfrost through which the underlying marks show faintly or not at all; best clue is all-white rump; bill shorter.

Behavior

Social, often in large twittering flocks; feeds on ground, weed heads, or trees, often around grain elevators, seed mills; very tame, trusting; agile at hanging feeders, feisty with own or other species; flight very undulating, with rattling "*chit-chit*"; perch call a protracted "*swee-eee-t*"; song a series of trills and twitters.

P. Sawatzky ©
1990

Range

Circumpolar; erratically migratory; Common breeds throughout northern boreal forest and tundra, Hoary on tundra above tree line and on highest Arctic islands; Common an irregular winterer in Pacific Northwest, most likely to appear in northeastern Washington and northern and eastern Idaho; Hoary much rarer, an infrequent companion of the Common in its incursions into the Northwest.

Food

Weed, birch, alder seeds, insects when abundant; small seeds at feeding stations; quickly learns to husk sunflower seeds either on shelves or in hanging feeders.

Nest

If you happen to be in the high Arctic in summer, look for a small cup of fine twigs, grass, plant stems, lined with plant down, feathers, hair; in tree, in low shrub, or on ground; often close together because birds are not territorial nesters; in Arctic, old nests might be relined and used again; nest surroundings messy with droppings.

Comment

The erratic redpolls are one of the most welcome callers at Pacific Northwest feeding stations, since they are unusual, unexpected visitors, and usually appear in large numbers. For feeding-station keepers much below the northern tier of states, the sight of a Hoary Redpoll in winter is a rare treat, and the farther south one goes, the higher it climbs on the list of "most-wanted" birds.

REF: A(W)—769–70; GO—318; NG—438; P(W)—342

Pine Siskin

Carduelis pinus

Finch family. "Siskin" from same echoic root as Dutch *sidskin*, "a chirper," or Russian *chizh*, "siskin" or "small bird"; *Carduelis* is Latin for "a goldfinch," from *carduus*, "thistle"; *pinus* is Latin for "pine."

Description

Much smaller than House Sparrow; body and head buff with darker brown stripes; darker wings and tail; yellowish wash at base of tail; yellow on inner third of flight feathers barely noticeable except when in flight or when wings raised, as in threat display; except between siskins, sexes indistinguishable; bill smaller and more pointed than other finches'.

Behavior

Very social, often in large flocks that swoop and swirl in swift synchrony, alternately bunching up and flaring apart; in spite of small size, reputed to be able to displace House Sparrows at feeder, using impressive raised-wing threat display; call a raspy, rising "*zweeee?*", a subdued "*tit-a-tit*," or a loud "*clee-it*" chirp; song a harsher version of goldfinch's melody.

Range

Erratically migratory; nests in northern and mountainous coniferous forest, irrupting in some winters to appear in great numbers well south of breeding range; nests and winters through much of Pacific Northwest, wintering in particular abundance in northwestern Washington.

Food

Seeds of small cones such as alder, birch, larch, cedar; forages in busy, acrobatic flocks through tops of trees; shares goldfinch's liking for dandelion and thistle; in season insects, buds; at feeder takes most small seeds, quickly shows preference for sunflower.

Nest

Adaptable, preferring conifer but will use shrubs and trees of any species, from three to fifty feet high; large cup of twigs, fibers, fine grass, lining of feathers, hair, rootlets; often messy because adults stop disposing of nestlings' feces after about nine days.

Comment

Like many northern finches, these erratic wanderers shift about on a continent-spanning scale, super-abundant one winter, scarce or totally absent the next. Invariably it comes in a bunch that tends to take over feeding stations when it appears, squaring off at much larger birds at the tray and pursuing them in the air. Although unable to bully Evening Grosbeaks, it feeds with them by dodging in and out, often picking up the bits dropped by the larger birds. Its sociability extends at times even to nesting in loose aggregations, foraging in flocks for the seeds it regurgitates for its nestlings.

REF: A(W)—752; GO—320; NG—434; P(W)—344

American Goldfinch

Carduelis tristis

Yellow color and singing ability like cage canary, hence also "wild canary"; less commonly "thistle bird" due to liking for thistle seeds; *Carduelis* Latin for "goldfinch", from root *carduus*, "thistle"; *tristis* is Latin for "sad," a singularly

-P. SAWATZKY -
-94 ©

inappropriate label for this embodiment of cheerfulness; older guides give generic name *Spinus*, from Greek *spinos*, "a linnet," the British name of the European cousin of our goldfinches.

Description

Smaller than House Sparrow; stubby tail, bill; in winter males and females uniform brownish olive, sometimes yellowish wash on head and neck; one or two white bars on dark wings; in early spring males acquire patches of yellow that spread as feather wear reveals summer body plumage of bright yellow with natty black cap, wings, and tail.

Behavior

Roves in flocks in winter and early summer; "bouncing" flight, wings flicked quickly for upward swoop, folded for downward, with rapid "*per-chic-o-ree*" or "*potato chip*" call with each "bounce"; song a bubbly succession of sweet trills punctuated frequently by a rising "*swee?*" whistle.

Range

Migratory; breeds and winters throughout Pacific Northwest; center of winter abundance is the shrub steppe and adjacent Ponderosa Pine zones where the Washington–Oregon border meets Idaho.

Food

Young fed on porridge of regurgitated seeds, with no "starter ration" of insects as provided by most other seed eaters; heavily reliant on thistle, dandelion seeds; black sunflower and smaller seeds at feeders.

Nest

Latest regular nester of all our songbirds, commonly July and even August; small, deep cup in shrubbery, tall weeds, or low tree, usually near water or swampy area, in open setting; body of plant fibers, lined with plant down, including cattail and thistle, rim bound with spider and/or insect webbing; often woven tightly enough to hold water; nest and supports messy with droppings.

Comment

Our "wild canary's" talent for mimicry is apparently essential to his love life, for he bonds to his mate by learning the notes of her song and "playing them back" to her, the couple thus developing a shared, unique vocabulary.

The goldfinch's late, extended breeding season is timed in part, if not altogether, to coincide with the seed-bearing schedule of thistle and other late-blossoming composite flowers. The seeds are essential food, their downy "parachute" fibers equally important for nest-building. These birds are frequent victims of the Brown-headed Cowbird, but the planted nestlings do very poorly on the finch gruel of straight seeds with no insect booster, and often succumb to malnutrition.

REF: A(W)—578; GO—320; NG—434; P(W)—344

Lesser Goldfinch
Carduelis psaltria

Smaller than American Goldfinch, hence "Lesser"; also called "green-backed goldfinch"; *Carduelis* Latin for "a goldfinch," from root *carduus*, "thistle"; *psaltria* Greek for "a lutist."

Description
Male has black cap, tail, and wings; dark olive-green back and rump; underparts bright yellow; white wing patch evident in flight; female has black wings and tail, all upper parts smokey olive-green, underparts washed-out yellow.

Behavior
Social in winter, may flock with siskins, American Goldfinches; often seen pulling fluffy seeds from weeds, especially thistles and dandelions; song similar to American Goldfinch, deemed by some to be less sweet and flowing; calls a rising "*tee-yee?*" and a falling "*tee-yer.*"

Range
Partially migratory; a black-backed form breeds in Rockies and scrub steppes of Southwest and is largely migratory; coastal green-backed is permanent resident from extreme southwestern Washington southward on west side of Cascades, through Coast Ranges to Baja California; prefers open woodlands, oak, and pinyon–juniper habitat; most abundant in northern California's Sacramento Valley.

Food
Seeds, especially dandelion, thistle, and other composite weeds; grass seeds, deciduous tree seeds; floral buds and berries; at feeder, sunflower seeds, millet; water an important attractant.

Nest
Small, tightly woven cup, rim and sides messy with droppings; in shrub, tree from two to thirty feet up.

Comment
Like the American Goldfinch, this roving winterer may or may not come to feeders, even though it may be present in the region. Bearing in mind that it usually avoids heavily wooded country, you may bait and wait in vain if that is where you live. This bird may also remain independent if there are lots of thistles and other weed seeds available. Thistle (niger) seed could provide the necessary enticement.

Knowing its affinity for water, laying on a nice, trickly fountain could be the key to getting this charming little bird to a winter feeder.

If all else fails, playing Vivaldi's "The Goldfinch" with its charming flute simulation of the bird's song might do the trick.

REF: A(W)—544; GO—320; NG—434; P(W)—344

Old World Sparrows

Family Passeridae

Passeridae is derived from Latin *passer*, "sparrow." The same root gives us "passeriformes," the name of the huge order of songbirds that includes, among many others, that most unsparrowlike, unmusical bird, the raven. A lot of references still put the House Sparrow in the Weaver Finch group.

The Passeridae are Old World sparrows, numbering 141 species native to Eurasia and North Africa. Two species were introduced to this continent, the House Sparrow and the very similar-looking Eurasian Tree Sparrow. The Tree Sparrow has not spread much beyond the environs of St. Louis, Missouri, where it was originally released in 1870. The House Sparrow is another story altogether.

Unlike many exotic plants, insects, fish, birds, and mammals that have become scourges by accident, carelessness, or covert entry, the House Sparrow was unleashed deliberately, not to say determinedly. It was brought in to control another introduced pest, the Canker Worm. This rescue operation took hold in the spring of 1853 when fifty were released in Brooklyn's Greenwood Cemetery, after two other attempts the previous year had failed. Thus began the bird world's most overwhelming invasion of a foreign species ever unleashed.

Many reintroductions followed, some for the sentimental ties with homeland England that they represented, some in yet more misguided efforts to eradicate insects cheaply, among them the Potato Beetle. Their effect on the worms and beetles was negligible, but their unanticipated impact on many native species of songbirds was incalculably harmful.

To their credit, not all our predecessors were motivated by self-interest or sentiment. Eminent bird biologist Elliot Coues vehemently opposed the House Sparrow, labeling it "public enemy number one." But his, and others', protests came too late.

Railroads proved to be a boon to these birds. Settlers questing westward on the newly built lines carried along cagefuls to be released at their destinations. They were often inadvertently carted hundreds of miles when they were shut into rail cars loading at elevators and stockyards. And the tracks, strewn with spilled grain, linked sparrow-friendly farms and villages easy flights apart along corridors through otherwise hostile wilderness. Whether in grain cars or by stages along the right-of-way, they appeared in Churchill, Manitoba, by 1930. Of twelve counted in 1931, all froze to death that winter, but later arrivals fared better and they are long established at this subarctic grain terminal.

With or without help, sparrows moved inexorably outward from New York, quickly achieving "abundant" status almost everywhere they settled. They were recorded in Seattle by 1897, in forty-four years completely spanning the continent.

The Perfect Partnership

During its peak in the second decade of this century, the House Sparrow was reckoned to be America's most abundant bird. In many areas it doubled the number of all other species combined. It flourished on the grains fed to domestic animals on countless small farms, and in villages where thrifty householders kept a cow and a small flock of chickens. But the draft horse was the sparrows' chief ally. Until after World War I it was the mainstay of public and private transportation in cities, the principal source of farm power, and an important adjunct to the logging business. Its droppings and spilled feed provided abundant and nutritious food, its barns nest sites and shelter from winter's cold.

North America has not been the only victim of the whirlwind takeover by the House Sparrow. It was taken to Australia in 1863–1864 (for "aesthetic reasons"!); to New Zealand in a number of transplants during 1859–1871; to South Africa from 1890–1897. Other introductions saw it loosed on South America, the Falkland Islands, Mauritius, and Mozambique, all coincidental with the arrival of European colonizers. In all of these locations it spread rapidly, in all it became a permanent resident at the expense of indigenous species. It now occupies two-thirds of the land surface of the earth.

Notwithstanding the success of the sparrow and starling here, North America has not been an ecological pushover for every exotic bird to hit its shores. By 1900 up to 150 species of birds had been released on this continent, and countless captives had escaped. But only 6 besides the House Sparrow have been successful: Starling, Rock Dove, Mute Swan, Ring-necked Pheasant, Chukar, and Gray Partridge. A few others have been able to establish themselves in restricted local habitats. The others vanished, victims of bad judgment by those who thoughtlessly dumped birds, pink flamingos among these, into environments they had no chance of coping with.

In environments it shares with humans, the House Sparrow has proven to be a master of adaptability, a talent that has not always been appreciated. Among the uncomplimentary names attached to it are "feathered rat," "avian cockroach," and "Woolco warbler." Shrilling at its world from an inner-city dumpster, it may be demonstrating that a strident voice is an advantage in an environment filled with traffic noise. It has learned to hunt insects at night under street lights.

The ultimate in adaptability was demonstrated by three that got into the Frickly Coal Mine in Yorkshire, England, in the summer of 1975 and stayed down at the 2,100-foot level until the spring of 1978. Two of them nested and hatched three young but they died.

"I'm With Him"

Away from people the bird has been notably unadaptable. It is rarely found far away from human habitation, and seems unable to hang on for long after farm homesteads are abandoned. A nest in a site more than several hundred yards from occupied buildings is unusual. Perhaps, in addition to food, it may well need the protection from predators that the close company of humankind affords. The one exception seems to be a shift to another protector. In a personal communication, C. Stuart Houston of Saskatoon observed that it often builds a nest at the base of a hawk's nest, sometimes miles from the nearest farm. It gains the same kind of "I'm with him" protection from the hawk that it gets from humans.

The House Sparrow's impact on native species has at least been limited to those that can tolerate closeness to us. Thus, the cheery House Wren, Eastern and Mountain Bluebird, Cliff, Barn, and Tree Swallows, and other desirables, have been seen as the most-mourned losers to the quarrelsome import.

A moment's reflection on human history suggests that the sparrow is more a symptom of a greater problem than a prime cause. The arrival of this brash exotic coincided with the beginning of the railroad age in North America and the consequent burgeoning of settlement. The wholesale habitat destruction that ensued guaranteed the dislocation of most wildlife. Given time, more native birds might have weathered the change and adapted to street and backyard life. But that niche was taken, even as the human immigrants arrived, by their avian tag-along, and the native birds were put to a double disadvantage. In the self-forgiving way we have of shifting blame, the House Sparrow takes the rap for what was very much a human offense.

The only type of habitat that is not decreasing is the human-altered kind. This should have continued to favor House Sparrows. But they suffered a marked decline after World War I, a loss that paralleled the drop in horse populations. The downturn has leveled out, but in many areas sparrow numbers continue a gradual fall. Farms are disappearing, and much livestock is concentrated in intensive-feeding animal factories. Most people now live in cities. The sprawling new suburbs, with their tightly built houses, are not as compatible to the tough little sparrow as were the leafy backyards, gardens, horse barns, and ramshackle cowsheds of yesteryear.

House Sparrow

Passer domesticus

Old World Sparrow family. Also "English" Sparrow; *Passer* is Latin for "sparrow"; *domesticus* is Latin for "house."

P. SAWATZKY ©
1990

Description

Chunky, dingy, short-legged; back and wings brown-streaked, breast plain dust-gray; male has black chin and bib; cap and rump gray; gray-buff ear patch; band of brown from eye widening around back of neck; markings of winter male much subdued, clearest in spring breeding season; female a subdued pattern of browns with lighter buff eye stripe.

Behavior

Social; forages in small flocks, may congregate at night roosts in large numbers; prefers to feed on ground; rather heavy flier; noisy, squabbling males battle over females; aggressive hang-about at feeders; voice a loud "*chir-rup*," often repeated monotonously; flocks may gather closely in bush or tree at certain times of day where, for an extended time, all seem intent on out-shrilling each other.

Range

Nonmigratory; universally, and exclusively, where human settlement has extended; occupant of streets, vacant lots, shopping mall parking lots, feedlots, and barnyards; breeds everywhere in Pacific Northwest where humans live.

Food

Grain, weed seeds, edible human refuse, insects; at feeders, favors small seeds, breadcrumbs, and cracked grain, but with a bit of time soon learns to handle sunflower seeds.

Nest

Hatful of dusty trash, straw, and feathers jammed into holes in eaves of buildings, in light standards, large signs, or birdhouses; often appropriates nests of Cliff Swallows; on rare instances builds a large, domed ball of grass with side entrance, high in tree.

Comment

A feeder heavily streaked with droppings is the sign of a clientele of House Sparrows, although native finches can also be messy. Opportunism is this scrappy little bird's middle name. I have watched them on hot summer days diligently working service stations and campground parking lots, pulling insects out of the radiators and bug screens on newly arrived vehicles.

No exception to the rule that undesirables must be prolific, the males begin competing for nest sites the autumn before the next breeding season, and pairs can be seen in March, or February in milder parts of the Northwest, hauling nesting material about the eaves and into Purple Martin and any other birdhouses they can get into. This head start, abetted by an incubation period as short as ten days, allows double- and often triple-brooding.

REF: A(W)—592; GO—296; NG—432; P(W)—346

CHAPTER 9

The Walk-In Trade

It rapidly becomes obvious to those who feed birds that some animals other than birds routinely answer the call of their hospitality, for better or worse. In the annals of bird feeding in America some quite unusual beasts have joined the regulars at the table. These have included deer, elk, and moose; black bears and raccoons; porcupines, woodchucks, and all the ground squirrels; mice, voles, and shrews; foxes, weasels, marten, and mink, for suet and for the rodents the seeds attracted; snakes, probably also for the mice; and, oftener than one might suspect, coyotes which, it turns out, can develop quite a liking for "spits"!

I haven't heard, but wouldn't be at all surprised to hear that feeding stations in the far north have been visited by polar bears, caribou, and musk-oxen.

A native animal relatively new to the urban setting is the raccoon, a shrewd scrounge with a keen nose for the goodies that bird feeders offer.

The two animals that attract the most attention and comment, however, are cats and squirrels. A close runner-up in some locations is the raccoon, well-established urbanite that it has latterly become. The cats that frequent feeders are, with very rare exceptions, simply free-ranging pets, and so are not treated in this chapter. They do, however, have their own intriguing behavior patterns, especially when playing out their role as half-time predators. For a discussion of domestic cats, and how to deal with them, see Mammal Problems in Chapter 5, The Downside.

Because mammals are so much a part of the feeder scene, it is essential to deal with them other than solely as nuisances to be discouraged or removed. They do, after all, have their own natural history, equally as fascinating as that of the birds.

As with the birds, reference sources are listed with each species account. My choices are Lloyd G. Ingles' *Mammals of the Pacific States* (1965) and a pocket guide, *Pacific Coast Mammals* (1987) by Ron Russo, indicated in the References section—REF—by I and R, respectively.

Opossums

Family Didelphidae

The ancestors of our scruffy, dim-witted, slow-footed "possum" are said to have walked through the Cretaceous Period with the dinosaurs, 80 million years ago. In the face of such awesome staying power, who should quibble about style?

One might add that possums also smell bad, emitting a rank scent from several glands. One, under the chin of the male, makes a yellow stain on the fur of his chest. The strong body odor might account for the fact that while almost any predator can easily run down a possum, they would rather not bother. Great Horned Owls catch them but, given a choice, prefer skunks.

"Possum and taters," a traditional dish of the Deep South, suggests that for some, at least, opossum is an acquired taste. Another southerner that relishes possum, with or without taters, is the alligator.

If you hassle a possum it will arch up on tiptoe, raise its tail straight up in the air, and, fur bristling, gape open its mouth to display an astonishing jaw-full of teeth and hiss loudly at you. If this works, and you back off, the opossum will withdraw at top speed in what is best described as a hurried walk. As it heads for the nearest thick cover, or a hole, it waves its tail in a circle as if using it to help maintain balance.

Writer Leonard Lee Rue, in *Fur Bearing Animals of North America*, notes that opossums come regularly to his feeders. He has seen them bluff out much larger raccoons in showdowns over food. If the bluffing fails, the opossum, while not a noted scrapper, will fight stubbornly and use its arsenal of teeth to good effect. In mating battles, the males fight viciously, often with severe injury and sometimes even death the result.

Only rarely, apparently, does the opossum "play possum" and go into its famous death act. Triggered by trauma and fear, it flops on its side, glassy-eyed, slack-jawed, drooling copiously and emitting a rank-smelling green mucous from its anal glands. In this state it remains "dead" even when picked up, poked, rolled about, or even chomped by a dog. There is no perceptible respiration, and heartbeat is barely detectable.

To what degree this is a state of catatonic shock, and to what degree a voluntary charade, is open to question. When it thinks the danger has passed, the opossum is able to arouse itself promptly and hasten away.

An enquiring biologist once did a simple measure of relative cranial capacity that considerably embarrassed the opossum. Using dried beans, he found that a raccoon skull would hold 150, a domestic cat 125, an opossum 25.

To compensate for its low IQ, the possum has a repertoire of survival-enhancing alternatives. Undeterred by a bad taste that turns off most other middling predators, the opossum feeds extensively on shrews and moles. It can also catch and eat poisonous snakes with no loss of appetite. Presumably because it evolved in the tropics along with a great many snakes, it is immune to the venom of rattlers, copperheads, and water moccasins. Researchers have injected opossums with sixty times the amount of venom that would be lethal to a similar-sized mammal, with negligible effect.

Like other "primitive" animals, the opossum is tenacious of life and can walk away from abuse and injuries that would kill most of its smarter contemporaries.

Distinguished as it is as North America's only native marsupial, the opossum's reproductive strategy is also unique. Two weeks after mating, the female produces a couple of dozen minute embryos so small the whole lot could fit into a teaspoon. In preparation for delivery, the female leans back against some support, her lower belly turned upward. She cleans out her pouch and licks a moist, flattened path through her belly fur from the pouch to her genital opening. When the young begin emerging she licks away the amniotic fluid that would otherwise drown the tiny embryos.

About all the embryos have for their next move is a set of well-developed front legs with claws that enable them to grasp their mother's fur. With no eyes, no rear limbs, most organs yet in rudimentary form, they begin a hand-over-hand journey up the moistened pathway to the pouch. Those that reach it search out one of the tiny nipples and latch onto it, employing mouth musculature that enables them to hang on and suckle.

Some of the young spill to the ground and are lost, some get to the pouch when all the nipples, usually thirteen in number, are taken. By the time weaning occurs some 100 days later, a healthy litter numbers about eight. Prior to weaning they emerge from the pouch, still attached to the nipples, which elongate to about 1½ inches shortly after suckling begins.

During the post-weaning period, the young may cling to their mother's fur as she forages. As they get bigger and more of a burden, she may leave them behind in her den. By the time they are ready to leave, they will have learned the rudiments of possum life, and will thereafter lead solitary lives except during brief mating sessions, and when females are tending young.

Common Opossum

Didelphis marsupialis

Also "Virginia" or "American Opossum"; in many references *D. virginiana*; "Opossum" from Algonquian "white animal"; *Didelphis*, "double womb"; *marsupialis*, "a pouch."

Description

Like a cat-sized rat; average weight of males about six pounds, females about four pounds; rough coat usually grizzled gray through which pale undercoat shows; face whitish with prominent "shoe-button" eyes; large, naked ears; long, tapering snout with piglike pink nose pad; long naked tail; legs and feet black, toes white; hind foot has fleshy opposable "thumb"; has fifty teeth.

Behavior

Solitary; strongly nocturnal; slow-moving, top speed a running walk; often "grins," exposing most of its teeth; when threatened, turns on an imposing threat posture; may hiss loudly or even growl; a good climber, uses prehensile tail as a "fifth hand."

Range

Prefers moist, lowland forest and farmland, not far from water; in pre-European settlement times ranged from South America north as far as Virginia and Ohio; now, through natural range extension, has spread northward as far as southern Ontario; first released in California and Oregon before turn of century, now found throughout Pacific Northwest wherever suitable habitat occurs.

Food

Omnivorous; preys on small mammals, birds and eggs, snakes, amphibians; insects, slugs, crayfish, carrion, garbage; fruit, berries, grass, clover, grain.

Nest

Uses old burrows, tree holes, brush and rock piles, buildings; makes nests of dry leaves and grass in each den; does not dig its own burrows.

Comment

Like some other animals, the humble possum has benefitted from the advent of European culture in America. It has even gone suburban in a big way, now rated as one of the major nuisance animals in Pacific Northwest cities, along with the Eastern Gray Squirrel and the Raccoon. Part of its success came after modern settlement, especially in the south and east of the continent, wiped out major predators such as cougars, wolves, bobcats, fishers, and the larger snakes. It turns out that the replacement coyote, noted for eating anything it can get into its mouth, does not care for possum. Now the most significant "predator" of the possum is the automobile, followed by men and dogs.

Although the possum is a good climber, it prefers to move about on the ground. For bird feeders who would rather not supplement the possum diet, keeping feeders and baths well off the ground, with squirrel baffles or metal-sheathed poles, are sufficient deterrents. Even more important is keeping garbage under tight-fitting lids, and not leaving pet food and water outdoors, especially overnight.

REF: I—76; R—63

Squirrels and Chipmunks

Family Sciuridae

Sciuridae is Latinized "shade-tail," from Greek *skia*, "a shadow," and *oura*, "tail," from tree squirrels' habit of stretching out on limbs with their tails over their backs, supposedly to shade themselves from the sun. On a bitter winter day it looks more like a warm fur muff.

Why at all should squirrels be treated seriously, even sympathetically, in a book about winter birds? First, for most of us they are an unavoidable fact of life. Second, squirrels are card-carrying native species toughing out our winters in ways that merit our sympathetic attention. They can be either worthy antagonists or fascinating guests, depending on whether we choose to fight them or feed them.

Arguably, rodents are the most successful order of mammals, and the squirrel family stands near the head of it. Squirrels are present in all the habitable continents except Australia, and fill widely varying niches wherever they occur. In the Pacific Northwest, the blocky, stolid marmot, the soft-eyed flying squirrel, and the skittering wee chipmunk are all squirrels. Some are among the world's most profound hibernators; others, like Red Squirrels, go all winter in high gear.

The Teeth Have It

Other admirable attributes notwithstanding, teeth are the rodents' key to success. Most prominent is a set of cutting chisels mounted at the front of the muzzle, giving most rodents a "buck-toothed" look, especially if, as in the case of beavers and porcupines, these teeth are deep orange.

The roots of these four incisors curve an astonishing distance into sockets in the jaws. Hollow-rooted and open at the bottom, they grow constantly throughout the life of the owner at a rate that compensates for normal wear and keeps them chisel-sharp. These features permit rodents to cut through extremely hard and abrasive material and not wear out their tools. Rats can bore holes in concrete and cut through metal sheathing around wires, and Red Squirrels can chisel apart rock-hard Lodgepole Pine cones.

Behind the incisors is a long, arched, toothless gap—the diastema—that permits the rodent to pull its lips shut behind its front teeth. Thus, it can chisel away without biting its lip, and the seal keeps concrete dust, metal filings, and cone debris out of the mouth. Behind the diastema are the grinding molars which, like our teeth, grow only so far and then stop.

Everything is mounted in a set of jaws hinged so that the lower can be switched instantly from cutting to grinding, with special sets of muscles to accomplish this change of gears. In the cutting mode, the lower jaw is shifted forward to engage the incisors, in which position the molars are disengaged. When the lower jaw is pulled back, the incisors are out of gear and the molars mesh into action.

Squirrels often exhibit an almost fiendish talent for choosing irreplaceable valuables for random gnawing. It is not vandalism, if that helps. Rather, the gnawing simply compensates for the soft diet of seeds that requires nowhere near the amount of toothwork that shucking the hereditary diet of cones or nuts demands. If the squirrel did not keep its front teeth ground down, they would grow to unmanageable lengths. Indeed, if accident or disease destroys one incisor, its opposite in the other jaw keeps growing longer and longer until the animal cannot feed at all and dies of starvation.

Many rodents, squirrels included, seem to love gnawing on old deer antlers, possibly gaining minerals as they hone down their teeth. Perhaps if you left a chunk of discarded antler, or a large bone, out where it could be chewed on by squirrels they would be less likely to vandalize your trim.

Compulsive Hoarding

There are a number of accessories and behaviors that various rodents have evolved to augment their teeth. Chipmunks hibernate in a nest built either right on, or very close to, their stash. At intervals of up to two weeks they begin to shiver violently to warm up. Awake, they take a drowsy bathroom break, eat a big snack out of stores, and then curl up again. Their hoard is often huge.

Lloyd G. Ingles's *Mammals of the Pacific States* records an underground cache including some 35,000 seeds from twenty different kinds of plants. Another account records a Least Chipmunk's nest with 478 acorns and 2,734 cherry pits in it.

In contrast, our largest squirrel, the woodchuck, stores its winter food as fat on its body. It rouses periodically to void urine; otherwise, it remains in deep torpor, its body stiff and chilled, its heart rate and respiration virtually undetectable.

Conceited as we humans are about our own intelligence, it is a matter of particular interest that squirrels have the largest relative brain weight of any small mammal. Bird feeders, all too familiar with the feeling of defeat that follows every attempt to keep squirrels out of their feeders, have suspected it all along.

The "Squirreliest" Squirrel

The tree squirrel that most typifies its family to many North Americans is the tough little Red. This noisy busybody is the most strident personality in the wild, the "squirreliest" of the squirrels. Except for rare moments of tranquillity, its moods vary from mildly agitated to wildly frenzied. In a human personality, its pugnacious hysteria would be intolerable, and accordingly it is judged harshly, and unfairly.

To better understand the behavior of Red Squirrels it helps to know that, familiar as they are in suburb and park, they evolved in the vast forests of the north. There they feed in summer on a great variety of buds, shoots, seeds, insects, mushrooms, eggs, and nestlings, and whatever else can be harvested or caught. But in winter the menu shrinks mainly to one item: the seeds of spruce.

The key to winter survival where the Red Squirrel evolved is therefore to be the sole, no-nonsense proprietor of a grove of spruce, the seeds of which can be harvested and stored for the winter. The competition is fierce; in city, farmyard, or boreal wilderness, it is a "no-vacancy" world until a property holder dies. A new claimant is invariably on hand to move in, establishing boundaries, patrolling them diligently, and giving its territorial cry. This is the loud, scratchy, rolling "*cheek-eek-eek-eek-eek-eek*" that greets the squirrel's human neighbors at dawn and keeps them reassured until dusk.

Established home ownership does not mean peace and quiet, of course. A Red Squirrel's life is a constant round of frantic skirmishing with neighbors as each repeatedly tests the boundary lines of the others. Homeless wanderers are invariably sent fleeing; in a fight, the psychological and tactical advantages overwhelmingly favor the owner on its home ground. The end of each conflict calls for a fresh burst of defiant territorial cries. There is never a dull moment in the life of a Red Squirrel, nor for those of us willing to be involved observers of its high-tempo existence.

About the end of August, a squirrel with a grove of cone-bearing spruce in its territory goes to work as if possessed, cutting bunches of mature but under-ripe cones from the tips of the twigs, letting them drop, and then scurrying below to store them. In two weeks it will cache as many as 15,000, an impressive mound if, as some squirrels do, it piles them in a heap before burying them. The singles it may "scatter hoard," burying them in ground litter. The bunches may go into a labyrinth of tunnels, preferably under a big tree in the center of its territory.

Burial keeps the under-ripened cones moist; otherwise they would dry out and open, spilling the precious seeds. It also keeps them out of view and in a more defendable stronghold against pilfering neighbors. Near such hoards will be piles of rust-colored "cone flakes" at stumps and logs where the squirrel perches in winter to shell out its meals.

A full cone hoard is enough to last a Red Squirrel for two winters. It instinctively "knows" that its life-supporting trees are capricious. As pointed out in the section on crossbills in Chapter 8, Knowing Your Winged Visitors, a bountiful seed crop is almost invariably followed by a "crop failure," and a winter of privation for squirrels.

Baby "Boom and Bust"

Red Squirrel family life is a trade-off between conflicting imperatives. Mating is brief and tempestuous, after which the male is driven off and returns to his own territory. The young are given all that solicitous single motherhood can offer. But in a foretaste of things to come, before weaning them the female will often shift her pups to a den near the edge of her territory. After weaning, she becomes less and less tolerant of them until her own territoriality reasserts itself and they are all sent off, and kept off, violently.

In the relative abundance of parks and suburbs, new squirrels have more options than their boreal cousins. But for those reliant mainly on the single-resource cone economy, the options are few. Should they be the progeny of the "baby boom" that follows a winter of cone abundance, they are a luckless lot. Driven into an overcrowded world, they face the winter of famine that invariably follows a year of plenty.

Most are foredoomed to perish, undernourished, easy pickings for predators as they flee distracted from one territorial defender to another. Even for the lucky minority that finds a place, the future is bleak; a store of dried mushrooms and rock-hard Lodgepole Pine cones is a poor substitute for a larder full of spruce cones.

The dispersal of surplus squirrels on the eve of a winter of privation is, ironically, a long-term benefit to their species. A few, a very few, will reach uninhabited pockets of plenty and beget new populations. They will thus play a small part in a grand plan, the dispersal of their species—a trade-off for the sacrifice of the many refugees that won't make it.

If the survivors could only talk, theirs would be tales of perilous runs over open ground, death-defying risks, hairbreadth escapes, and desperate battles. They would be among the rare ones, survivors, thanks to a combination of luck, speed, and dauntless spirit. It is small wonder that their descendants are scrappy and strong, and that they will defend their home with the last spark of energy in their tough little bodies.

REF: I—196; R—27

Chipmunks—Skedaddlers Extraordinaire

Chipmunks are in the family Sciuridae, genus *Eutamias*. Why, in a book dealing with a hobby that is so strongly associated with winter, would one discuss an animal that sleeps off winter in hiding?

Chipmunks, part of the ground-dwelling contingent of the squirrel family, also belong to that group of animals that deal with winter by opting out. But although they hibernate, after a fashion, they are late turning in, arise early, and are often up and about during mild spells. The length of their winter, and yours, of course depends on which of the Pacific Northwest's vastly differing climates you live in.

If you feed birds all year round, of course, you could soon be on a first-name basis with entire families from one or more species.

There are a half dozen members of the genus *Eutamias* occurring in varying degrees of abundance in the Pacific Northwest. Depending on the habitat that you and the chipmunks share, the species most bird feeders are likely to encounter are the Least, the Yellow Pine, and the Townsend's. Present but less likely to enter your life are the Lodgepole, the Sonoma, and the Red-tailed.

Stripes Do Not a Chipmunk Make

Confusion might arise between chipmunks and the two species of Golden-mantled Ground Squirrels where their ranges overlap. All bear conspicuous lengthwise stripes on their backs. The Sierra Nevada squirrel lives in the montane pine and fir forest of Oregon, Idaho, northern California, and extreme southeastern Washington. The Cascades squirrel lives up in the pine, fir, and spruce forest of the Cascade Mountains in Washington and southern British Columbia.

These ground squirrels are larger than chipmunks and have relatively shorter tails. The best diagnostic feature is a lack of face stripes. If the face is striped, it is a chipmunk.

Another identifying clue are cheek pouches; chipmunks have them, the ground squirrels do not. For such a small animal, these pouches have amazing capacity. One "chip" is on record packing eight hazelnuts, four in one cheek, three in the other, one in the teeth. The observer commented that it would likely have had four in both cheeks except that it would not have been able to jam the load through its burrow entrance.

Applied Charm

Chipmunks are bold, pretty, and pert. At back step and picnic table, they quickly turn their cute ways to good use in training humans to feed them on demand. Their capacity for handouts is limitless; what they do not sit up and nibble on the spot, they stuff into their bulging cheek pouches and scamper off with, a comical process their benefactors find endlessly entertaining. Good climbers, but not essentially arboreal, they are just as happy at feeders gleaning fallout off the ground.

Unfortunately, these endearing little skedaddlers often vanish just about the time they have thoroughly captivated you. Cats know a lot more than they let on about such disappearances, chipmunks apparently being especially vulnerable to them.

Chipmunks and the aforementioned ground squirrels provide interesting contrasts in winter preparation strategies. When weed seeds ripen and acorns fall, both animals put them away, the ground squirrel by eating them and laying on fat, the chipmunk by stashing them in a secure hideaway.

Hibernation

Come winter, both animals hole up in a burrow with a sleeping chamber below the frost line. The ground squirrel is the true hibernator and goes into a profound torpor. The chipmunk is a lighter sleeper. Both arouse themselves every week or two for a groggy bladder break to get rid of metabolic wastes. The chipmunk takes time for a substantial snack before turning in again.

The differing hibernation techniques explain chipmunks' compulsive hoarding instinct. Given a source of preferred food, be it natural or from a feeder, they commence harvesting it as if possessed, cheek pouches bulging on the collecting half of each shuttle to and from their hideaway.

By the time winter comes, or the source is exhausted, they may have enough in store for twenty chipmunks. Ron Russo, in *Pacific Coast Mammals*, cites the discovery of a food cache containing 67,970 items "with 15 different kinds of seeds, corn, and a piece of bumblebee." Like King Midas with his gold, chipmunks often sleep right on top of their food hoard during winter.

Of the three species mentioned above as being less widespread through the Northwest, the Sonoma is a denizen of chaparral, redwood forest, and drier examples of Yellow Pine forest in north-central California. The Red-tailed occupies the spruce–fir forests of the Continental Divide up to timberline, thus appearing in extreme northeastern Washington and much of Idaho. The Lodgepole inhabits Lodgepole Pine, chaparral, and red fir forests in northwestern California and southwestern Idaho.

The other three more likely to be guests at your feeder are given the full species treatment after the squirrels.

Red and Douglas Squirrels

Tamiasciurus hudsonicus and *T. douglasii*

Also "chickaree"; "Squirrel" from Greek *skiourus,* compounded from *skia,* "a shadow," plus *oura,* "tail," descriptive of animal's using tail as a shade from the sun; *Tamias* from Latin "steward" or "one who stores," plus *sciurus,* "shade tail"; *hudsonicus* is Latinized "of Hudson" (Bay), where first type specimen was obtained; *douglasii* is from David Douglas, Scottish plant collector who explored the Pacific Northwest and British Columbia in the 1820s and 1830s.

Description

Trim, muscular body about six inches long, fluffy tail about same length, with dark subterminal band; light eye-ring prominent in all seasons in both species. Red: in winter, coat paprika-rufous, especially bright in tail and along back; belly, throat, and chin silvery gray; in summer, body olive-brown, underparts white, with black line on side separating them; rain-forest forms much darker, slightly smaller than interior forms. Douglas: in winter stiff upright hairs on ear tips more obvious; grizzled on upper body and tail; indistinct back band and tail reddish brown, sides grayish olive; belly pale yellowish gray; flank stripe indistinct; in summer olive-brown above, distinct black flank line, tail reddish brown; belly and feet bright orange; overall, Douglas is slightly smaller and darker than the Red.

Behavior

Hyperactive, excitable, inquisitive; when alarmed, runs and climbs with explosive speed; at rest on haunches, coils tail closely over back and neck; noisy; territorial call a scratchy, rattling *"chrrrrrr"* usually delivered from elevated point; alarm call a sharp, strident *"k'cheek!-k'cheek!"*, often accompanied by agitated drumming of hind feet; drives other squirrels off territory in wild pursuits; often chases birds from feeder and vicinity.

Range

Red: Truly northern, right across Canada throughout boreal forest to tree

P. Sawatzky ©
1990

limit, southward wherever there are woodlands; northwestern Washington and northwestern Oregon, all of Idaho; Douglas: south from Canadian border through Coast, Cascade, and Sierra Nevada mountains.

Food

In summer, buds, shoots, fruit, seeds, insects, nuts, mushrooms, and occasional eggs and nestlings; in winter, stored acorns, maple samaras in deciduous forests, and spruce, pine, fir, and hemlock cones in coniferous forests; at feeder eats anything, but prefers sunflower seeds, baked scraps, peanuts.

Nest

Favors tree holes, but will accumulate bulky ball of shredded grass and bark in buildings, rock piles, burrows, or in open branches where it is called a "drey."

Comment

In the hyperkinetic world of the Red and Douglas Squirrels, territorialism can generate nerve-wracking standoffs in the presence of a feeder. The unlimited supply of rich food escalates trespass beyond the resident's ability to drive away the interlopers, unless he or she is overwhelmingly dominant. Everyone edges in on the goodies, tension mounting, adrenalin pumping. They fume, shriek, and growl, cramming frantically for a few seconds until another scuffle explodes in which there might well be significant bloodshed. I wouldn't be at all surprised to learn that Red Squirrels suffer from ulcers and hypertension.

Total peace is impossible, but with management the tension can be eased somewhat and the birds, at least, will benefit. If the main feeder is the focus of constant mayhem, several other, preferably hanging, feeders, can be deployed nearby. These will give the smaller birds, and perhaps even the beleaguered resident squirrel, a place to feed—out of the crossfire as it were.

REF: I—195; R—29

Eastern Gray and Western Gray Squirrels

Sciurus carolinensis and *S. griseus*

Also "black" squirrel; "Squirrel" from Greek *skiourus*, from *skia*, "a shadow," plus *oura*, "tail," from animal's habit of resting with tail over back as a shade; *Sciurus* is Latin for "shade tail"; *carolinensis* is Latinized "of Carolina," where first type specimen was described; *griseus* is Latin for "gray."

Description

Eastern: Twice size of Red and Douglas Squirrels; body eight to twelve inches, tail same or longer; in most cities a jet black variant dominates; gray phase has grizzled gray coat with rusty shading on head and flanks; short white tuft behind each ear, light buff eye-ring; longest hair tips on tail frosty; belly silver-white; in some local populations a grizzled buff-ocher color dominates. Western: Somewhat larger than Eastern; "salt-and-pepper" coat; tail very full, hairs white-tipped; belly white. In young of both species coat is smooth and shiny, roughening with age. An all-black variant occurs in both species.

Behavior

Both species much calmer, quieter, and slower-moving than Douglas Squirrel; both species, in sitting position, curl tail against back and neck in graceful "question-mark"; when moving, both species float it out behind; when agitated, thrash tail in circular, spasmodic jerks; sometimes tolerate other Grays at feeder; alarm call a grating, protracted, nasal "*raaaa-aaak*," repeated monotonously; also a short, muted "*whuck!*"

Range

Eastern: Introduced; originally southeastern states; released in city parks, campuses in Pacific Northwest (Seattle in 1925), expanding into countryside. Western: Native; strongly associated with oak woodlands; occurs north from Mexican border through Sierra Nevada and Coast Range of California, into western Oregon and Washington, stopping just short of Canadian border; range diminishing due to loss of oak woodlands, and assumed competition from Eastern Gray.

Food

Buds, shoots, bark, tree seeds, flowers, nuts, fruit, fungi; occasionally eggs and nestlings; buries nuts singly, accurately unearths them from under a foot or more of snow; omnivorous at feeder, but prefers sunflower seeds, peanuts, baked goods; Western relies primarily on acorns, secondarily on pine nuts.

Nest

In tree hole or building; nest (drey) in branches high in tree, a round, untidy clump of leaves and grass with entrance in side; may preempt and "improve" a woodpecker hole.

Comment

A strong trend that sees the black variant of the Eastern Gray Squirrel become the most dominant strain in cities has not emerged in Seattle.

The Eastern is a traveling animal, introduced to many places far beyond its historic limits. Most of these are urban locations where it thrives, well fed on a mixture of natural foods such as acorns and maple and ash samaras, and human refuse. Protected from most of its predators, it multiplies and expands its territory. One of the few species to reverse the trend that has seen many Eurasian animals successfully colonize much of the New World, the Eastern Gray was introduced into Great Britain in the 1890s. It is blamed for severe depletion of the native Red Squirrel, and has become such a nuisance that the government, as of March 1994, launched a nationwide extermination drive.

In Washington the state Department of Wildlife classifies them as "a serious nuisance" in many areas of Tacoma, Seattle, and Everett. It claims that the imports have flourished to the point of driving out native squirrels, especially the Western Gray, which the state is thinking about declaring endangered. It urges bird feeders to place feeders where squirrels can't gain access to them, and to use a catch pan to keep seeds from dropping to the ground.

As bird feeders are well aware, this is much easier said than done. Grays can jump higher and farther than Reds or Douglases. Their persistence and acrobatic skill are legendary, especially when tackling devices specifically intended to foil them. For bird feeders fuming about being outsmarted by a "dumb" animal, or who feel conscience-bound not to aid an animal that is either harmful or intolerably destructive, some countermeasures are outlined in Chapter 3, Feeders and Shelters, and Chapter 5, The Downside.

REF: I—193; R—30

Fox Squirrel

Sciurus niger

"Fox" due to reddish color of coat; "Squirrel" from Greek *skiourus*, compounded from *skia*, "a shadow," plus *oura*, "tail", hence "shade tail"; *niger* is Latin for "black," because one color phase is black.

Description

Very similar to and somewhat larger than Eastern Gray Squirrel; body ten to eleven inches long, tail equal length; color can range from reddish tan through grizzled gray to black; underparts rust yellow to orange; some all-gray animals have very little to no rusty shading; some grays have very dark heads, white noses, and white ears.

Behavior

Agile, graceful when climbing; more deliberate in movements than Gray; more likely than Gray to forage on ground away from trees, especially into corn fields; collects nuts in fall and buries them singly in shallow holes.

Range

Introduced from southeastern United States into parks, campuses, estates in Northwest; present in many urban areas; may extend range outward from original introductions, in some instances displacing native Western Gray Squirrel.

Food

Shoots, buds, grain, fruit, green bark, acorns, conifer seeds, fungi, insects; at feeder, sunflower seeds, peanuts, nuts.

Nest

Hole in tree, building; builds large, leaf-and-twig nests high up in trees secure enough to withstand most winter gales.

Comment

It is said that the Fox Squirrel is displacing the native Western Gray as it expands its range from cities like Seattle and San Francisco. It is not always welcome once it becomes plentiful and the novelty of having them around wears off. I was told by a resident of Walla Walla that someone had released five of them in a park there, and that in a few years they had multiplied into a minor plague.

REF: I—193; R—28

Northern Flying Squirrel

Glaucomys sabrinus

Occasionally "Canadian" Flying Squirrel or "fairydiddle"; "Northern" as distinct from "Southern" (*Glaucomys volans*); "Flying" descriptive of ability to glide short distances; "Squirrel" from Greek *skiourus*, "shade-tail"; *Glaucomys* is Greek for "gray mouse"; *sabrinus* is Latin for "river nymph," refers to Severn River west of Hudson Bay where first type specimen was described.

Description

Smaller than Red or Douglas Squirrel; body 5 to 7½ inches, tail slightly shorter; weighs from 2.5 to 5 ounces; large, dark eyes; very soft, gray-buff fur, cinnamon along back, shaded to light buff underparts; glide membrane dark-bordered; tail noticeably flat, especially on bottom surface.

Behavior

Strictly nocturnal, from hour or more after dusk to hour before dawn; swoops rapidly from tree to tree, gliding at an angle of about thirty to forty degrees; occasionally lands on the ground; scampers up tree when alarmed and immediately turns to head-down launch posture; agile, but not as athletic, particularly on the ground, as Red or Gray; often tolerant of each other at feeders; quiet, voice a soft chatter.

Range

Throughout boreal forest as far north as there are sizable trees; needs either mature conifer or mixed woodlands; does well in wooded parks and well-treed urban areas; in Pacific Northwest found in Yellow Pine, red fir, spruce, hemlock, and redwood biomes through Coast, Cascade, Rocky, and Sierra Nevada highlands, in Blue Mountains, and along coastal lowlands well into northern California.

Food

Primarily lichens, fungi, buds, blossoms, berries, insects, sweet sap; occasionally eggs, nestlings; forages on ground for mushrooms, which it adds to its winter food caches in den or nearby hollow trees.

Nest

Often uses abandoned woodpecker holes or natural cavities, may occasionally also use building or birdhouse; bed of finely shredded grass, bark; outside nest is a big ball ("drey") of moss, grasses, lichen, sometimes in disused bird nest or drey of Red or Gray Squirrel.

Comment

Many years before I ever saw a real live Northern Flying Squirrel I would occasionally find their light, fluffy, uniquely flattened tails on the ground amongst

tall trees, testimony to the previous owners' particular vulnerability to cats and owls. They are the main prey item of the Northern Spotted Owl.

People living in well-treed regions often have no idea that they are kept company, well after dark, by these shy little gliders. One reason they go unnoticed is that they do not venture out until a couple of hours after sunset, and they retire while it is still dark. It is thought that the reason for this is that their chief natural predators, owls, begin hunting at dusk. By staying out of sight during this period, the squirrels gamble on the chance that most owls will already have eaten by the time they venture forth.

Anonymous midnight scurryings on my cottage roof were clarified when I placed a small light bulb, with an inside switch, over the window feeder. Turning it on when the squirrels were munching out did not seem to bother them in the least, and neither did my obvious presence a few inches on the other side of the glass. At such close quarters it was easy to be captivated by their soft-eyed, furry appeal. It is also easy to understand why these gentle creatures have in the past been tamed and became much-loved familiars in cabins and forest-fire lookout towers.

REF: I—195; R—31

Least, Yellow Pine, and Townsend's Chipmunks

Eutamius minimus, E. amoenus, and *E. townsendii*

"Least" from small size compared to other chipmunks; "Yellow Pine" named after the tree; "Townsend's" after American explorer/naturalist J. K. Townsend (1809–1851); "Chipmunk" an Anglicized Algonquian name; *Eutamias* (formerly *Tamias*) is Greek/Latin for "true steward," referring to zeal for storing food; *minimus* is Latin for "least"; *amoenus* is Latin for "pleasing"; *townsendii* is Latinized "Townsend."

Description

All three very similar in appearance, the major common field marks being the bold, lengthwise striping on the back and on the sides of the face; small size, and long, slender tail; pointy face; beady, light-ringed eyes; large ears.

Least: Smallest, weighing from 1.2 to 1.9 ounces; body length from 4 to 4½ inches, tail 2¾ to 3½ inches; coat may have an overall grayish cast.

Yellow Pine: Slightly larger, body 4 to 5¼ inches, tail 3 to 4¼ inches, and colors and patterns brighter than Least; coat more reddish than Least, its flanks noticeably cinnamon.

Townsend's: Largest of all western chipmunks, weighing from 2.5 to 4.3 ounces; body 5½ to 6 inches, tail 3½ to 5 inches; coat overall darker brown than other chipmunks.

Behavior

All are quick-moving, dainty, beady-eyed alert; dart about on ground, usually (especially Least) with long tail held straight up; readily climb trees, low bushes, and feeder poles, but seek refuge in ground-level hideaways; diligent food hoarders; hibernate, but are early spring risers and may venture out briefly during extended mild spells in winter; voice a clear, high "*chip-chip*" and low, steady "*chuck*" or "*wok*," with ventriloquistic quality making them hard to pinpoint if the animal is hidden; in alarm, Least issues a slightly rasping "*churrrr*" followed by a trill issued in flight. Townsend's is shyest, preferring to remain hidden in its habitat of dense forest undercover; also the most arboreal of the chipmunks, climbing well up into large conifers.

Range

On maps, ranges may seem to overlap considerably; however there may be less direct mixing due to habitat preferences, which separate the species on the basis of altitude and vegetation types as well as latitude and climate.

Least: Wide adaptability to great variety of drier habitats, from low sagebrush scrubland, rain-shadow side of mountain ranges right up to alpine tundra; in Pacific Northwest in central Washington, central and eastern Oregon, central and southern Idaho, northeastern California.

Yellow Pine: In open, dry, Douglas fir–Yellow Pine zone in northeastern California, central and western Oregon, eastern Cascades and northwestern Washington, most of central and southern Idaho.

Townsend's: Favors wetter habitats; Yellow Pine, hemlock, fir forests; because much of this habitat has been logged, it has shown ability to adapt to the tangle of slash and emergent brush in clear-cuts; only chipmunk found throughout the Olympic Peninsula.

Food

Seeds, nuts, bulbs, greens, insects; at feeders, fond of sunflower seeds, grains, baked scraps, dried fruit; opportunistically predatory on eggs, nestlings.

Nest

A ball of shredded grass and fibers, deep in a neat, hidden burrow in a rock, trash, or brush pile, or under root tangle or building; nest often built near or on the main underground food cache; Townsend's may build tree nest.

Comment

Cute though they are, chipmunks occasionally horrify their admirers by revealing their latent taste for blood. They get this honestly, since all the squirrels are potentially carnivorous, even cannibalistic. They have been seen to grab baby birds from their nests and, with matter-of-fact relish, nibble them alive. Having for many years simultaneously hosted two species of chipmunks along with many nesting birds, I can verify that the birds that nest around my dooryard seem to achieve normal fledging success. Perhaps most parent birds can fend off chipmunks. Or maybe the sunflower seeds I furnish, plus the abundant supply of grasshoppers and other insects around the place, make it unnecessary for the chipmunks to fill out a food group with nest robbery.

REF: Least: I—181; R—36

    Yellow Pine: I—185; R—37

    Townsend's: I—186; R—38

Wood Rats

Family Cricetidae

This family includes the New World mice and their relatives. Although wood rats superficially resemble Norway Rats, these native wild rodents aren't related at all to the vermin that share back alleys and basements with humankind. Their habits are quite different, and their long tails are covered with hair in contrast to the naked, scaly tails of rats. In the case of the Bushy-tailed, the tail is quite a generous, hairy brush.

These soft-furred, lustrous-eyed scurriers have a certain quirky charm. They are attracted to odd, bright-colored, or shiny objects that they carry off, a droll prank unless your watch happens to be amongst the purloined trinkets. The loot is added to the pile of trash that is the focus and chief marker of their territory. It is a food storehouse, an eating platform, and a loft where green leaves can be dried before being stored away. A labyrinth of tunnels running through it also serves as a diversionary escape route. The actual nest is usually elsewhere, in a rock crevice, burrow, or some other stronghold.

Things That Go Thump in the Night

Wood rats are nocturnal and furtive, but not necessarily silent; when agitated they drum or thump with their hind feet and tail. In a cottage they make a lot of racket tipping things over, dragging them about, or dropping items on their way out. Being awakened in the dead of night by spooky thumps, crashes, and scuffing noises coming from under the bed is hair-raising if you don't know the source.

Unfortunately, they abruptly lose their image of charm when one gets into an unoccupied human dwelling. Territorial, it first sprays everything with what must be copious quantities of overpoweringly pungent urine. Intensely task-oriented, it chews upon, shreds, drags about, and otherwise inflicts amazing damage to the contents in a remarkably short time. Given an entire winter with a cottage to itself, it may relocate its nest indoors, complete with three-foot-high rubbish pile in a bedroom closet. Probably most of the mattress, the clothing, and as much of the drapes as it can reach will be shredded to make the inside of the nest nice and comfy, and to decorate the pile.

The effect of long-term wood rat tenancy inside a small building is to make it uninhabitable for humans without major cleaning and deodorizing.

One can feed birds and live happily with the prospect that it could attract wood rats if advance precautions are taken to exclude them from buildings and vehicles. Take a look at Chapter 5, The Downside, for more thoughts on living with animals that are tolerable neighbors but intolerable house guests.

Bushy-tailed Wood Rat

Neotoma cinerea

"Wood Rat" from habitat association; also "pack rat" from habit of packing trinkets away from campsites and cottages; *Neotoma* from Latin *neo*, "new," and *toma*, "sharp", allusion to teeth of a new genus of rodent; *cinerea* from Latin *cinis*, "ashes", hence "ash-colored."

Description

Long-tailed, ground squirrel-like; body eight to ten inches, tail five to eight inches; fairly prominent, finely furred ears; tail hairy; soft fur a tawny gray. Region also home to Dusky-footed (*N. albigula*) and Desert (*N. lepida*) Wood Rats, animals very similar in appearance to Bushy-tailed except that tail hair is very short and fine.

Behavior

Solitary, nocturnal; territorial; builds large mound of sticks, bones, foliage, dried manure, and, where obtainable, human discards such as tin cans, bottles, et cetera, placing mound in rock crevice, under log, against or in large tree, on rock outcrop, et cetera; when alarmed or aggressive, drums and thumps hind feet; sprays marker points through territory with strong-smelling urine; "steals" bright or novel objects from cabins and campsites to add to its pile.

Range

Widely distributed through Washington, Oregon, and Idaho, and in northern and northeastern California; found in wide variety of habitats, preferring transitional zones including arctic alpine, sagebrush scrub, Yellow Pine forest, Lodgepole Pine forest, and northern juniper woodland. Bushy-tailed range overlaps that of the Dusky-footed in the Cascades in Oregon, and in northern California. The Desert intrudes into southern Idaho and southeastern corner of Oregon.

Food

Chiefly plant material, including roots, bulbs, shoots, seeds, needles of conifers, fungi, and berries; doesn't eat grass; will frequent feeders for grain, sunflower and other seeds.

Nest

Fine, shredded plant fibers in a rock pile, crevice, burrow, or similar secure den; also builds a pile of litter near den, three feet or more high, of branches, bones, and trash.

Comment

Like many rodents, the wood rat stashes food, using its territorial mound to dry and cure moist plant material before storing it. In autumn it caches large piles of twigs and dried vegetation for its winter food supply.

REF: I—267; R—58

Raccoons

Family Procyonidae

"Some people think of raccoons as wonderfully intelligent creatures, affectionate, playful, and downright adorable. To others they are vicious, devious, and downright destructive vermin." Thus Des Kennedy, writing of his life amongst the creatures of British Columbia's Denman Island in his book *Living Things We Love to Hate*, sums up the diverse emotions generated by the masked bandit the Algonquian-speaking peoples called "*arakun.*"

It should be noted that Denman Island, which is just off the east side of Vancouver Island in the Strait of Georgia, has not been blessed, or cursed, with raccoons just yet. A determined group of residents has banded together to keep it that way. A bad example exists on neighboring Hornby Island where opossums were liberated, presumably by hunters brain-damaged on "houn'-dawg" hunting adventures from the American southland.

A similar lame-brained effort to manage wildlife for the benefit of trappers saw coons loosed on the Queen Charlottes. There are no cougars, wolves, or lynxes in the Charlottes, and most other natural raccoon pathogens have been left far behind. With no natural controls, the inevitable population boom sees coons inflicting massive damage on nesting seabird populations and other native animals.

The adaptable, omnivorous coon has turned humankind into an aid, making itself at home in farmyards and suburban developments. Here it dines well on garbage, pet food, and other back-step freebies, and on succulent garden produce. It quickly becomes a night raider of any bird feed it can reach. For accommodations, it settles into fireplace chimneys, culverts, ventilation ducts, garden sheds, attics, and crawl spaces, most of which are superior to the traditional den tree. My personal experience includes being awakened one night in my suburban home by the sound of a large coon purposefully ripping the shingles off my roof to get into the attic. I interrupted his work with a well-aimed billet of firewood.

Altogether, for the upwardly mobile coon, life in the city is much superior to what it was back in the old swamp. It follows that the urban coon is bigger and healthier, and raises more young than its country cousin.

Although originally and exclusively North American, the raccoon has been introduced—either deliberately or as escapees from fur farms—into France, Germany, Ukraine, and a number of places in Siberia.

As well as their value as bearers of thick fur on a good-sized, durable hide, raccoons have found undeserved favor as pets. While very young, a coon is the most engaging of companions—cute, inquisitive to a degree, intelligent, cuddly, and full of endearing sounds and mannerisms. However, while it may be as tame as you please, it is not domesticated. Any young coon will, if given the liberty of the house, become a thorough nuisance, climbing, prying, poking, and pilfering into places no dog, cat, or small child could ever get at.

At about twelve weeks of age, this cute little bandit becomes assertive; restrained or chastised, it may explode into a clawing, biting, shrieking bundle of highly intense aggression, exactly as it would in dominance battles with its littermates. The fury subsides as abruptly as it erupts, leaving its loving owners shaken and, probably, bleeding. Thereafter, vicious outbursts lurk just below the veneer of tameness and trust. Anyone who has raised a raccoon or two almost invariably has the scars to prove it. Sterling North, author of the best-selling book *Rascal*, was unnerved when "Rascal" turned on him, and he finally returned him to the wild.

Emergency wards and clinics in suburbs across the country get raccoon-bite victims every summer. These are often men who unwisely attempted to get physical with a coon in a shed, loft, flue, or some other disputed turf. The assisting family dog might at the same time be car-pooled to the vet for repairs. But at least as often the victims are children who were approached by coons or who enticed them close. The incentive is always food; what the children mistook for friendliness was simply a bold approach by a wild animal in search of an easy meal. If the kids try to grab or pick up the coon it defends itself, sometimes with very bloody, traumatizing results.

To the pain and shock of attack and physical hurt is added the possibility that the animal was rabid or afflicted with encephalitis. The etiology of rabies is well known; encephalitis can be transmitted from raccoons to dogs, but not to humans, for whatever comfort there is in that.

Northward Bound

Coons are members of the family that includes coatimundis, ringtails, and kinkajous, all of them subtropical to tropical animals. It may be that the resemblance between the goggled faces of the raccoon and the Giant Panda is not coincidental; there is evidence that indeed they are related.

In the south of its range, the raccoon stays up and about all year-round. But as a southern animal moving ever northward, the vanguard has had to adapt to survive the long famine that northern winters impose. Like other food generalists—badgers, skunks, and bears—it simply sleeps through its problem.

Raccoons have an enormous capacity for food, tucking away four pounds or more a day where supplies permit it. Under the right conditions they will be rolling fat by fall. Although they grow torporous in their winter dens, they do not hibernate. Their heart rate if anything speeds up during cold weather, driving a metabolism that costs about 0.75 ounce of body weight per day. A mild spell may bring them out to shuffle about for awhile before turning in again.

In the northern parts of their range, snow depth is critical: anything deeper than six inches is too difficult to get around in, and they are virtually compelled to retire. During a long, cold winter a coon may lose up to 50 percent of its autumn weight. If a coon's supply of fat runs out before the snows of spring recede below the crucial six inches, it dies. A high percentage of young coons do not make it through northern winters.

It is interesting to note that the arrival of raccoons in the suburbs has helped to draw in another furtive visitor, the cougar. The Pacific Northwest supports a good population of these big cats, which now and then show up in town. These appearances trigger alarm, headlines, and usually the death of the cougar. Thankfully, confrontations that end with people getting hurt or killed are extremely rare.

These out-of-place cougars may be roving youngsters seeking territory, or they may be adults that have learned to hunt the acreages. Here the aforementioned coons, and deer, are both plentiful and less wary than their truly wild counterparts. The fare is rounded out by domestic cats and dogs. In several western American cities, Denver among them, cougars are several generations into suburban living, breeding well within the sprawling semi-rural developments wherever patches of sufficient cover or rough terrain provide denning refuge.

Raccoon

Procyon lotor

Also "coon"; "Raccoon" from Algonquian *arakun* or *arathune*, variously interpreted as "scratcher" or "scratches-with-hands"; *Procyon* from Latin *pro*, "before," and *cyon*, Greek for "dog," supposedly linked to the group of stars that rises in the summer sky just before the dog star, Sirius; *lotor* from Latin "to wash," from animal's perceived habit of "washing" its food.

Description

Size of a very large domestic cat; low-slung, heavy-furred, with a thick, black-ringed tail; black facial "mask" made very prominent by light muzzle and broad, very light brow lines over mask; erect, light-edged ears; stands with arched back higher than shoulders; coat a grizzled gray, brown, or tan, sometimes with a ruddy cast to it; alike in motion to a very fat cat; average weights for males fifteen to eighteen pounds, for females twelve to fifteen pounds, heavier in fall than in spring; young-of-year appreciably lighter, occasional adult males much heavier.

Behavior

Males solitary, females and young-of-year social; runs with a rolling, hump-backed gait; readily climbs, and relaxes in, large trees; can descend trees head-first; frequently sits on haunches, especially when feeding or grooming; individuals conditioned to feeding by humans can become very bold, aggressive scroungers; a slow runner, when pursued takes refuge in a tree, burrow, hedge, culvert; when cornered, by dog or human, a very tough, determined fighter;

produces great variety of sounds, including a coughing growl, buzzy snarl, hiss, musical churring call, soft chattering, high squeaks, purring; front paws handlike in dexterity; famous for habit of captive animals' "washing" their food.

Range

Throughout temperate North America except for driest parts of Southwest United States, south through Central America; in many areas introduced to provide furs and/or hunting sport; favors woodlands and farmlands adjacent to water; has learned to prosper in cities; found throughout Pacific Northwest except in upper mountain levels and interior dry lands.

Food

Omnivorous; in the wild frogs, insects, small mammals, birds and eggs, fish, snails, clams, crayfish, fruit, nuts, roots, bulbs; forages in shallow water by rapidly dabbling about with both front paws; in cities feeds on garbage, garden produce (especially sweet corn in the "milk" stage) and whatever wild food (baby rabbits, mice, grubs, eggs, et cetera) may be available; at feeders prefers sunflower seeds and suet.

Nest

Hollow tree or log, disused woodchuck or fox den, rock pile, cave; around dwellings, in attics, lofts, barns, sheds, disused machinery, culverts, chimneys; females bear litters of three to five in a nest of grass, leaves, wood chips, or paper, cloth, and other discarded materials.

Comment

As a feeder of birds in several very different locations, all of which have raccoons in varying levels of evidence, I make a point of keeping my distance. I take pains to store garbage, seed, and suet out of reach, and maintain my buildings in as raccoon-proof shape as possible. If a coon broke into one of my buildings I would live-trap and deport it.

The place where the raccoons in my life have been most numerous is rural Manitoba where, thanks to the cold winters, they are strictly mild-weather visitors. To sustain an arms-length truce I keep feeders as coon-proof as possible. Thus far I have never had to destroy one, but from time to time, in a live trap intended for stray cats, I find a very dejected-looking raccoon. Following the indignity of being inspected (through the wires) and weighed (in the cage), it is freed. My intent is that the unpleasant experience will make it avoid the yard thereafter.

Most coon lore repeats unquestioningly the fact that they always "wash" their food. This is supported by captive animals that habitually dunk food into water and manipulate it about in a motion that looks much like purposeful scrubbing. Thus, millions of zoo visitors will swear that coons won't eat unless they can wash their food first, even if it's something like a soaking-wet frog just out of the pond.

Others, privy to the habits of wild coons, say the habit is much less pronounced in them. They also observe that wild coons rub dry food between their paws, and captive ones without access to water do the same thing. Wild coons also rub their front paws together in a kind of compulsive reflex even when there is no food involved.

For an animal that evolved to make a living feeling about for prey in the shallow margins of rivers, ponds, and swamps, crayfish must have become, early on, a major staple of diet. Raccoons have slim, sensitive front toes much more heavily stocked with nerve receptors than our own fingers. Crayfish have horny pincers and a powerful grip, as anyone who has been caught by one can attest.

Dabbling about, blindly poking your delicate fingers into crayfish lairs under muddied water is a sure way of getting repeatedly pinched. To avoid the nasty pincers but keep in contact with the crayfish, a rapid, hand-to-hand buffeting would keep it disoriented until the claws could be pinned down prior to a quick disabling bite. This rapid, double-handed batting motion, repeated out of context as an evolved reflex, in or out of water, is at the root of the "washing" myth.

REF: I—357; R—77

Appendices

Appendix 1: Recipes for the Gourmet

The following recipes call for rendered beef fat, either suet or trimmings. Remember to save the cracklings; they are excellent broken up and scattered on your feeder shelf along with the seeds. For buying and handling suet, see Suet under Feeds in Chapter 2, Seeds and Feeds. Below is a mere sampling of bird recipes—entire books have been published on the subject; see the Bibliography for these.

Cascades Bird Pudding

This versatile mixture can be put in a net bag or plugged into holes in a suet log or between the scales of a big pine cone. Thanks to a good friend in Cle Elum for this recipe.

2 cups whole rolled oats
1 cup rendered suet
1 to 2 tablespoons sugar (or honey)
½ cup peanut butter

Cook the oats in water until thick. Remelt suet (don't overheat) and pour it into the hot oats. Add sugar and peanut butter; stir to even consistency and let cool. Hang out of reach of squirrels, because the scent of the peanut butter will attract them more than pure suet.

Protein Pemmican

This mix adds a sweet energy kick from the fruit, and the protein could help a robin, Varied Thrush, or other partially insectivorous bird make it through the winter.

3 parts rendered suet
1 part meat—lean burger, moist cat or dog food, unspiced bologna, et cetera
Raisins, chopped fruit, dried wild berries

Remelt suet; mash up the meat and stir it into the suet. Add fruit and stir mixture as it cools to get a consistent blend. Experiment with fruit to determine how much of any given kind you can add; too much, and the cooled block won't hold together.

Bread Pudding Block

> *Rendered suet*
> *Stale bread, doughnuts, crackers, et cetera, and/or cornmeal*

Remelt suet; crush or grind up baked goods and stir them into the suet. Stir again as the mixture begins to cool to get a uniform mix. Pour into molds and let set. Experience will dictate just how much of any given baked product can be used and still have the block hold its shape.

Baron von Berlepsch's "Bird-stone"

Von Berlepsch, one supposes, was a European gentleman of the early twentieth century recognized as an authority on birds. "Bird-stone" is a term coined by old-time bird feeders for rendered, hard suet.

I found the baron's recipe in a booklet written in 1923 by R. Owen Merriman, published by the National Parks of Canada. It reminds us that ours is not the first generation to care for the birds.

Expect a strange look from the nature shop clerk when you lay the following list of ingredients on the counter.

> *4.5 ounces white bread, dried and ground*
> *3 ounces meat, dried and ground*
> *6 ounces hemp (the seeds, of course)*
> *3 ounces crushed hemp*
> *3 ounces maw**
> *1.5 ounces poppy-seed flour*
> *3 ounces white millet*
> *1.5 ounces oats*
> *1.5 ounces dried elderberries*
> *1.5 ounces sunflower seeds*
> *1.5 ounces ants' eggs*
> *3 ounces chopped nuts (various)*
> *3 ounces chopped green (unroasted) peanuts*
> *2 ounces ground bone***
> *2 ounces sharp sand (for grit)****

To the total quantity of dry food, add about one and one-half times as much melted beef or mutton suet. Mr. Merriman helpfully suggests: "It will be found convenient to dry the bread before grinding it, but to grind the meat before drying it."

*"Maw" is the seed of the opium poppy, commonly used as food for cage birds.

**Bone meal, or perhaps cuttlebone, would do nicely here.

***I would serve the sand as a side dish. I know birds don't have teeth, but the mere thought of that sand in the mixture puts my fillings on edge.

Appendix 2: Feeders and Shelters

Roosting Box

Big is not necessarily better, because it is also less snug. This is about bluebird-nestbox size—five by five by eight inches. Tuck in a small forked branch or two for perches, and add an inch or so of sawdust to the floor. Note that the hole is best located low down in the box.

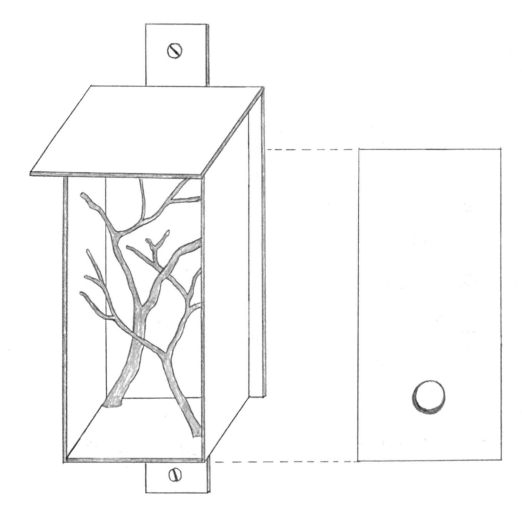

Window Shelf and Hopper

These dimensions are approximate only; actual size depends in part on the width of your window. In mild climates a roof should be added to prevent rain or melting snow from pooling on the shelf and soaking up into the hopper.

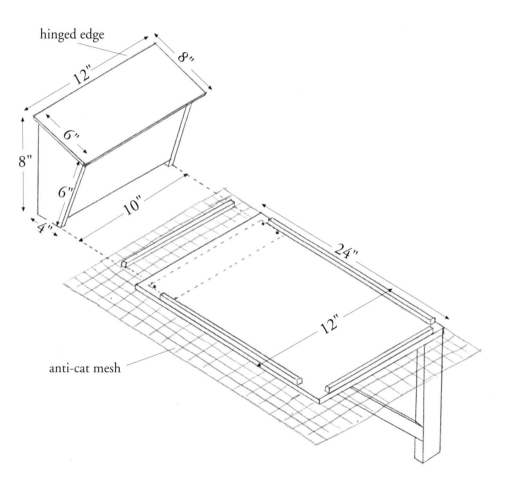

Roofed Table

This can be any size; the one shown here is about two by three feet. The deck, roof, and corner braces on the legs are quarter-inch plywood, the gable pieces half-inch ply. The edges around the deck can be either one inch by one inch or one inch by two inches. The deck supports are one inch by two inches, the legs two inches by two inches.

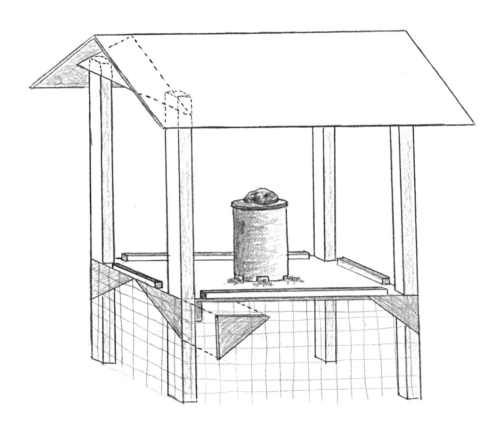

Flat-topped Double-decker

The suggested dimensions provide hopper-supplied lower decks protected from rain by the larger, flat upper deck, which also doubles as a fair-weather feeder shelf. Make sure the edge around the filler hole is waterproof; a generous bead of caulking compound under the edge pieces and at the corners will do this, plus a double coat of good paint. The filler hole cover can be part of a tin can, or a piece of ply with a screw through one corner, adjusted just tight enough to hold the lid in place but permitting it to be slid aside for filling.

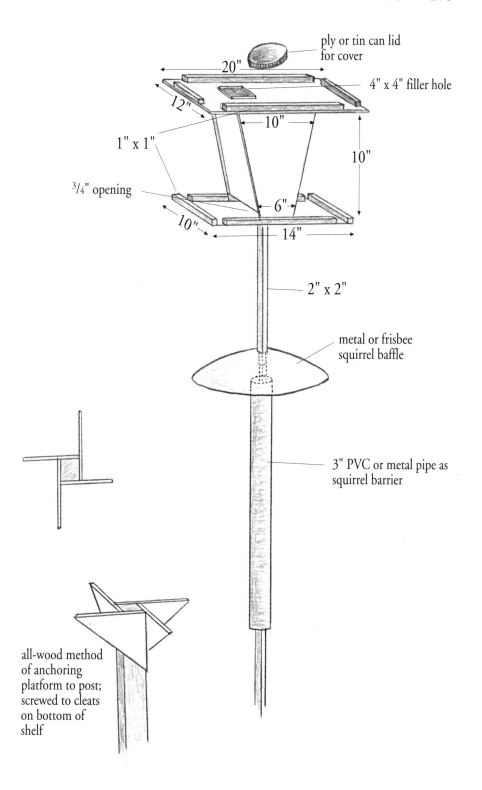

ply or tin can lid
for cover

20"

4" x 4" filler hole

12"

10"

1" x 1"

10"

3/4" opening

6"

10"

14"

2" x 2"

metal or frisbee
squirrel baffle

3" PVC or metal pipe as
squirrel barrier

all-wood method
of anchoring
platform to post;
screwed to cleats
on bottom of
shelf

Appendix 3: Naturalist Organizations

National

Project FeederWatch
Cornell Laboratory of Ornithology
159 Sapsucker Woods Road
Ithaca, NY 14850

National Audubon Society
700 Broadway
New York, NY 10003-9562

Regional

National Audubon Society
Western Regional Office
555 Audubon Place
Sacramento, CA 95825

National Audubon Society
Washington State Office
P.O. Box 462
Olympia, WA 98507

Bibliography

BIRDS

Field Guides

Harrison, Colin. *A Field Guide to the Nests, Eggs and Nestlings of North American Birds.* New York: Collins, 1978.

Harrison, Hal H. *A Field Guide To Birds' Nests (east of the Mississippi River), Peterson Field Guide Series.* Boston: Houghton Mifflin Co., 1975.

Peterson, Roger Tory. *A Field Guide to Western Birds.* 3d ed. Boston: Houghton Mifflin Co., 1990.

Robbins, Chandler S., et al. *Birds of North America, Golden Guide Series.* New York: Golden Press, 1983.

Scott, Shirley L., ed. *National Geographic Society Field Guide to the Birds of North America.* Washington, DC: National Geographic Society, 1987.

Udvardy, Miklos D.F. *Audubon Society Field Guide to North American Birds (Western Region).* New York: Alfred A. Knopf, 1977.

General References

Bent, Arthur Cleveland. *Life Histories of North American Birds.* New York: Dover Publications, 1964.

Boswall, Jeffery. *Birds for All Seasons.* London: BBC Publications, 1986.

Burton, Robert. *Bird Behavior.* New York: Alfred A. Knopf, 1985.

Choate, Ernest A. *The Dictionary of American Bird Names.* Boston: Harvard Common Press, 1985.

Corral, Michael. *The World of Birds.* Chester, CT: Globe Pequot Press, 1989.

Ehrlich, Paul, et al. *The Birder's Handbook.* New York: Simon and Schuster, 1988.

Forsyth, Adrian. *The Nature of Birds.* Camden East, ON.: Camden House Publishing, 1988.

Kilham, Lawrence. *On Watching Birds.* Chelsea, VT: Chelsea Green Publishing Co., 1988.

Mace, Alice E., ed. *The Birds Around Us.* San Francisco: Ortho Books, Chevron Chemical Co., 1986.

Martin, Brian. *World Birds.* Enfield, Middlesex, England: Guinness Superlatives, 1987.

Miller, Millie, and Nelson, Cyndi. *Early Bird—Western Backyard Birds.* Boulder, CO: Johnson Books, 1991.

Page, Jake, and Morton, Eugene S. *Lords of the Air.* Washington, DC: Smithsonian Books, 1989.

Pasquier, Roger. *Watching Birds.* Boston: Houghton Mifflin Co., 1980.

Perrins, C., and Middleton, A., eds. *The Encyclopedia of Birds.* New York: Facts on File Publications, 1985.

Proctor, Noble. *Song Birds.* (With cassette.) London: Quarto Publishing, 1988.

Root, Terry. *Atlas of Wintering North American Birds.* Chicago: University of Chicago Press, 1988.

Weidensahl, Scott. *The Birder's Miscellany.* New York: Simon and Schuster, 1991.

Regional References

Ennor, Howard R. *Birds of the Tri-Cities and Vicinity.* Richland, WA: Lower Columbia Basin Audubon Society, 1991.

Evanich, Joseph E. *The Birder's Guide to Oregon.* Portland: Portland Audubon Society, 1990.

Haras, Willie. *Wings Across Georgia Strait.* Comox, BC: Lindsay Press, undated.

Lewis, Mark G., and Sharpe, Fred A. *Birding in the San Juan Islands.* Seattle: The Mountaineers, 1987.

Littlefield, Caroll D. *Birds of Malheur National Wildlife Refuge, Oregon.* Corvallis, OR: Oregon State University Press, 1990.

Mark, David M. *Where to Find Birds in British Columbia.* New Westminster, BC: Kestrel Press, 1984.

Nehls, Harry B. *Familiar Birds of the Northwest.* 3d ed. Portland, OR: Audubon Society of Portland, 1989.

Bird Feeding and Attracting

Burton, Robert. *National Audubon Society North American Birdfeeder Handbook.* New York: Dorling Kindersley, 1992.

Campbell, Scott D. *Easy-to-make Bird Feeders for Woodworkers.* New York: Dover Publications, 1989.

Dawe, Neil, and Dawe, Karen. *The Bird Book.* (Packaged in small, clear, plastic window feeder.) New York: Workman Publishing, 1988.

DeGraaf, R., and Witman, M. *Trees, Shrubs and Vines for Attracting Birds.* Amherst: University of Massachusetts Press, 1979.

Dennis, John. *A Complete Guide To Bird Feeding.* New York: Alfred A. Knopf, 1978.

————. *Summer Bird Feeding.* Northbrook, IL: Audubon Workshop, 1990.

Harrison, Kit, and Harrison, George. *The Birds of Winter.* New York: Random House, 1990.

Kress, Stephen. *The Audubon Society Guide to Attracting Birds.* New York: Charles Scribner's Sons, 1985.

Mahnken, Jan. *Feeding the Birds.* Pownal, VT: Storey Communications, 1983.

Schnek, Marcus. *Your Backyard Wildlife Garden.* London: Quarto Publishing, 1992.

Vriends, Matthew M. *Feeding and Sheltering Backyard Birds.* Hauppauge, NY: Barron's Educational Series, 1990.

Witty, Helen, and Witty, Dick. *Feed the Birds.* (Mesh suet bag included.) New York: Workman Publishing, 1991.

Mammals

Ingles, Lloyd G. *Mammals of the Pacific States.* Stanford: Stanford University Press, 1965.

Russo, Ron. *Pacific Coast Mammals.* Berkeley: Nature Study Guild, 1987.

INDEX

ABOUT THE AUTHOR

Bob Waldon brings to his authorship a lifelong fascination with nature and the outdoors, an interest he sustained during a twenty-five-year career in the newspaper and publishing business in Winnipeg, Manitoba. He and his wife, Carole, spent summer vacations canoeing historic fur trade routes in Canada's northland. They also found time for sailing, cross-country skiing, and, of course, bird feeding. These interests in time led Bob to the environmental movement; he is a former president of the Manitoba Naturalists' Society and the Canadian Nature Federation.

At a time of life when most people contemplate retirement, Bob left the publishing business to launch a new career. For five seasons he served as an interpretive naturalist at Riding Mountain National Park in Manitoba. He also became a natural history columnist and book reviewer. These several interests in time combined to produce a series of regional books on feeding wild birds; this is the fifth of that series. The regions covered by the first four books are the Canadian Prairies, Ontario, Upper Midwest United States, and British Columbia.

Bob and Carole now divide their time between 160 acres of excellent deer and chickadee habitat in Manitoba, and a home in Alert Bay on northern Vancouver Island.

ABOUT THE ILLUSTRATOR

Peter Sawatzky's career developed from a blending of his fascination with wildlife and his profession as a painter and commercial artist. In 1973 he was first introduced to woodcarving and saw in this medium both a creative challenge and a means of earning a livelihood as a full-time artist.

As a carver Peter has won international recognition and a growing list of awards and exhibition credits. He works mainly with American basswood, using traditional hand tools almost exclusively and working as much as possible from a single block of wood. He recently branched out into bronze castings and, characteristically, mastered every step of the process, including the actual casting with a furnace of his own.

Never having set aside his interest in the graphic arts, Peter was pleased to accept the offer from his longtime friend Bob Waldon to do the illustrations for this series of books on feeding wild birds.

Peter lives in Glenboro, Manitoba, with his wife, Karen, and their teenage children, Jeremy and Erin.

THE MOUNTAINEERS, founded in 1906, is a nonprofit outdoor activity and conservation club, whose mission is "to explore, study, preserve, and enjoy the natural beauty of the outdoors ...." Based in Seattle, Washington, the club is now the third-largest such organization in the United States, with 14,000 members and four branches throughout Washington State.

The Mountaineers sponsors both classes and year-round outdoor activities in the Pacific Northwest, which include hiking, mountain climbing, ski-touring, snowshoeing, bicycling, camping, kayaking and canoeing, nature study, sailing, and adventure travel. The club's conservation division supports environmental causes through educational activities, sponsoring legislation, and presenting informational programs. All club activities are led by skilled, experienced volunteers, who are dedicated to promoting safe and responsible enjoyment and preservation of the outdoors.

The Mountaineers Books, an active, nonprofit publishing program of the club, produces guidebooks, instructional texts, historical works, natural history guides, and works on environmental conservation. All books produced by The Mountaineers are aimed at fulfilling the club's mission.

If you would like to participate in these organized outdoor activities or the club's programs, consider a membership in The Mountaineers. For information and an application, write or call The Mountaineers, Club Headquarters, 300 Third Avenue West, Seattle, Washington 98119; (206) 284-6310.

Send or call for our catalog of more than 300 outdoor titles:

The Mountaineers Books
1011 SW Klickitat Way, Suite 107
Seattle, WA 98134
1-800-553-4453